# A Guidebook to The Bible

# Harper ChapelBooks

# A Guidebook
# to
# The Bible

*By Alice Parmelee*

Harper ▲ ChapelBooks

**HARPER & ROW, PUBLISHERS, NEW YORK**

# A GUIDEBOOK TO THE BIBLE

*To Mary*

# *Preface*

THE Bible is a greatly honored but often neglected book. Part of this neglect is due to the difficulty of understanding it, for even in its modern English translations it remains an ancient book which does not yield its full richness to the casual reader. The present volume is an attempt to tell how the Bible was written so that the average reader may see it, not as a forbidding and incomprehensible collection of sacred Scriptures, but as a living record of men's lives and thoughts. In this book are stories about the men who wrote the Bible and the times in which they lived. Here also are incidents in its amazing journey down the centuries to our own day. Stories such as these take the Bible out of the graveyard of dead literature and help us know it as a timeless book filled with beauty, entertainment, wisdom, and spiritual insight.

In recent years scholars have added many new chapters to our knowledge of the Bible until today more is known about it than ever before. This book has no new facts or theories to impart, but it tries to organize our present knowledge into a connected story and so make Biblical scholarship available and interesting. My aim has been to follow the highroad traveled by the majority of competent scholars and to avoid the byways of unproved theories. On the basis of the most widely accepted scholarship I have attempted to recreate the vanished days in which the Bible was written and to summon its ancient authors from oblivion. In bringing into sharp focus what time has rendered hazy, I have tried to be faithful to the known facts and to indicate where reliable history ends and theory and imagination sketch in the outlines.

In preparing this book I have incurred a debt of gratitude to the host of scholars who have surveyed and charted the entire field of the Bible. Without the immense labors of translators, historians, writers of commentaries, archaeologists, and Bible students this guidebook could not have been written. There is hardly a sentence in it that does not depend on their work.

The King James Version has been used for the quotations, but these have been kept to a minimum. This book is not a substitute for the Bible and it will have failed of its purpose unless it leads the reader on to the Scriptures themselves. The list of Bible readings at the end is designed merely to illustrate the text. It is hoped that the following pages may give the modern reader a key with which he can unlock for himself some of the vast treasures of the Bible and possess his great literary and spiritual heritage.

ALICE PARMELEE

*March 3, 1948*

# Contents

ix

## PART II: THE NEW TESTAMENT

## Contents

# PART I

*The Old Testament*

# 1

## *Unraveling the Old Testament*

### The Search for Origins

"HOW shall I catalogue it?" wondered a young librarian as she opened the Bible. On her index card was space for the author's name and the publication date. What facts could she find to record? Well she might wonder, though the volume itself looks ordinary enough in its modern dress of printed paper bound in black cloth. Standing on a shelf among modern novels, schoolbooks, and biographies, the Bible usually seems just a little more solemn and a little less interesting than they. Could it be printed and bound to show at a glance what an extraordinary book it is? Doubtless this is impossible, but people have tried to do it, nevertheless, as is shown by the treasured volumes kept today under glass in libraries and museums. Kings have had the Bible bound between gold covers set with precious stones. Artists have adorned its pages with delicate illuminations of breath-taking beauty. Scribes have literally dipped their pens in liquid gold and written its words on purple-stained vellum. But the majesty and truth and incomparable power of the Bible still defy visible expression. As the young librarian knew, there is far more here than meets the eye. The little black cloth volume is a disguise indeed.

In the first place, the Bible is not a single book at all. It is

3

divided into two parts: the Old Testament and the New Testament. But even the Old Testament is not a single book. From Genesis to Malachi it contains thirty-nine books, some of which, like Ruth or Haggai, are only a few pages long, while others, like Genesis and Psalms, are nearly as long as an average book.

Is this little library of the Old Testament similar to a one-volume edition of Shakespeare and does it contain the collected works of a single author? Some people believe that this is indeed the case and that God Himself is the actual Author of each word in the thirty-nine books. This theory raises difficulties. We cannot believe that the men who wrote the actual words were as unthinking as a teletype mechanically spelling out a message. The authors left too much of their own personalities on every page for us to believe that they were automatons when they wrote the Bible. The background of their days, their different ideas about God, their individual responses to life — all these colored their words and sometimes, it must be admitted, obscured their message. Filled as the Bible is with the infinite variety of human life, we yet find amid its many-colored hues the pure white light of a revelation from God. On some pages this light shines brighter for us than on others, perhaps because our understanding of spiritual things is limited by our personal experience. No doubt also, to some Bible writers there was granted deeper spiritual insight than to others, and some were more willing channels of divine revelation. It seems reasonable then to suppose that God used not only the pens of people like ourselves to spell out His message, but that He also used their minds, their experiences, and their personalities. With the clearest words at his command each writer put down as much of the divine message as he was able to understand. In reading the Bible we are always aware of its two poles: the human and the divine. We see men's groping efforts to find God, but we also see God's revelation of Himself to men. A New Testament writer summed it up in a phrase: "God, who at sundry times and in divers manners spake in time past unto the fathers by the prophets . . ." (Hebrews 1:1).

No doubt it was their divine quality which caused the thirty-nine books to be chosen from the entire body of Hebrew literature and at length brought together between the covers of one book. Certainly it is the human aspect of the books that gives them their fascinating variety. Here are poems and legends, songs and folklore, statistics and genealogies, orations, hymns, proverbs, and novels. The books are written in many moods and in many styles. The cadences and the rhythm of the sentences change from book to book and sometimes even within one book. There can be no question about it that the Old Testament is the work of many authors. It was doubtless in the process of being written during a period of a thousand years.

If it is impossible in cataloguing the Old Testament to give the name of its author because there was not one but many, or the date of its publication because this was gradual, extending over many centuries, we can perhaps catalogue the Old Testament book by book. Here again we run into difficulties. We have the titles, all thirty-nine of them, and, though they are not the original titles, they will do very well for our purpose. It is with the authors' names that our problem begins, for we find no title pages and few clear statements of authorship. In the days when every word of the Bible was thought to be from God few people cared to discover who had written the various books. Moreover, ancient peoples did not share our curiosity about authors. Our first question about a book is: Who wrote it? Woe betide anyone today who prints a section of another's work without using quotation marks and obtaining permission from the copyright holder! In Old Testament days all this was different. Authors apparently did not bother to sign their own work and few people seem to have asked: Who wrote it? As for copying, that was freely done without regard to quotation marks, which had not been invented, nor copyrights, which did not exist. Today what is considered literary theft was then really a high literary compliment, for who would laboriously copy another's work by hand unless he considered it to be of great merit? All this shows why cataloguing the Old Testament books is not a simple matter of listing, but becomes a complicated puzzle.

Traditions grew up about the authors of the thirty-nine books. Some of these traditions were probably founded on actual fact. The names of such prophets as Amos, Hosea, Isaiah, and Jeremiah may have become attached to their works at such an early date that these traditions of authorship are fairly reliable. Others seem less credible. Moses was supposed to be the author of the five famous books with which the Old Testament opens. If we read the first two chapters of Genesis carefully we shall note a strange fact. Here are two stories of creation, but they are two different stories! Did one man write both? In the last chapter of Deuteronomy we read the story of the death of Moses and we ask ourselves: "Did Moses write about his own death?"

We notice, moreover, that the five books are richly varied in content. There are ballads and laws, census lists and lyric poetry. Could Moses have been a master of so many literary forms? When the truth begins to dawn on us, the whole theory that Moses was the author of the first five books collapses like a house of cards, and we see that this great Pentateuch must be the work of many men. We begin to question also the theory that David was the author of the Book of Psalms and that Solomon composed Proverbs. Having discarded the old theories, we shall find evidence that hardly a single book as it now stands in the Old Testament was written by one person. Even in such books as Amos, Hosea, and Isaiah we shall discover additions by later hands.

Each book is a marvelously complex creation into whose making went the craftsmanship, insight, and genius of many men. It is fascinating to note where changes in style and differences in ideas occur and to realize that here one man must have put down his pen and another probably began to write. There are times when we wish ancient authors had not copied so freely from other writers and that editors and redactors had not mixed so many new ideas with the original texts. We often feel that if we could get back to the original documents we would be closer to a true understanding of God's message to men. But this is probably not so. All who worked on these books were trying to make God's message clear. The literary historian and the textual critic may lament the ancient documents plowed under when the Old Testament books were put in final shape. For those who love the heritage of Israel the contributions of all her prophets, writers, and editors are valuable.

The Old Testament is like an ancient city where men have lived for centuries. Studying the books to discover their various authors is like excavating an old city. Successive layers of debris, rubble, and broken pottery are dug up, each layer showing to those who understand such evidence the history and life of its own period. In much the same way, unraveling the books of the Old Testament brings fascinating information to light. It helps us to see the steps in Israel's religious progress from the crude superstitions of her earliest days to the sublime visions of her great prophets. Most important of all, in the process of unearthing the origins of the Bible its people begin to live for us as they never did before and its message becomes real to us.

We shall make our way back through more than three thousand years to the days when the oldest things in our Bible were composed, and we shall hunt for the first writings, for their authors, and for the story of how the books came into being. This is a difficult search and we shall need to follow every possible clue. Language experts, archaeologists, historians, theologians, and scholars supply us with many a lead in our hunt and there are plenty of clues to be found in the pages of the Old Testament itself.

From first to last this library of thirty-nine books contains the story of a great people. Here are their moments of exaltation, their royal splendors, their dark wrongs, the ringing words of their prophets, the imperishable songs of their poets. In unraveling the Old Testament our first clue is the people themselves out of whose experiences these amazing books came. If we can discover who the people were and what made them different from all other ancient peoples, we shall be well on our way to understanding the Book which is their highest creative achievement.

## 2

# The People Behind the Book

## THE HEBREWS AND THEIR NEIGHBORS

THE people who gave us the Old Testament join the pageant of history under the leadership of Moses, and from then on we can trace their fortunes. Bitter conflicts with the Canaanites and Philistines marked the years of their settlement in Palestine and the formation of their little kingdom under Saul and David. Solomon reigned unwisely and his successor saw a fatal division split the kingdom into North and South. The Northern Kingdom of Israel was conquered by the Assyrians in 722 B.C. Judah, the Southern Kingdom, survived as an independent nation only until 586 B.C. when Jerusalem was captured and destroyed and its people led captive to Babylon. This was the beginning of the dispersion of the Jews which has been a factor in world history until the present day. At length some of them returned to Palestine and rebuilt the Temple in Jerusalem in 516 B.C., but they were henceforth a subject people under the domination of some world power, first Persia, later Greece, and then Rome.

These people have been given various names: Hebrews, Israelites, and Jews. They came originally from the vast reaches of the Arabian desert, the nursery of the great Semitic race. The Hebrews belonged to this virile race and were re-

9

lated to such other Semites as the Canaanites and the Phoenicians. Long before the time of Moses, migrating bands of Hebrews must have come out of the desert with their wives and children searching for better pastures for their flocks, and fields where they might plant crops. The ancient world seems to have been alive with migrating tribes seeking to escape from the hardships of the desert. The stories of the patriarchs: Abraham, Isaac, and Jacob, paint a picture of the lives of these nomad tribes in the dimly-known centuries before their real history began.

The fertile lands they coveted stretched in a giant crescent from the Euphrates to the Nile. Green pastures and well-watered farming country must have seemed a veritable paradise to eyes accustomed to the bare expanse of desert. But the nomads found the green lands already occupied. The Egyptians, Akkadians, Hittites, Babylonians, Phoenicians, and Canaanites, all well-organized and powerful peoples, controlled the fertile lands. Though the nomads made many an armed attack they could not overthrow the empires of antiquity. Some of the Hebrews must have settled down in small family or tribal groups within the boundaries of the great powers.

In those far-off days of tribal migrations the people we now call the Hebrews had not yet received their name. It is true that a word similar to Hebrew, namely, *Habiru*, occurs frequently in cuneiform documents found within the boundaries of the ancient empires, but it is fairly certain that *Habiru* did not originally refer to the Hebrews. It seems, rather, to be a word denoting aliens or foreigners of any race. In the Mari Tablets written in North Mesopotamia about 2000 B.C., alien soldiers employed as mercenaries are called *Habiru*. Among the tablets unearthed at Nuzi there are labor contracts dating back to the fifteenth century B.C. These contracts concern the employment of foreigners who are called *Habiru*.

The most famous letters surviving from antiquity are three hundred or more clay tablets discovered in Egypt at Tel el-Amarna. Here in the fourteenth century B.C., Ikhnaton (Amenhotep IV) built his capital and here he stored letters from his vassal rulers and governors in Syria and Palestine. The Tel el-Amarna tablets are of clay incised with the cuneiform writing used in international correspondence. In one letter the Egyptian governor of Jerusalem wrote this report to Pharaoh: "The Habiru are capturing the cities of the king—all are lost." These fourteenth century *Habiru* may have been a group of mercenaries revolting against Egyptian rule. On the other hand, the word may name an invading tribe, and, if this second interpretation is correct, the Amarna letters would contain the first known mention of the Hebrews. Though it is not certain exactly when the word *Habiru* narrowed down from its original meaning of alien and began to denote one particular race, it is probable that the people we now call Hebrews received their name from the word *Habiru*. Thus their very name stands for the long period of tribal migrations when groups of Hebrews emerging from the desert were eager to accept any employment offered to aliens or foreigners within the great empires, for this gave them a foothold in the fertile lands.

From the peoples of the Tigris-Euphrates region among whom the Hebrews probably lived as *Habiru* they learned many things, and Genesis is full of memories of those days. In the story of Adam and Eve we read that "a river went out of Eden to water the garden; and from thence it was parted and became into four heads . . . and the fourth river is Euphrates." Eden itself, then, was located in fertile country, not in the desert cradle of the race. An old Babylonian legend forms the basis of the story of Noah and the flood. Abraham is said to have come from the city of Ur not far from the place where the Tigris and Euphrates rivers join before they flow into the Persian Gulf. Moreover, scholars tell us that some of the laws in Deuteronomy are similar to laws in the famous code of Hammurabi of about 2000 B.C. Centuries passed before these stories and laws and memories were written down in the form in which we now read them in the Bible, but the Hebrews never forgot one of their first contacts with a civilization higher than their own. Of all the streams that flowed into the Bible one of the most ancient is the stream of legend, myth, law, and remembered experience that issued from Babylonia.

From time to time groups of Hebrews migrated to the banks of the Nile. They may have gone as traders bringing goods along the caravan routes that linked the Euphrates to the Nile. Many were probably driven to Egypt by famine, as were the brothers of Joseph. In Egypt the Hebrews gazed with awe at the mighty pyramids, already centuries old. They talked in the market places with men who in agriculture and government, in building and art, in morality and religion had achieved the highest civilization yet known. Some of the ancient and often crumbling things from Egypt in our museums today the early Hebrews may have seen when they were fresh and new: the woven materials, the carved furniture, the alabaster jars, the exquisite jewelry, the painted frescoes. They may actually have handled some of the papyrus documents which, after thousands of years, still survive as fragile evidences of one of man's mightiest achievements.

It was the Egyptians who first learned how to cut the stem or pith of the papyrus reed into thin strips and paste them together to make a sheet of paper. Ink they manufactured from soot mixed with gum and water. They cut their pens from split reeds. As for writing itself, the Egyptians experimented with pictures and signs until at last, long before 3000 B.C., they devised the oldest alphabet in the world. The Egyptian scribe, however, preferred to write with his pictures and signs and it remained for another people to develop the alphabet.

Under Moses the real history of the Hebrews began. Curiously enough, we are not sure exactly when this happened. Scholars differ in their calculations of when Moses lived by as much as six hundred years. Many historians think that Rameses II, who died about 1225 B.C., was the Pharaoh who oppressed the Hebrews. Tentatively we date the Exodus about 1250 B.C., remembering that this date is surrounded with uncertainty and may have to be revised if future discoveries bring to light new evidence to contradict it. Whenever he lived, Moses was one of the greatest of the Hebrews. He was their liberator, their lawgiver, and, most important of all, he was the man who first taught them that they were God's people. In this idea lay the seed of Israel's great religious development. Tradition says Moses was brought up by an Egyptian princess and educated in the royal household. His name is the Egyptian word for "son" and it occurs frequently on Egyptian tombs and in the names of some of the Pharaohs like Thutmose. Egyptian influence must have permeated Moses' thinking and through him exercised a strong influence upon Israel's early life.

The Euphrates and the Nile flow through the Bible, depositing on its pages some of the fruits of their civilizations. During the earliest years of Hebrew history and indeed throughout the centuries while the Old Testament was being written, there was constant influence upon the Hebrews from all her neighbors. From the Canaanites, whom they found living in Palestine and among whom they settled, the Hebrews learned how to plant vineyards and raise crops. They learned from them many of the arts and crafts of both peace and war and they even adopted part of the Canaanite religion. The local Canaanite gods of agriculture were called Baalim. In order to assure the fertility of their lands the Hebrews worshiped the local Baal with pagan rites on the "high place" until the prophets taught them that Yahweh was the only God.

Recently there was unearthed at Ras Shamra on the North Syrian coast the library of a large temple school which flourished there about 1400 B.C. When its clay tablets were deciphered some were found to contain epic poems belonging to a Canaanite cult. The remarkable parallels between this cult and Old Testament literature and ritual show us that Israel's religion was not unique in its origin. It sprang from the common matrix of religious ideas and practices of the ancient world. Not in their source but in their amazing development lies the glory of Israel's religious conceptions.

Most important, perhaps, of all they learned from others was the alphabet. Though their method of writing came from the Egyptians, the Hebrews did not derive their alphabet from Egyptian hieroglyphic or hieratic writing but from the Canaanite-Phoenician alphabet which they found in use in Palestine when they arrived. The clay tablets of Ras Shamra were written in this alphabet. The Hebrews adopted the Canaanite-Phoenician alphabet and used it when they wrote the Old Testament. The seafaring Phoenicians carried this alphabet to the shores of Greece, little realizing that it was the most valuable part of their cargoes. The Greeks breathed life into its consonants by devising vowels. The Romans, Arabs, and Indians all made use of this alphabet, and today it is the alphabet of our typewriters and printing presses.

Though very old, the Canaanite-Phoenician alphabet has a still older ancestor. This was discovered in the crude marks scratched in the sandstone at Serabit el-Khadim. Here in the Sinai peninsular were located copper mines and also the ancient turquoise mines which supplied the jewelers of Egypt. Between 1850 and 1800 B.C. Pharaoh Amenemhet III employed Semitic tribes akin to the Hebrews to work these mines. The mine foremen were Semites also. They must have been fascinated by the way the Egyptian scribes kept records at the mine. Perhaps on his day off a foreman decided to try his hand at writing. Egyptian picture and sign writing called hieroglyphic was far too complex a system for him to master in an afternoon, but it did suggest signs to him. These he developed and used for words in his own Semitic language. Only thirty-seven different words in the Sinaitic writing have been found. Most of them concern prayers and offerings made to Ba'lat, the goddess of the turquoise. The ingenious mine foreman carved inscriptions for his fellow workers which said such things as: "For favor, a votive offering to Ba'lat." Such perhaps is the origin of the first purely alphabetical writing in the world.

Scholars believe that even the name which the Hebrews used for their God was borrowed from a foreign people. From the time of Moses many of the Hebrews called their God Yahweh. This name seems to have been originally the name of the god of the Kenites, a tribe living in Midian, south of the Dead Sea. Here Moses found refuge when he was forced to flee from Egypt, and here he married one of the Kenite women. He must have learned the name Yahweh from the Kenites, and when he returned to his people in Egypt he taught them that God's name was Yahweh.

When they wrote Yahweh's name, the Hebrews used only four consonants, because their alphabet, as we have seen, did not include vowels. The four consonants were J H V H. As "J" was pronounced like "Y" and "V" like "W" we usually write the four consonants: Y H W H. In Hebrew these four consonants are the famous Tetragrammaton and are written thus: יהוה. With no vowel sounds indicated it could not have been easy to learn to read ancient Hebrew, but everyone who could read at all surely knew that Y H W H was to be pronounced Yahweh. This name became so sacred that people did not dare speak it aloud for fear of sacrilege. In reading the scriptures they passed over Y H W H in silence and substituted ădōnāi or "Lord" in place of it.

About four hundred years ago a curious mingling of Y H W H or J H V H and *adonai* occurred. Christians made the mistake of attaching the vowels of *adonai* to the consonants J H V H and as a result of this they coined the artificial word Jehovah. Centuries of use have hallowed this splendid name and we now find it difficult to realize that its majestic syllables were unknown to the ancient Hebrews who, when they pronounced God's name at all, probably said "Yahweh."

What did the word "Yahweh" originally mean to the Hebrews? Possibly its meaning was derived from the verb "to be." This seems to be one aspect of the meaning of Yahweh in the well-known story of the burning bush in the third chapter of Exodus, when God revealed His name to Moses. But the recently deciphered Ras Shamra tablets throw new light on the derivation of Yahweh and indicate that it may come from the same root as the word "to speak."[1] The idea of God speaking to them runs like a golden thread through all the records of Israel's religion. Yahweh spoke to Moses out of the burning bush. After Moses had taught the Hebrews that Yahweh had chosen them to be His people, they always thought of Him as One who spoke to them. Their deepest concern was to hear His words and learn His will. Finally, there arose among them prophets through whom the Lord spoke to His people.

Fascinating as it is to discover in Hebrew life, thought, and literature the influences of foreign peoples, we shall not find in these the clue to the greatness of the Bible. The things Israel borrowed from Egypt and Babylonia, Canaan and Phoenicia were not what really mattered. Myths and laws, customs and skills, ways of thinking and ways of worshiping: all these were the common denominators of an ancient international civilization. To explain the uniqueness of the Bible we shall have to find what it was that Israel did not share with her neighbors, what it was that she alone possessed.

There was granted to Israel as to no other ancient people to love and serve and understand her God. Power, conquest, and art were the gifts other nations received. Israel was given spiritual things. Her great men were neither administrators and builders like the mighty Pharaohs, nor conquerors like the kings of Assyria, but prophets who spoke the words of God. Empire and wealth were not for Israel. Her true glory lay in her fellowship with God. This was deep and rich and enduring. Her high adventures, her bitter failures, her sorrows, her songs became factors in her growing understanding of God. The things she borrowed from others: Babylonian myths, Egyptian ideas, Canaanite ritual, all these she purified of their crude paganism and recreated afresh to the glory of God. She fashioned her literature out of the durable fabric of her religion and embroidered it with the brightly colored pattern of her life. In all the events of her history Israel saw the hand

---

[1] See Raymond A. Bowman, "Yahweh the Speaker," *Journal of Near Eastern Studies*, Vol. III, no. 1 (1944).

of God. History was to her "the mighty acts of the Lord." In words that live today she proclaimed her certainty that Israel belonged to Yahweh, the God of the whole world. She learned to know Him as a God of justice and love who requires righteousness of men. In this lay the splendor of Israel and her claim to greatness.

Israel learned these tremendous truths in the vanished centuries while she was writing the Old Testament. From its pages there seems to blow a wind from God, and on the wind we hear that ancient cry in which she proclaimed her faith:

> Hear, O Israel: The Lord our God is one Lord.
>
> DEUTERONOMY 6:4

The wind still brings us the voice of the Law and the voices of the prophets. We hear the command which still, after twenty-five centuries, demands our obedience:

> Thou shalt love thy neighbour as thyself.
>
> LEVITICUS 19:18

The prophets continue to challenge us with their question:

> What doth the Lord require of thee?
>
> MICAH 6:8

And we still humbly try to shape our lives by kindness, mercy, and justice.

The centuries have proved that Israel was endowed with extraordinary spiritual insight. The answers she found to many of life's problems remain valid answers, and the books in which she bequeathed us her heritage surpass all ancient literatures in moral and spiritual grandeur. Weighed on the scales, the Old Testament outbalances a pyramid, an alphabet, and countless ancient armies.

# 3

## The Oldest Writings in the Bible

### SONGS AND POETRY

W E shall not find the oldest writings of the Bible conveniently grouped together in the beginning of Genesis, for the editors of the Old Testament books were not interested in chronological development. The surviving remains of the earliest Hebrew literature are like fossils in a rock, imbedded in much later writings. Perhaps the very oldest fragment that has come down to us from the days of desert warfare and tribal struggles is Lamech's Boast. Lamech lived long before Moses and tradition states that he and Zillah were the parents of Tubalcain, the man who is said to have discovered the art of smelting metals. Perhaps when Lamech made his wild boast he was brandishing in his hand one of the first of those metal weapons which as time went on became more complex and cost mankind so much anguish. However this may be, Lamech's savage cry of revenge belongs to a very early period of Hebrew development.

> Adah and Zillah, hear my voice;
> Ye wives of Lamech, hearken unto my speech:
> For I have slain a man to [for] my wounding,
> And a young man to [for] my hurt.
> If Cain shall be avenged sevenfold,
> Truly Lamech seventy and sevenfold.
>
> GENESIS 4:23, 24

Before we reach the end of the Bible story, we shall read of One who learned this old song from the Scriptures in the village school at Nazareth and used its words to carry a far different meaning.

> Then came Peter to him, and said, Lord, how oft shall my brother sin against me, and I forgive him? till seven times? Jesus saith unto him, I say not unto thee, Until seven times: but, Until seventy times seven.                                        MATTHEW 18:21, 22

Between the unlimited revenge of Lamech and the unlimited forgiveness of Jesus lies the long road from savagery to the highest moral standards the world has ever known. The entire development of man's experience as recorded in the Bible is between these two extremes. Though it is disappointing to find that one of the oldest fragments in the Bible is the song of a swaggering desert chieftain with blood on his hands, nevertheless, Lamech provides us with a fixed starting point from which to measure progress. Though more than thirty centuries separate us from Lamech, we realize that even now there are Lamechs among us. Indeed, beneath its surface, we shall find the Old Testament to be an almost contemporary book. Humanity is still struggling to advance along the road from Lamech to Jesus.

Another literary fossil is Miriam's Song of Victory at the Red Sea. If the authorities who date the Exodus about 1200 B.C. are correct, this brief song must come from that time. The tribes in Egypt had escaped from bondage only to be pursued by Pharaoh's army. In panic the Hebrews fled on foot over the exposed sea or lake bottom. Thundering behind them came the Egyptian chariots. But the chariot wheels stuck in the moist, soft sand and the returning waters drowned the Egyptian army. As if by a miracle the Hebrews were saved. Miriam snatched up a timbrel and led a wildly cheering crowd of women in a dance of victory. As they danced they shouted:

> Sing ye to the Lord, for he hath triumphed gloriously;
> The horse and his rider hath he thrown into the sea.
>                                        EXODUS 15:21

This was a turning point in Israel's history. From then on

the Hebrews knew that Yahweh was their God and that they were His people. The moment of their great deliverance was the moment when their religion came alive. No one present could forget the excitement of the hour, and the song itself became a part of their faith in Yahweh's power to help them. When those who had been children on that day became grandfathers, they taught their grandchildren the words of the song. In this way the oldest hymn to God in the Old Testament was preserved. This brief song composed by Miriam rings up the curtain on Israel's religion and prepares for the first act at Mount Sinai when the tribes entered into a covenant with Yahweh and pledged their allegiance to the God who had delivered them.

When the Hebrews entered the Promised Land of Canaan, they found it inhabited by a people with a far higher civilization than their own. As we have seen, the Canaanites possessed a well-developed system of writing. They were farmers and merchants, scholars and soldiers. The Hebrews found that fortified cities blocked their invasion. Armies equipped with iron weapons fought against them. Horse-drawn chariots, ancestors of the modern tank, terrified the Hebrew infantry. It required daring to enter the struggle at all. Morale played a decisive part. The Hebrews, encouraged by their experience at the Red Sea and by the teachings of Moses, believed that their enemies were Yahweh's enemies and that He would fight for them. They constructed a wooden box called the Ark and in this they believed that the Lord was present. They carried the Ark into battle singing:

> Rise up, Lord, and let thine enemies be scattered;
> And let them that hate thee flee before thee.
>
> NUMBERS 10:35

When they brought the Ark back to their camp they chanted:

> Return, O Lord, unto the many thousands of Israel.
>
> NUMBERS 10:36

The invasion and conquest of Palestine was a prolonged struggle lasting possibly for several centuries. Though fighting continued during the period of the rulers called "Judges," the Hebrews began to settle down, building houses of mud or sun-dried brick like those of their Canaanite neighbors. They tilled the soil and planted crops. They engaged in simple manufacture and commerce. Except in the south where shepherds grazed their flocks on the Judean hills, the Hebrews exchanged the ways of desert nomads for the life of a settled people. Warfare, however, constantly interrupted their lives. One episode in the wars against the Canaanites is celebrated in the great Ode of Deborah. Though this Ode must have been composed in the troubled years between 1200 and 1000 B.C., it is one of the finest songs in Hebrew literature.

> Hear, O ye kings;
> Give ear, O ye princes;
> I, even I, will sing unto the Lord;
> I will sing praise to the Lord God of Israel.
>
> JUDGES 5:3

With this mighty overture proclaiming Israel's faith in her God the keynote for the action is sounded and the story begins. It tells how the Lord who dwelt in Mount Seir marched forth to battle for His people. They were threatened by Canaanite armies which held the countryside in terror. Highways were deserted and caravans crept along hidden paths. The tribes were roused for battle, and those living near the plain of Esdraelon joined the army of Israel. We notice that the more remote tribes of Reuben, Gilead, Dan, and Asher felt safe in their isolation and remained at home. Israel was far from being a united nation at this time.

Ranged against the Israelites was the Canaanite army led by Sisera. At Megiddo they fought a battle in which, according to the Ode, more than Israelites fought against the Canaanites.

> They fought from heaven;
> The stars in their courses fought against Sisera.
>
> JUDGES 5:20

A sudden rain storm swelled the river Kishon into a raging torrent, and Sisera's chariots and horsemen became mired. Seeing the battle going against him, Sisera fled and sought refuge in the tent of a Kenite woman named Jael. She received him with desert hospitality, but in the night she drove a tent peg through his head.

Far away in Sisera's palace his mother anxiously watched through her latticed window for her son's return.

> Why is his chariot so long in coming?
> Why tarry the wheels of his chariots?
>
> JUDGES 5:28

Her ladies replied that Sisera delayed in order to divide the spoils of war. The booty would include rich garments, and the ladies took pleasure in imagining the bright dyes and rich embroideries. But Sisera's chariot never came, for Sisera lay dead at Jael's feet.

This superb paean of triumph ends on a note of confidence that all Yahweh's enemies will perish like Sisera. The author ascribed his poem to Deborah, one of the leaders in the struggle, but we believe it to be the work of some great but unknown poet who, with consummate literary skill, portrayed the life, the battles, and the warlike faith of those far-off days.

A century or so later Saul, Israel's first king, was defeated in battle. The battlefield was at Mount Gilboa and the enemy was the Philistines, those inhabitants of the seacoast who bequeathed their name to Palestine. When Saul learned that his son Jonathan was dead and that the battle had gone against him, he died, like Roland of a later day, by falling on his own sword. News of the calamity reached David and he poured out his grief in a noble lament.

> The beauty of Israel is slain upon thy high places:
> How are the mighty fallen! . . .
> Saul and Jonathan were lovely and pleasant in their lives,
> And in their death they were not divided:
> They were swifter than eagles,
> They were stronger than lions.
> Ye daughters of Israel, weep over Saul . . .
> How are the mighty fallen,
> And the weapons of war perished!
>
> II SAMUEL 1:19-27

If this is a genuine poem by David it is one of the few

ancient Hebrew writings to which we can attach a definite name and date. Saul died in 1013 B.C. and the elegy must have been composed under the shadow of that shocking disaster.

Other ancient fragments scattered through the Old Testament books are: the Blessing of Noah, the Song of the Well, Joshua's Command to the Sun and Moon, some of the ancient laws, and a number of old riddles. All these fragments must have circulated orally for many years and have been recited around campfires and at city gates until their form was polished and their rhythm became perfect.

The next step in their preservation was taken when someone collected these popular songs and sayings and wrote them in a book. This is not merely a theory, for there is definite evidence in the Bible that the Hebrews had at least two old anthologies of poetry and song. One was entitled the Book of Jasher. We are fairly certain that it contained David's elegy, for the title of the book is mentioned just before the opening line of the elegy. Joshua's command to the sun and moon to stand still also came from this anthology as we learn from the question:

> Is not this written in the book of Jasher?
>
> JOSHUA 10:13

The second anthology, called the Book of the Wars of the Lord, doubtless contained Miriam's Song and the Ode of Deborah. Thanks to these two anthologies, we now possess examples of the beginnings of a great national literature. What became of the two books we do not know. Long ago all copies of them must have perished, perhaps in the burning of some ancient city. But before these two collections disappeared Lamech's Boast and Miriam's Song, Deborah's superb Ode and David's moving Lament, the Incantations to the Ark, and similar ancient verses had been copied in new volumes and thus saved from the oblivion that swept away all other pieces of early Hebrew literature. In these fossil remains we see the Hebrews learning to express their deepest feelings. In these songs we hear, as it were, the orchestra tuning up for the symphony which is to follow.

## 4

# The Father of History

## THE FOUNDING OF THE KINGDOM

THE Greek historian Herodotus who lived about 500 B.C.
is usually called the Father of History, for the writing of
history is thought to have begun with him. The title, however, rightly belongs to another man. He lived in Jerusalem
during the reigns of David and Solomon, about 1000 B.C., five
hundred years before Herodotus. It was only recently that
scholars discovered the true father of history, because the book
he wrote suffered a strange fate. It remained in plain sight
throughout the centuries, but people who read it did not realize what they were reading. Many of us have read I and II
Samuel without knowing that some of its chapters are from
the oldest history book in the world.

In studying I and II Samuel scholars noticed a curious thing:
They found two accounts of Saul being made king.[1] They saw
that David was twice introduced to Saul.[2] They read two
similar stories of how David spared Saul's life.[3] To their
amazement they read in one chapter how David killed Goliath
and in another chapter how Elhanan killed him also.[4] Now
Goliath was certainly not killed twice!

---

[1] I Sam. 10:17-24; 11:15.
[2] I Sam. 16:14-23; 17:55-58.
[3] I Sam. 24:3-7; 26:5-12.
[4] I Sam. 17; II Sam. 21:19.

"Surely," they said, "these must be clues showing that the Books of Samuel are made up of two separate narratives written by two different authors." Thereupon the scholars became detectives and searched in the text of Samuel for further evidence of two authors. They found two widely different styles and vocabularies and points of view, and it was not long before they disentangled the two or more strands woven together to form the Books of Samuel. The oldest of the strands they found to be an ancient narrative telling the story of the founding of the Hebrew kingdom. It began with the Philistine war which threatened Israel's existence. In the midst of this danger Saul became king and succeeded in uniting the tribes of Israel against the Philistines. Though he was defeated at Mount Gilboa and died there, David succeeded him as king, freeing Israel from Philistine domination and establishing his capital at the mountain fortress of Jerusalem. The central part of the narrative[5] tells of the chief events of David's reign and by itself forms a biography of Israel's most popular king.

Once the old narrative embedded in the Books of Samuel had been discovered, the search for its author began. Scholars were convinced that only an eyewitness could have written many of the stories which take us into the royal court itself and into David's presence. The question of authorship narrowed down to this: who in David's court could have written this book? In those days few but priests were able to write. The two priests who were most often with David were Abiathar and Ahimaaz, and either may have been the author. Today the majority of scholars favor the theory that Abiathar was the author. One of his ancestors was Eli, the old priest of Shiloh, whose voice the child Samuel once thought he heard in the night. Abiathar's father was probably Ahijah, the high priest in Saul's reign. Thus Abiathar came from a family closely associated with the beginnings of the Hebrew monarchy. Abiathar himself became David's priest and loyal friend while David was an outlaw living in the cave at Adullam.

---

[5] II Sam. 9-20.

From I Samuel 22:20, where Abiathar enters David's story, the narrative is alive with the vividness of an eyewitness account. After David's death Abiathar supported Adonijah's claim to the throne rather than that of Solomon. Angered by this Solomon banished Abiathar from his court.

> And unto Abiathar the priest said the king, Get thee to Anathoth, unto thine own fields; for thou art worthy of death: but I will not at this time put thee to death, because thou barest the ark of the Lord God before David my father, and because thou hast been afflicted in all wherein my father was afflicted.
>
> I Kings 2:26

In the village of Anathoth the aging priest Abiathar probably spent the rest of his life, remembering his years of power at David's court and pondering the history of the Hebrew monarchy. It may be that his years of exile afforded him the necessary leisure in which to write The Founding of the Kingdom.

Abiathar's biography of the king is a portrait drawn from life. This is not a picture of an ideal king and a picturesque court, but an honest, objective record of David's reign. Abiathar shows us that David was often generous and chivalrous, but he also shows us that David was an Oriental monarch in a cruel age. The stories are not always pleasant to read, for they contain fratricide, adultery, murder, and treason. Abiathar gives us the harsh facts as he saw them, neither praising nor blaming the royal family.

From every point of view the old narrative in the Books of Samuel is a remarkable achievement. Long before it was written the Egyptians had inscribed accounts of their conquests on monuments, and the Hittites had kept annals of their empire, but all of these are little more than lists of events and in no sense history books to compare with The Founding of the Kingdom. As far as we know, this volume, written by a Hebrew priest around 1000 B.C., is the oldest book of history in the world. With no models to follow Abiathar, or whoever the author was, created the art of history writing.

Moreover, his book marks the emergence of Hebrew prose writing. So far, the oldest things we have found in the Bible have been poetry. The Founding of the Kingdom is our earliest example of the extensive use of Hebrew prose. We should expect its style to be crude, undeveloped, and poor in quality. This, however, is not the case. Abiathar was a gifted writer. His descriptions are sharp and clear, his characters move before our eyes and speak in lifelike words, his stories are dramatic. In Hebrew literature there is no finer style than his, and one must search long through the literature of mankind before finding anything to equal the vigor and simplicity of The Founding of the Kingdom. The oldest surviving example of Hebrew prose is also one of its best.

Even if he were not the father of history and the master of an incomparable prose, the author of The Founding of the Kingdom would deserve undying fame for preserving the story of Nathan. He must have been present one day in the palace when Nathan, the prophet, suddenly appeared and boldly denounced King David. Shortly before this, David, desiring to marry Bathsheba, had ordered her husband Uriah to be sent into a dangerous battle with the Ammonites so that he might be killed. For this crime Nathan denounced the King in the name of Yahweh saying:

> Wherefore hast thou despised the commandment of the Lord, to do evil in his sight? thou hast killed Uriah the Hittite with the sword, and hast taken his wife to be thy wife, and hast slain him with the sword of the children of Ammon.

II Samuel 12:9

We gasp as we read Nathan's daring words. One does not challenge an Oriental despot thus. David's anger flared up when Nathan exposed his crime and the attending guards must have reached for their swords, waiting for the inevitable order to seize the prophet and execute him. But for all his criminal acts David possessed greatness of character. In Nathan's impassioned words he heard a new note: the Lord will not tolerate crime. He requires upright conduct even of kings. This was a revolutionary idea in a day when Yahweh was worshiped by men with bloodstained hands.

David is faced with a turning point in man's spiritual history. Will he understand the challenge and accept it? The story moves swiftly forward to its simple and momentous climax.

And David said unto Nathan, I have sinned against the Lord.
II SAMUEL 12:13

The guards must have relaxed their grip on their weapons and the puzzled courtiers shrugged their shoulders. "Odd and not like David," they would have said. Abiathar, the priest and writer, could not forget this episode in which David acknowledged that his murder of Uriah was a sin against God. He dimly sensed its importance and decided to record it in the book he may even then have been writing. In this he showed himself to be gifted with the moral and spiritual insight for which Israel became famous. Long before Israel's great prophets began to preach righteousness, Abiathar recorded a moment in history when a king confessed his sin against Yahweh. It is to the glory of this ancient history by Abiathar that it contains this cry of David's which pierces the cruelty and injustice and moral blindness of antiquity and acknowledges that in the worship of God there must be righteousness.

## 5

# The Epic of Israel

## THE J NARRATIVE

SOMETIME between the years 950 and 850 B.C., a man sat in a quiet room in Jerusalem writing upon a roll of papyrus. His pen was cut from a reed and this he dipped from time to time in a small clay pot of ink. Now and again he laid down his pen and walked across the room to consult some old document stored in a jar on his shelf. The man was so absorbed in his work that he did not notice the hubbub rising from the narrow street outside. A caravan was passing loaded with articles manufactured in Egypt: bronze dishes, ivory furniture, and papyrus rolls like the one on which he wrote. The laden donkeys uttered their complaining brays, unaware that they were near the end of their long journey from the Nile. From the market place rose the sound of voices speaking many languages, for Jerusalem, which was the capital of the Kingdom of Judah, was also a center of world trade. A detachment of the palace guard marched down the street, their iron weapons clanking. A group of children began to sing one of the old victory songs of Israel. But the man writing on the papyrus roll paid no attention to these distractions. His whole being was focused on one idea and his pen raced to put that idea into words. As the sentences formed themselves on the long strip of papyrus and the stories began to take shape, the writer must have felt a glow of satisfaction. He saw his idea of history beginning to live in words. He was forging the scattered stories, the legends, and the memories of his race into an enduring record. How enduring that record was to prove would have astonished him. After nearly three thousand years we read his book today and find many of its stories as fresh and alive as though they had been written yesterday.

We do not know who the writer was, but from hints in his book we can piece together a number of facts about him. He was a man of Judah, living, no doubt, in Jerusalem. As his name for God was Jahveh (Yahweh), we call this writer the Jahvist or simply J. The book he wrote is known as the J Document, a title that fails to indicate the vividness and the drama of his superb Epic of Israel.

Though J's book no longer exists as a separate volume, it still survives and can be found and read in the books of Genesis, Exodus, Leviticus, Numbers, and Deuteronomy. It runs throughout the entire Pentateuch and probably continues on into Joshua and Judges, forming the oldest strata of continuous writing in the opening books of the Bible. Only the ancient fragments are older, and though The Founding of the Kingdom is a hundred or more years older, it is not in the Pentateuch. A table of contents was an unknown convenience in J's day, but we can make one for his book. Though we are uncertain about the extent of the J epic it probably contained these stories:

> The Creation of Man
> The Garden of Eden
> Cain and Abel
> Noah and His Ark
> Abraham and the Promise
> Isaac and Jacob
> Joseph's Adventures
> Moses and the Exodus
> The Invasion of Canaan
> Stories of the Judges

The table of contents shows at a glance the scope of the epic. Beginning with the creation of the earth J unfolded, against the vast panorama of world history, the story of Israel's rise and her triumph under Yahweh. Nothing like this had ever been done before.

J did not invent the stories that served to carry his long history forward. The plan is his and the masterful telling of the stories, the grace and charm of the narrative are due to his literary genius, but the stories themselves he borrowed. They were already centuries old when he began to write. Like Shakespeare who, it is said, did not invent his plots but took them from old chronicles and early plays, so J took the materials for his history from the songs and legends of his people. Some, no doubt, came from written documents like the Book of Jasher or the Book of the Wars of the Lord, others were legends his grandfather had told him, still others he had heard as a boy standing motionless and wide-eyed in the crowd gathered at the city gate to listen to a storyteller. Not a few were stories taken from Israel's Babylonian and Egyptian heritage. Through the years J collected his material which, like a heap of colored beads, remained separate and miscellaneous until J found the thread upon which to string each one carefully and in order.

The thread was his idea, or perhaps we would call it his faith. He saw Yahweh's hand at work in the affairs of men shaping them according to a divine plan. History was to him the working out of Yahweh's will for Israel. In all that happened, in Abraham's migrations, in Joseph's sojourn in Egypt, in the rescue of the infant Moses from death, J saw Yahweh behind the events, guiding them according to His purposes. It was this magnificent conception which gave form and unity to the Epic of Israel. It accomplished the author's purpose of teaching men that Yahweh was the God of Israel. The first readers of the epic surely caught J's vision of Israel marching forward through the centuries toward a glorious destiny under the banner of God.

The unknown author wrote with consummate skill and he must be classed with Abiathar as a master of Hebrew prose. Who can forget the characters he drew? There was dignified Abraham, ambitious Jacob, cunning Esau, brilliant Joseph, inspired Moses. After reading about these people they become as real to us as people we actually know. If we give J our whole attention and imagination he can paint for us scenes, like those of women drawing water at the well, which are as vivid as a motion picture. He was a prince among storytellers. His plots move swiftly, the details are concrete, and the dialogue is pointed and dramatic. Even in translation J's style is both noble and simple, majestic and yet direct. It is no wonder that stories from the Epic of Israel have captivated people for nearly three thousand years.

## 6

## A Religious History of Israel

### THE E NARRATIVE

TWO hundred years after the father of history wrote The Founding of the Kingdom and a hundred years or more after J completed his Epic of Israel, another literary genius appeared. He lived about 750 B.C. after the United Kingdom of Saul, David, and Solomon had been split into North and South. J belonged to the tribe of Judah which became part of the Southern Kingdom, but the new writer lived in the Northern Kingdom and belonged to the tribe of Ephraim. Bethel instead of Jerusalem was his city, and there is every reason to believe that he was one of the priests who officiated in Bethel's Temple.

On feast days he used to watch the crowds pouring into the Temple. He often took part in the ceremonies, chanting the words of the ritual as smoke ascended from the burning sacrifice upon the altar. Ever since the days of Abraham his people had burned sacrifices to their God Elohim upon such altars. They believed this pleased Elohim, for had He not greatly favored Israel throughout the centuries?

Dozens of legends and stories of the old days were stored in the priest's memory. Some he had learned from his mother; others he had studied in ancient books when he was preparing to be a priest. He knew, for instance, that Abraham pitched his tent at Bethel near where the Temple now stood, and here also Jacob dreamed his dream of the angels of God ascending and descending. He liked to think of Joseph, the young man who made good in that far-off land to the south where a great river flowed. In all these stories the priest of Bethel saw proof that Elohim had been with His people since the dawn of history, guiding them, protecting them, and giving them a country for their inheritance. He had made of them a strong nation. Now King Jeroboam II sat upon the throne of Israel; the Temple was filled with worshipers; the future seemed secure. Pride in his people and gratitude to Elohim filled the heart of the priest of Bethel and he longed to share his patriotism and his faith with his fellow Israelites. He wanted others to see in history the evidence of Elohim's dealings with His people. Accordingly, he set out to write a Religious History of Israel.

As we do not know this priest's name, we take the initial letter of his word for God, Elohim, and of his tribe, Ephraim, and call this writer E and his Religious History of Israel the E Document.

E's history is really a serial story in many parts, beginning with the Abraham legends and probably ending with the history of King Saul. In his long story, as in the Epic of Israel, the centuries come and go, and with them the patriarchs, Moses, the Judges, and Saul, but Elohim or Yahweh remains the central figure, dominating the history of Israel and giving it meaning.

There are two masterpieces in E's history. One is the story of the sacrifice of Isaac, where the author makes us see the little boy, the bundle of wood, the knife, and the ram caught in the thicket, and makes us feel sympathy for Abraham, the brokenhearted father. The second masterpiece is the Joseph story. This reaches its climax when Joseph, then the most powerful official in Egypt, tells the brothers who had once sold him into slavery who he really is. It is a tense moment. The brothers, remembering their treatment of Joseph years before, are terrified, for now Joseph has them completely in his power. Here are the words E puts in Joseph's mouth:

Now therefore be not grieved, nor angry with yourselves, that ye sold me hither: for God did send me before you to preserve life . . . So now it was not you that sent me hither, but God . . . God hath made me lord of all Egypt.

GENESIS 45:5, 8, 9

There speaks the priest of Bethel who saw in everything that happened to the people of Israel the guiding hand of God.

E's Religious History of Israel was a splendid achievement, completed while the Northern Kingdom of Israel still enjoyed prosperity and power and the future seemed assured. Even then, an uncouth prophet was preaching in the streets of Bethel, warning Israel of her approaching doom. But men did not heed this prophet named Amos. They preferred to read of the triumphs of their ancestors in the Religious History of Israel and to offer the traditional sacrifices at Bethel's altars. Amos' cry for righteousness fell on unheeding ears. Meanwhile, beyond the horizon a cloud was gathering and, as Amos had predicted, the storm broke. The Kingdom of Israel was attacked by the mighty Assyrian army and in 722 B.C. it was conquered and annexed to the Empire of Assyria. Towns were pillaged and temples were burned; many of the Israelites were carried away into captivity and their homes were given to strangers. From that time on, the land that had been Israel's became a subject province of Assyria inhabited by a mixed population.

When this disaster overwhelmed North Israel and many ancient documents were lost or destroyed, somehow E's Religious History of Israel managed to survive. Perhaps a trader discovered it in the library of Bethel's ruined Temple. Thinking he might be able to sell it to a learned man in Jerusalem, he may have packed it in one of his bales and brought it by caravan to Jerusalem.

There the E Document must have been eagerly read by the priests of Judah who found many of its stories of the patriarchs, Moses, and the Judges similar to the stories in their own Epic of Israel. But the priests noticed that some of the stories were slightly different from their versions. The style and point of view of the two histories were different, as was perhaps only to be expected in works written a hundred or more years apart. In spite of all their differences, it was plain that both J and E worshiped the same God and saw His hand guiding Israel. The priests in Jerusalem treasured the old E roll and made copies of it. Perhaps they required all candidates for the priesthood to study it and, no doubt, professors lectured on the two histories, noting such differences as these:

| J | E |
|---|---|
| THE EPIC OF ISRAEL | THE RELIGIOUS HISTORY OF ISRAEL |
| Yahweh (Jahveh) | Elohim |
| Judean traditions | Ephraim (northern) traditions |
| Patriotic and national | Priestly point of view |
| Dramatic | Logical and systematic |
| Crude stories | More polished and refined stories |
| Yahweh appears in person | Elohim reveals himself through dreams and angels |
| Grandeur of style | Elaborate style |
| Simple | Detailed |
| Example of J: | The way E writes of the same incident: |
| And the Lord said unto Jacob, Return unto the land of thy fathers, and to thy kindred; and I will be with thee. | And the angel of God spake unto me in a dream, saying, Jacob: and I said, Here am I. And he said . . . I am the God of Bethel, |
| GENESIS 31:3 | where thou anointedst the pillar, and where thou vowedst a vow unto me: now arise, get thee out from this land, and return unto the land of thy kindred. |
| | GENESIS 31:11-13 |

For many years the priests struggled with the difficulty of having two histories of Israel, until someone suggested that it would be more convenient to have the J Document and the E Document combined in a single roll. The man who prepared the new edition in which J and E were joined did a skillful piece of work. Sometimes he chose a story from one document, probably discarding a parallel one from the other. Again he gave the same story from both J and E side by side. He even wove together a story from J and the same one from E in such a way that they formed a single narrative.

Here is an example of how the editor dovetailed two slightly different stories of the same event. Many people read this story without noticing the conflicting details. The portions in roman letters are J's story and, when read by themselves, form a complete account of how Joseph was sold by his brothers to Ishmaelites traveling to Egypt. E's narrative is based on different traditions in which Reuben protects Joseph and Midianites steal him from a pit. It is here printed in italics.

And Joseph went after his brethren, and found them in Dothan. And when they saw him afar off, even before he came near unto them, they conspired against him to slay him. *And they said one to another, Behold, this dreamer cometh. Come now therefore, and let us slay him, and cast him into some pit, and we will say, Some evil beast hath devoured him: and we shall see what will become of his dreams.* And Reuben[1] heard it, and he delivered him out of their hands; and said, Let us not kill him. *And Reuben said unto them, Shed no blood, but cast him into this pit that is in the wilderness, and lay no hand upon him; that he might rid him out of their hands, to deliver him to his father again.*

And it came to pass, when Joseph was come unto his brethren, that they stript Joseph out of his coat, his coat of many colours that was on him; *and they took him, and cast him into a pit: and the pit was empty, there was no water in it.* And they sat down to eat bread: and they lifted up their eyes and looked, and, behold, a company of Ishmeelites came from Gilead with their camels bearing spicery and balm and myrrh, going to carry it down to Egypt. And Judah said unto his brethren, What profit is it if we slay our brother, and conceal his blood? Come, and let us sell him to the Ishmeelites, and let not our hand be upon him; for he is our brother and our flesh. And his brethren were content. *Then there passed by Midianites merchantmen; and they drew and lifted up Joseph out of the pit,* and sold Joseph to the Ishmeelites for twenty pieces of silver: and they brought Joseph into Egypt.

*And Reuben returned unto the pit; and, behold, Joseph was not in*

---

[1] This should probably be Judah. In dovetailing the two accounts the word Judah, which originally stood here, was changed to the Reuben of our present versions.

*the pit; and he rent his clothes. And he returned unto his brethren, and said, The child is not; and I, whither shall I go?* And they took Joseph's coat, and killed a kid of the goats, and dipped the coat in the blood; and they sent the coat of many colors, and they brought it to their father; and said, This we have found: know now whether it be thy son's coat or no. And he knew it, and said, It is my son's coat; an evil beast hath devoured him; Joseph is without doubt rent in pieces. And Jacob rent his clothes, and put sackcloth upon his loins, and mourned for his son many days. . . . Thus his father wept for him. *And the Midianites sold him into Egypt unto Potiphar, an officer of Pharaoh's, and captain of the guard.*

Genesis 37:17-36

By 650 B.C. there was a new history of Israel built with bricks from the J Document, written sometime between 950 and 850 B.C., and from the E Document of about 750 B.C. How we wish we now had the two original rolls so that we might prove our theories! The J E edition of Israel's history long remained popular, so popular, indeed, that priests and writers continued to copy and revise it, adding new chapters whenever they saw fit. In spite of countless editors and copyists whose work obscured the old outlines, we believe that today we can trace the oldest strata of continuous writing in the books from Genesis to Samuel and that this is the J E history of Israel. Of the other adventures that befell this history we shall speak in a later chapter. But now we shall turn from the writing of history to the writing of prophecy.

# 7

## The First Book of Prophecy

### AMOS

IT was a feast day in Bethel and the city streets were filled with people on their way to the Temple to offer sacrifices. The King of Israel, Jeroboam II, was expected to be present, and Amaziah, the high priest, would officiate. Perhaps the historian whom we call E rolled up his writing on that day to take his place with the other priests in the elaborate ritual accompanying the feasts and burnt offerings. The time, as nearly as we can determine it, was the year 760 B.C.

On almost every face in the crowd there was a smile of satisfaction. Never had Israel been so powerful among the nations as she was during these "boom" years. Rich men rubbed shoulders with haughty officials. Ladies of fashion who had just risen from their ivory couches paraded down the street in all their silk finery. Sounds of feasting, drinking, and merrymaking arose from all sides. Only occasionally was there a pitiful sight to be seen. Here was a man weeping because he must sell his daughter into slavery in order to provide food for his family. There were children whose pale faces showed evidences of hunger and wretchedness. All was not well in Israel. False weights were used in the market place. Injustice presided over the courts of law, and a person in trouble could find no kindness. Serious wrongs existed in Israel and there were dishonesty and cruelty everywhere. But few people on that feast day noticed injustice and wretchedness. They were intent on winning Yahweh's favor, and they believed this could be done by offering Him burnt sacrifices. So far as we know, the men and women of Israel were blind to the importance of upright, honest living. No voice had yet proclaimed to them that sacrifices cannot buy Yahweh's favor.

As the prosperous men and women of Bethel swept along the street toward the Temple, they may have noticed a stranger standing on a corner watching them with keen, unsmiling eyes. He was evidently a shepherd lately come to town from the hills of Judah, for he wore a sheepskin garment and in his strong, toil-stained hands he carried a shepherd's staff.

"A country yokel!" sneered one of the passers-by, little knowing that here was a man destined to be remembered for centuries as one of the truly great men, not only of Israel, but of all humanity.

The stranger in Bethel on that feast day in 760 B.C. was Amos. There was a burden on his mind. Yahweh had spoken to him and, true prophet that he was, Amos felt impelled to deliver His message.

He began to speak to a little group of curious people gathered close about him to hear. His first words created a sensation.

> Thus saith the Lord; For three transgressions of Damascus, and for four, I will not turn away the punishment thereof.
>
> AMOS 1:3

"Good!" shouted the people.

They were delighted to hear that Yahweh was angry with their old enemy Damascus. Few of them noticed the full implication of the prophecy they cheered so heartily. If Yahweh announced that He would punish Damascus, He must be a god whose power extended not only over Israel but over other nations as well. In the excitement of cheering Amos, the crowd did not realize that his words were to cause a revolution in their theology. The old idea of Yahweh as Israel's own, exclusive, national God could no longer survive after Amos began to teach that Yahweh was supreme over all nations.

The crowd pressed closer to listen to the new soothsayer or prophet, for they liked his opening words. Surely he would go on to tell them other things they enjoyed hearing. But Amos was a prophet of quite another sort.

The crowd applauded when Amos declared Yahweh's anger against the children of Ammon for their atrocities. They agreed that Yahweh should be angry against Moab for burning "the bones of the king of Edom into lime." But a roar of protest greeted the climax of Amos' prophecy:

> Thus saith the Lord; For three transgressions of *Israel,* and for four, I will not turn away the punishment thereof.
>
> AMOS 2:6

People were aghast. How could Yahweh punish His own people Israel? What had they done to make Him angry? Surely they had not failed to offer sacrifices. There had never been such a vast crowd in Bethel as was here today to please Yahweh with offerings. The shouts of disapproval died down as men and women strained to hear why their God was angry with them. In the hush Amos thundered the Lord's denunciation:

> Because they sold the righteous for silver, and the poor for a pair of shoes.
>
> AMOS 2:6

Some of the bystanders merely laughed. It was ridiculous to suppose that Yahweh cared about such trifling matters as foreclosing a mortgage and selling a man into slavery. What if this involved a little cheating and a bribe or two to the judge? Everyone did these things. If there was anything wrong in them and Yahweh was angry, surely the Temple sacrifices would placate Him.

The crowd shifted away from the prophet who said such uncomfortable things, but Amos continued to preach wherever men would listen to him. He tried to make them understand that Yahweh could not be bribed with any offering, for He was a righteous God. This idea, which is a commonplace today, was a strange, new doctrine then and men could not understand it. "Hear what the Lord says," pleaded Amos:

> I hate, I despise your feast days . . . Though ye offer me burnt offerings and your meat offerings, I will not accept them: neither will I regard the peace offerings of your fat beasts. Take thou away from me the noise of thy songs; for I will not hear the melody of thy viols.
>
> AMOS 5:21-23

Who ever heard of God not being pleased with all the elaborate ritual of their religion? The very idea was preposterous. From the crowd someone shouted: "Well, what does Yahweh want, then?" Amos answered in words Yahweh had given him:

> Let judgment run down as waters, and righteousness as a mighty stream.
>
> AMOS 5:24

Amos left no doubt in any mind that it was righteousness, not ritual, which the Lord wanted.

> Seek good, and not evil, that ye may live; and so the Lord, the God of hosts, shall be with you, as ye have spoken. Hate the evil, and love the good, and establish judgment in the gate.
>
> AMOS 5:14, 15

Amos also made it perfectly clear that Yahweh was Lord of all nations:

> Are ye not as children of the Ethiopians unto me, O children of Israel? saith the Lord.
>
> AMOS 9:7

The city of Bethel was now in a turmoil. Men argued shrilly about Amos in the market place, and on every hand his revolutionary phrases were repeated. Amaziah, the high priest, was troubled when he saw that attendance at the sacrifices was falling off. It began to look as though men were taking the new teaching seriously. To Amaziah, Amos' ideas were theologically unsound and his preaching a sacrilege. The situation was getting out of hand. With his own ears Amaziah heard Amos say:

> The sanctuaries of Israel shall be laid waste; and I will rise against the house of Jeroboam with the sword.
>
> AMOS 7:9

The high priest knew that the moment had come to act. This was even worse than sacrilege, it was sedition and the King must stop it. There was no telling what would happen if Amos convinced people that Yahweh had deserted Israel's king.

After sending an urgent warning to King Jeroboam, Amaziah took matters into his own hands. The priest confronted the prophet. He forbade Amos to prophesy in Bethel and rudely ordered him to go home to Judah. Amos calmly defended himself declaring that his authority to prophesy came from the Lord Himself.

> And the Lord took me as I followed the flock, and the Lord said unto me, Go, prophesy unto my people Israel. Now therefore hear thou the word of the Lord.
>
> AMOS 7:15, 16

When he had delivered the Lord's messages in Bethel, Amos set out for his home in Tekoa, a mountaintop village lying a day's journey to the south. There he dictated to one of his followers the prophecies he had spoken in Israel. On all sides the barren Judean hills stretched toward the horizon and only the bleating of sheep broke the silence. In a rude mud hut the scribe bent over his scroll and wrote swiftly to keep up with the pace of Amos' dictation. There was rhythm and form and tremendous power in the prophecies. They abounded in judgments on national and international affairs and they were alive with comments on city life and country ways. The scribe knew that Amos was one of the great men of the time, but he probably never fully realized that his roll of prophecy would create a new epoch in history and literature and religion.

The Book of Amos was the first Old Testament book to be completed. Abiathar's history and the J Document are older, but in our Bible these are no longer separate books. Amos was the first book of prophecy and it ushered in the prophetic movement of the eighth century B.C. which established a high-water mark in spiritual history. Hosea, Micah, and Isaiah were to follow Amos in teaching that God is righteous and that He demands righteousness of men.

When the scribe finished writing the book, he added at the beginning of the scroll a title and a date:

> The words of Amos, who was among the herdmen of Tekoa, which he saw concerning Israel in the days of Uzziah king of Judah, and in the days of Jeroboam the son of Joash king of Israel.
>
> Amos 1:1

In order to make the date more precise a later scribe added: "two years before the earthquake," little dreaming that in a far-distant day when these prophecies would still be read, men would pause and ask: What earthquake?

Amos' prophecies survived and were treasured. His book was studied and copied and edited again and again. Sometimes the notes a scholar jotted down in the margin were incorporated in the text of the next edition. Perhaps the oracles against Tyre and Edom (Amos 1:9-12) were added in this way. It must have been after Jerusalem fell in 586 B.C. and the Hebrews went to Babylonia as exiles that someone added the sentences now found at the end of the book:

> And I will bring again the captivity of my people of Israel, and they shall build the waste cities.
>
> Amos 9:14

In the main the book is believed primarily to contain the prophecies of Amos himself, whose words after twenty-seven centuries still have meaning for us in our personal lives, our social dealings, and our international affairs.

## 8

# The Golden Age of Prophecy

## HOSEA, ISAIAH, MICAH

AMOS did not stand alone. With him there dawned in
Israel an age of prophecy made glorious by Hosea, Isaiah,
and Micah. To these four spokesmen of the Lord the eighth
century was far from being a golden age. The minds of the
prophets were attuned to the holiness and righteousness and
love of God; no wonder that they saw the evils of their day as
a dark stain against that holiness. Their century was sick and
they knew of no remedy effective enough to cure it but upright
living and true worship. The kingdoms of Israel and Judah had
by their sins offended the righteousness of Yahweh, and destruction surely awaited them unless the prophets could open men's
eyes and make them see their danger and act. The prophets
threw themselves into their unpopular task of reproof and warning. Prophecy is not "history written beforehand" and the
prophets were not cheap soothsayers and fortunetellers. Nor
were they dreamy mystics enjoying a beautiful vision. Rather,
they were practical men fired with a vision of God's reality and
righteousness and inspired to put that vision into words.

Their mission was heartbreakingly difficult. "Thus saith the
Lord" they declared to the deaf and unheeding ears of Israel.
Israel had her eye upon the grim reality of tribute money, for-

eign envoys, Egyptian chariots, and Assyrian armies. She hardly
listened when Isaiah said:

> Now the Egyptians are men, and not God;
> And their horses flesh, and not spirit.
>
> ISAIAH 31:3

Would Israel never see that the mightiest reality in the world
is God and that men and nations only break themselves when
they oppose God's will?

As the great eighth-century prophets utter "Woe" and "Hear
ye" we seem to be listening to the thunder of approaching doom.
In our day the social injustices and the political and international catastrophes of their century have faded into history
so that we often fail to understand exactly what they mean by
their references to obscure issues. But the main points of their
message remain clear and valid today, long after doom overtook
both the Northern and the Southern kingdoms. The centuries
have tested the quality of the prophets' inspiration and accorded
to these four men, and to the prophets who followed them, a
supreme place in human history. With them there began to
shine upon Israel a glory and a splendor that raised her life
above that of her ancient neighbors and endowed her literature
and her religion with deathless values.

Among the crowd in the streets of Bethel where Amos first
spoke his prophecies there may have been one young man who
was profoundly moved by what he heard. As he listened he
forgot the jeers of the crowd and the uncouth appearance of
the prophet, for the words of Amos stirred his mind and heart
and kindled a strange new spirit within him. When the voice of
Amos ceased, the succession of the prophets passed to the young
man who had perhaps listened to him in the crowd. The young
man was Hosea, son of Beeri. Hosea might well have become
merely a follower of Amos, content to repeat the prophet's teaching about the justice of God and to work for the social reforms
this teaching demanded. But an even greater destiny than this
awaited Hosea. Beside the idea of the justice of God, Israel's

religion needed a second pillar to support it. God was austere and terrible, if men knew only His justice. No one had yet seen deeply enough into God's nature to perceive His love. To Hosea it was granted to discover this profound truth. Amos and Hosea thus became the architects of the two chief pillars of prophetic religion: the justice and the love of God.

All that we know of Hosea comes from the one short book bearing his name and written by him or by an immediate follower. To the casual reader the book is disappointing, for we understand only occasional phrases, and its references to ancient events puzzle us. In much the same way references to today's events will puzzle someone in the year A.D. 4600 who may happen to read one of our newspapers! The translators have had a difficult time with Hosea's book, for its text has suffered from poor transmission and frequent editorial changes. Moreover, Hosea's ideas are not preserved in their logical order, but are set down in short, often disjointed, sentences. They give the impression of a chaotic collection of rough notes jotted down by one of Hosea's followers and never worked up later into a finished literary whole. But Hosea's contribution to religion is so important that his book has received careful study.

Something about Hosea the man himself can be discovered from his book. He was a native of the Northern Kingdom of Israel and his intimate knowledge of priestly life and the religious situation of his day indicate that he may have been a priest. He was undoubtedly a well-educated man, thoroughly acquainted with the political and international affairs of the years 745 to 735 B.C. and wise enough to make sound judgments upon them. All this seems to show that Hosea was a city man, but his book abounds in country sights and events. He spoke of such things as the lion, the panther, threshing, sowing, nettles, the early and the latter rain, and the swollen country brooks. His mission left him no time to develop these fleeting images, but, had he not been a prophet, Hosea's seeing and understanding eye and his deeply-feeling heart would surely have made him a poet.

Concerning the events of his outward life this book contains only one story, that of his marriage to Gomer, narrated in the first and third chapters. Gomer is described as an immoral woman, and we read that after she had left his home and taken other lovers Hosea bought her back for the price of a common slave. As many factors of this story are puzzling, some people think it may not be the actual history of the prophet's tragic marriage, but a story Hosea told as a parable to illustrate the heart of his message. We shall, perhaps, never know whether or not Hosea's great prophetic teaching rose out of some bitter tragedy such as Gomer's unfaithfulness to him; but many scholars believe that personal suffering was the cost of Hosea's tremendous message.

Hosea took the idea of the marriage relationship to describe the relationship of Yahweh to His people Israel. Hosea said that God was like a loving husband and Israel was His wife. In an age when men cringed before Yahweh and feared His anger, this was a new and startling teaching. People believed their relation to God was little better than that of a slave bowing and trembling before a powerful, Oriental despot. This new teaching that they, as members of Israel, were loved by God as a wife is loved by her husband was a strange new doctrine. But what of Israel, the wife? Like Gomer, Israel had been unfaithful, for she had adopted the religious practices of other nations and worshiped strange gods. The state of Israel's political disorders and her dangerous international situation were all, Hosea said, evidences of her unfaithfulness to the God who loved her.

Most of Hosea's utterances are concerned with Israel's unfaithfulness, which lies like a dark shadow on every page of this book. But the very darkness of the shadow implies an intense brightness on the other side. There would have been no shadow at all if Hosea had not seen on the other side of Israel's faithlessness the radiance of the love of God.

At times the radiance breaks through, as in these words of

tenderness in which Hosea pictured God as the Father of Ephraim or Israel:

> When Israel was a child, then I loved him, and called my son out of Egypt . . . I taught Ephraim also to go [walk], taking them by their arms: but they knew not that I healed them. I drew them . . . with bands of love: and I was to them as they that take off the yoke on their jaws, and I laid meat unto them . . . How shall I give thee up, Ephraim? how shall I deliver thee, Israel? . . . I will not execute the fierceness of mine anger, I will not return to destroy Ephraim: for I am God, and not man; the Holy One in the midst of thee.
>
> HOSEA 11:1, 3, 4, 8, 9

Hosea's influence on the prophets who followed him was immense. We can trace his ideas in Isaiah, Jeremiah, and Ezekiel. Centuries later Hosea's teachings were so well known that Jesus chided [1] the Pharisees for not understanding the meaning of Hosea's great sentence:

> For I desired mercy, and not sacrifice; and the knowledge of God more than burnt offerings.
>
> HOSEA 6:6

"Mercy" here includes the ideas of goodness, kindness, and love. By "the knowledge of God" Hosea meant understanding of God's love and a loving relationship to Him. Here, then, in this eighth-century prophet we see the beginning of that idea of God's love and fatherly care which, though strange and new to the ancient Israelites, has now become a cornerstone of faith to Christians who pray, "Our Father Who art in heaven."

The third great prophet of the eighth century was Isaiah, who was born about 760 B.C. while the streets of Bethel still echoed with the prophecies of his fellow countryman Amos. Both prophets were men of the Southern Kingdom of Judah, but they belonged to different social groups. Amos was a shepherd of Tekoa, while Isaiah was an influential statesman of Jerusalem. Isaiah may even have been a member of the royal family, entitled by birth to the high position of royal counselor he held during

---

[1] See Matt. 9:13; 12:7.

the reigns of four kings. It was a period of international turmoil in which the little Kingdom of Judah stood in danger. Through all those dark years when kings grew fainthearted and officials plotted intrigue, Isaiah never deviated from his prophetic mission. He continued to preach the message God had given him, reminding men that their truest safety lay in establishing a right relationship with God.

"In the year king Uzziah died," which would have been about 740 B.C., Isaiah tells us that he received his call to be a prophet. The story in which he records this intense spiritual experience is an Old Testament classic. One day as he was worshiping in the Temple at Jerusalem, a vision of God enthroned in holiness and glory came to him and he cried out in terror that he, a sinful man, should thus behold his Lord.

> Woe is me! for I am undone; because I am a man of unclean lips . . . for mine eyes have seen the King, the Lord of hosts.
>
> ISAIAH 6:5

He saw flying toward him a seraphim bearing a live coal from the altar. With this the heavenly being touched Isaiah's lips as a sign of forgiveness. Then the voice of the Lord came to him saying: "Whom shall I send and who will go for us?"

Isaiah replied: "Here am I; send me." And the Lord said: "Go, and tell this people."

For about forty years Isaiah was the Lord's voice in Jerusalem performing his task with shining eloquence and high courage. Through all his prophecies echoes the song he heard the seraphim sing:

> Holy, holy, holy, is the Lord of hosts:
> The whole earth is full of his glory.
>
> ISAIAH 6:3

God is holy, Isaiah said, and He demands holiness of men. Like his predecessors Amos and Hosea, Isaiah preached about right living, which for him was part of the true worship of God. He drew up an indictment against Israel for her sins, charging her with cruel injustice, callous enjoyment of wealth, and rampant idol worship. With many a telling phrase he makes us see what life was like in those remote days. He felt that he was speaking for God when he said:

> Put away the evil of your doings from before mine eyes; cease to do evil; learn to do well; seek judgment, relieve the oppressed, judge the fatherless, plead for the widow.
>
> ISAIAH 1:16, 17

Though Amos had already proclaimed the Lord's sovereignty over the whole earth, men had not accepted the revolutionary doctrine. They feared the Assyrians were waging war, not only against them, but against their God. They trembled lest the Assyrian deities should overcome Yahweh. Isaiah tried to show his fellow countrymen that the empires of the earth are merely instruments in the Lord's hands. Assyrian armies could not wage war against Him: rather, it was He who used them as a rod to punish His own people. It was useless, Isaiah explained, for Israel to look to Egypt for help. There was nothing to be gained from foreign alliances. True safety lay in doing God's will and trusting in Him.

Probably the unique note in Isaiah's prophecies was his confidence in God which shines brilliantly against the dark perils of those years. On a day when Jerusalem was threatened with a siege, King Ahaz went out to inspect the city's water supply. The prophet met him "at the end of the conduit of the upper pool in the highway of the fuller's field." One can almost see the meeting of the two men, the King weighed down with fear, the prophet confident in God. Isaiah rebuked the King for his lack of faith, saying in words that ring down the ages:

> If ye will not believe, surely ye shall not be established.
>
> ISAIAH 7:9

Year by year Isaiah watched the Assyrian armies approaching nearer to Jerusalem, seizing Carchemish, Damascus, and Samaria on their way. But he continued to believe that the whole earth was the Lord's and he taught:

> For thus said the Lord God, the Holy One of Israel; In returning and rest shall ye be saved; in quietness and in confidence shall be your strength.
>
> ISAIAH 30:15

Tradition states that Isaiah died a martyr to his faith in the reign of the half-heathen king, Manasseh. Whether this is true or not, it seems certain that after his death his teachings were not forgotten, though at that time one would have searched in vain through Jerusalem for the book of his prophecies. Here and there some of his followers must have treasured a sheet of notes they had taken of his majestic speeches. In Isaiah 8:16 there is a hint that the prophet trained a group of disciples and had his prophecies written down for their instruction. Possibly one of the disciples possessed the original story of Isaiah's call to be a prophet written in his own hand. Of course this is all pure conjecture, but within the limits of possibility, nevertheless. No doubt during the evil days of King Manasseh faithful disciples worked in secret to record Isaiah's sermons. Before long there must have existed a series of little books, each about the length of Amos or Hosea, and each collected by one of Isaiah's followers. In time the books of this miniature library were brought together, edited, and published in one scroll which might well have been called: Collected Prophecies of Isaiah. Today scholars believe they can identify some of the original booklets which went into the making of the first edition of the Book of Isaiah.

This first edition of Isaiah was considerably shorter than our present book. In the first place, it lacked many of those pictures of the coming of a Messiah and of a happy future when God will be worshiped in all the earth. These shafts of sunlight were added later to the original work of Isaiah and are no less valuable to us than the words of the great eighth-century prophet. No doubt Isaiah himself would have proudly spoken such words as these for the Lord:

> They shall beat their swords into plowshares, and their spears into pruning hooks: nation shall not lift up sword against nation, neither shall they learn war any more.
>
> ISAIAH 2:4

> The people that walked in darkness have seen a great light . . . For unto us a child is born, unto us a son is given.
>
> ISAIAH 9:2, 6

Most scholars believe that the first edition of Isaiah consisted only in the chapters 1 to 40 of our present book. As the standard roll of antiquity was too long for Isaiah, scribes of a later day realized that they needed something to fill the space after the words: "For there shall be peace and truth in my days." They found what they could conveniently use in the prophecies of a sixth-century Hebrew prophet and poet. It is for this reason that a new voice begins to speak to us at the fortieth chapter of Isaiah. Our Book of Isaiah is thus an anthology of prophetic writing, fitly named for the great eighth-century prophet of Jerusalem, the friend of kings, the spokesman of God.

Whether or not Isaiah ever met his humble fellow countryman, Micah, we do not know. Both preached in Judah during the same period, but, while Isaiah was an aristocrat, Micah was a peasant who distrusted the ways of city men. Micah may have visited Jerusalem, only about twenty miles distant from his native village of Moresheth, but his sympathies were with those who lived in the country. All about him he saw misery and the pinched faces of hungry children. This was not due to poor crops, for Moresheth stands in the midst of rich farm lands. The sufferings Micah saw were caused by wealthy landowners who robbed the farmers of their fields and forced them to work for starvation wages. Often these landowners lived in Jerusalem where they spent their ill-gotten wealth on luxuries. No wonder Micah denounced Jerusalem and warned of its approaching destruction. Like all the prophets he demanded justice. He poured out his indignation upon the greed of the rich, the rulers, the judges, and the priests.

Micah's prophecies were collected in the first three chapters of the book bearing his name. Though the remaining four chapters are probably the work of an unknown prophet, they contain several famous passages, chief among which is the challenging question and answer:

What doth the Lord require of thee, but to do justly, and to love mercy, and to walk humbly with thy God?

MICAH 6:8

As time went by, men's consciences were stirred by this question. Though the prophets themselves often preached to deaf ears, and banishment and martyrdom fell to their lot, a change was on the way. Jeremiah reports that Micah's denunciations moved King Hezekiah to repent. Israel stood in need of reform. This was not long delayed, for in the seventh century a book was to appear which ushered in a religious and moral reformation. Though it was not a book of prophecy, we can see in it the influence of Amos, Hosea, Isaiah, and Micah. Their words at length bore fruit. The spirit of the prophets triumphed.

# The Book Found in the Temple

## DEUTERONOMY

IT was payday for the carpenters, builders, and masons at work on the repairs of Jerusalem's Temple. The year was 621 B.C., the eighteenth year of the reign of King Josiah. Shaphan, the king's scribe or secretary of state, was on his way from the royal palace to the Temple. It was his duty to be present when the high priest Hilkiah opened the collection box of the Temple and distributed the money it contained to the workmen for their wages.

As Shaphan hurried along the streets of the city he saw many signs of the heathen worship of his day. There were altars to Assyrian gods in the very Temple itself. Everywhere people practiced idolatry. Superstition and witchcraft flourished. From the shrine of Tophet, in the valley of Hinnom just outside the walls of Jerusalem, Shaphan saw smoke rising and he shuddered. Here was the altar where men offered their first-born as a sacrifice to appease the wrath of Molech. To this barbaric level had Israel fallen in that evil and desperate day. It seemed as though the lofty moral and spiritual teachings of the prophets had been completely forgotten and that Israel was doomed to occupy a place of dishonor among the peoples of antiquity. Manasseh and Amon, who had reigned from 693 to 638 B.C., were half-heathen kings and it was their foreign policy to flatter their Assyrian overlords by adopting Assyrian cults and religious practices. When Amon was murdered his eight-year-old son Josiah ascended the throne of Judah. Now, at the age of twenty-six, Josiah decided to stamp out the evils of his father's and his grandfather's reigns. It was for this reason that in the year 621 B.C. the Temple was being repaired and put in order for the worship of Yahweh.

When Shaphan reached the Temple he found everyone highly excited.

"See," exclaimed Hilkiah, forgetting his high-priestly dignity and rushing toward the scribe, "I have found the book of law in the house of the Lord!"

He thrust a dust-covered scroll into Shaphan's hands. Workmen had just found it behind a loose stone in a recess of the building. Why had it been put there instead of in the Temple library? What did the book contain and why were the priests so excited about it? There was something strange about the whole affair, and Shaphan decided to take the scroll to the King at once.

He paid the workmen their wages and hurried back to the palace with the roll under his arm. The King was curious about the dusty book and ordered his scribe to read it to him. Shaphan read to the end, rolled up the scroll, and waited breathlessly for the King to issue his royal command concerning the extraordinary book. Shapan looked up and to his amazement saw King Josiah rise slowly and deliberately from his throne and, in the ancient gesture of sorrow and remorse, rend his clothes.

What sort of book was it to cause such excitement at the Temple and such an act of repentance by a king? The scroll was none other than the first edition of our Book of Deuteronomy, probably the most significant book ever written by a Hebrew. In majestic and sonorous language it laid down Israel's religious and moral laws. Comparing the lofty demands of these laws with the low moral and spiritual level to which Israel had fallen, we can understand why the young King, his high priest, and his secretary of state were dismayed and shocked, and why the King's first response was a gesture of repentance.

Though the Bible tells us nothing about the real author of Deuteronomy, it is possible to build up his story from the known conditions of the time. We hope that he was present on the day his book was taken from its hiding place and that he lived long enough to see it made into the law of the land, the spiritual and moral constitution of Israel. He was doubtless a priest in Jerusalem during the evil days of Manasseh's reign. The teachings of the prophets had influenced this priest deeply and, when he saw altars to heathen gods being set up in the very Temple itself and smelled the incense offered to foreign idols, he knew the time had come to act. It would have meant certain death if he had spoken openly against the abominable religious practices introduced by Manasseh. Had not Manasseh ordered Isaiah put to death? The priest gathered about him a few like-minded men who admired the prophets and treasured their sayings. In secret these men made their plan. They determined to draw up a new constitution for Israel consisting in her good old laws, which the priest would rewrite in the new prophetic spirit. It was an ambitious undertaking for the little underground movement. When the document was finished the group dared not publish their book but hid it until the time was ripe for its discovery on the memorable payday in 621 B.C.

Josiah did far more than rend his garments. He immediately called a public assembly of officials, priests, prophets, and common people. The roll was read and in the hush that followed the King rose and solemnly promised to keep the Lord's commandments and to obey all His laws as written in the book. For their part, the people "stood to the covenant," ratifying the King's vow. Thereupon a wave of reform swept through the land. The nation desired to become "a holy people unto the Lord." Altars to heathen gods were torn down. Idols were smashed. All objects connected with pagan cults were thrown into bonfires. The shrine in Hinnom was destroyed. At Jerusalem the Temple, now rebuilt and cleansed of impurity, became fit for the dwelling place of God and the one center for His true worship. Men taught their children the watchword of the whole reform:

Hear, O Israel: The Lord our God is one Lord: And thou shalt love the Lord thy God with all thine heart, and with all thy soul, and with all thy might.

DEUTERONOMY 6:4, 5

The scroll found in the Temple touched off not only religious reforms but social ones as well. It contained a primitive bill of rights. Under the new laws of Deuteronomy there was more justice for everyone. Women, foreigners, and the poor were protected and the rights of slaves and employees were recognized. It was a triumph for the message of the prophets.

The style in which Deuteronomy was written matched its noble spirit. Its author was a master of eloquent, majestic prose which stated his message with power. His words glow with the new prophetic fire. He believed that his book represented the teachings of Moses and he wrote it in the form of an oration by that great lawgiver and liberator. No wonder that the book was soon venerated as a sacred document, a holy book, and that Deuteronomy became the seed of the Bible. From this time on the religion of Israel became more and more the religion of a book.

Deuteronomy was often edited, revised, and amended. It was read and studied so much through the centuries that its style and teachings influenced many a later Hebrew writer. Its Greek translators gave it the title Deuteronomy, meaning the Second Giving of the Law by Moses. It was a living force six hundred years after its discovery when, in the Christian era, New Testament writers quoted or referred to it more than a hundred times. Today we find in Deuteronomy, not only the first sacred book out of which grew the idea for the Bible, but one of the cornerstones of our laws and our religion.

## 10

### Editing Israel's History

JOSHUA, JUDGES, SAMUEL, KINGS

INSPIRED by Deuteronomy, Josiah's reforms of 621 B.C. made Jerusalem the religious capital of the kingdom, the holy city of Israel. Shrines and altars throughout the country were torn down in order to stamp out heathen cults with their evil practices. Only at the altar in Jerusalem's Temple might people offer sacrifices to Yahweh. Here people from the villages and towns of Judah came every spring to celebrate the Passover. Often they must have brought with them documents and books of many kinds, for they knew the priests at the Temple were collecting a library of Hebrew literature and would be glad to purchase volumes they did not already have. The shelves of the Temple library must have held many torn and ancient rolls, as well as new volumes in which the ink was hardly dry. What would we not give to be able to browse in that library today! We would handle reverently the book that caused a reformation: the first edition of Deuteronomy. We would gaze at the prophecies of Amos, Hosea, Isaiah, and Micah, all written in the handwriting of their disciples. The most venerable rolls in the collection would be the Book of Jasher and the Book of the Wars of the Lord. If the priests had been able to save the original manuscript of Abiathar's Founding of the Kingdom with its eyewitness account of David's reign, we would find ourselves looking at a roll then almost four hundred years old! The two splendid old epics of Israel by J and E were nearly as old, though their combined version had been completed only recently.

At the time of which we write, about 600 B.C., we might have found certain shelves in the library empty. These were the shelves where the historical records of the kingdoms of Israel and Judah were usually kept. They were in constant use at that time. In another room of the Temple a group of priests had spread these rolls of history upon their desks and they were bending over them patiently deciphering the writing of long dead royal scribes and historians, and forgotten Temple recorders. The priests read with their pens poised and fresh rolls on the desks beside them. They belonged to a guild of writers who were engaged in bringing out a new edition of Israel's history based on the old records. Now and again one of them would pause in his reading to copy out a passage he wanted to include in the new history.

These priestly writers had excellent sources to work with. They doubtless had a complete set of the Chronicles of the Temple going back to the date of its foundation. The Record of Solomon's Reign (I Kings 11:41) was filled with a wealth of detail. The History of the Kings of Israel and its companion volume, the History of the Kings of Judah (II Kings 13:12, 21:25) contained official reports of the reigns of all the kings. Probably biographies of Elijah and Elisha completed the list of documents. From these ample sources of Hebrew history the priestly historians were gathering material for their new book.

They were inspired by the teachings of Deuteronomy and hence they are often pompously named Deuteronomic historians. It is hardly fair, however, to call them historians, for they were not attempting to make an objective record of past events. If their book is judged by historical standards it falls short. Actually these men were religious teachers. They tried to use the facts of history to prove that the ideals of Deuteronomy were true. They believed that if the king and the nation walked in the ways of Yahweh and kept His statutes and commandments they would prosper. History proved this to them. Accordingly, they set out to tell the story of the nation, from the accession of Solomon to the reign of Josiah, from the point of view of Deuteronomy. They marshaled the kings of four centuries, thirty-eight royal personages in all, and caused them to pass in review before the reader. Of each ruler they asked: was he loyal to Yahweh and did he worship exclusively in Jerusalem? These were definite teachings of Deuteronomy and each king was tested by them. If his record gave a "yes" to the questions, the king was judged "right in the eyes of the Lord." If the king worshiped Baal and offered sacrifices to idols he was said to have "done evil in the sight of the Lord."

The priestly historians warn their readers that they are not giving the full picture of any king. Over and over again they insert sentences like this:

> The rest of all the acts of Asa, and all his might, and all that he did, and the cities which he built, are they not written in the book of the chronicles of the kings of Judah?
>
> I KINGS 15:23

When the priests finished their book it formed a companion volume to Deuteronomy. Originally one book, it was later divided into two parts and called I and II Kings. On its pages the history of four hundred years teaches the ideals of Deuteronomy. But the Books of Kings are not in themselves true history. The day came, however, when the old chronicles and histories of Israel and Judah perished, doubtless in the flames that destroyed the Temple when Jerusalem fell to the Babylonians in 586 B.C. In some way I and II Kings was fortunately saved. But for this book of religious instructions we should know little of the royal personages of Judah: Solomon the magnificent, who built the Temple; Rehoboam the unwise, who lost half a kingdom; Asa, who deposed his mother because she worshiped idols; Jehoshaphat; Athaliah, daughter of Ahab and the

infamous Jezebel; Amaziah; Jotham; Hezekiah, the good king
who listened to Isaiah; Manasseh, the evil king who worshiped
Assyrian gods; and Josiah the reformer. In our sample roll
call we must mention among Israel's kings: Jeroboam the revo-
lutionist; Omri the great and Ahab his son; Jehu, who drove
furiously; Jeroboam II, in whose reign Amos preached; and
Hoshea, who saw Israel destroyed.

So successful were the Books of Kings that other priestly historians with the teachings of Deuteronomy in their hearts decided to issue new volumes of history. The destruction of the
Temple and captivity in Babylonia did not quench their enthusiasm to record the history of Israel's early period from the conquest of Canaan to the accession of Solomon. Somehow they
managed to save the old scrolls they needed: the J and E epics,
the hero tales, and account of Samuel, and Abiathar's Founding
of the Kingdom. All these they may have transported across
the weary miles of the old caravan route to Babylon, for it was
probably there that the Deuteronomic editions of Joshua,
Judges, and I and II Samuel were first issued about 550 B.C.

Following the pattern established by the authors of Kings, all
these books contained much old material from the ancient
scrolls, reworked and edited from the new point of view. Joshua
contained the old J E stories of the conquest of Canaan rewritten
in the style of Deuteronomy. The hero Joshua became the
mouthpiece of the priestly historians and they caused him to
exhort men to:

> Love the Lord your God, and to walk in all his ways, and to keep
> his commandments, and to cleave unto him, and to serve him with all
> your heart and with all your soul.
>
> JOSHUA 22:5

For the Book of Judges the priests did little rewriting. The
ancient stories of tribal leaders and judges were of exceptional
literary brilliance. These tales the priests reset, like old family
jewels, in new settings. The new settings consist of introduc-
tions and conclusions pointing out the religious meaning of the
stories. The priests saw an ebb and flow in the history of this

period which they believed was due to the nation's sins. When the Israelites disobeyed the Lord, He punished them by allow-ing their enemies to overwhelm them. Then they cried out in distress and the Lord sent them a deliverer. At the death of the deliverer or "judge" the cycle of irreligion, disaster, repentance, and restoration began again. In the hands of sixth-century writers the superb old stories of Deborah, Gideon, Jephthah, and Samson became the means of teaching that God's hand is at work in history.

Following Judges came I and II Samuel. It covered the period dominated by Samuel the kingmaker, Saul, Israel's first king, and David the conqueror of Jerusalem. The priestly historians had plenty of source material for these rulers, and we are greatly indebted to them for copying word by word into their book, Abiathar's Founding of the Kingdom. But for them we might have lost the first history book in the world.

When I and II Samuel was finished, about 550 B.C., it closed the gap between Joshua and Judges on one side and I and II Kings on the other. It fitted into place like a keystone in the arch of Israel's history. These Deuteronomic editions now spanned six centuries of history and added their evidence to the teachings of Deuteronomy itself. This series of books of re-ligious instruction based on history passed through many edi-tions. For three hundred years the series was often revised and enlarged. About 200 B.C. the books were canonized, or declared to be sacred writings, and thereafter no significant changes were made in their text. This series preserved a great deal of early Hebrew literature and history. It also profoundly affected Jewish religion. It has been said that history was a kind of sacrament to Israel. In the "outward and visible" facts of his-tory Israel saw the face of her God. No wonder, then, that this historical series was not classified as history but was named the Former Prophets. Christianity rang with echoes from the pages of these books, and their stories and ideas became one note in the theme song of our religion and our civilization.

## 11

# Voices of Triumph and Despair

## ZEPHANIAH, NAHUM, HABAKKUK, LAMENTATIONS

ALARMED cries often penetrated to the hushed rooms in the Temple at Jerusalem where the priests were writing. Sometimes the authors of Deuteronomy must have paused to listen to disquieting rumors brought to them from the city gates. Frequently the priestly historians heard the tramp of soldiers marching through the streets. The hundred years from 650 to 550 B.C. was a time of political turmoil. Empires rose and were vanquished; kingdoms perished; proud cities fell; and from innocent lips came cries of anguish. Through these years of crisis the writers of Deuteronomy and the historical series from Joshua through Kings kept steadily at their work. The events of their times must have affected them deeply, but they mentioned little contemporary history in their books. There are, however, four small books in the Old Testament which vividly tell how the troubles of those years affected all the Hebrews. These books are: Zephaniah, Nahum, Habakkuk, and Lamentations.

Some of the members of the little underground group who had written Deuteronomy may have been in the crowd that listened to Zephaniah, for he preached in Jerusalem early in Josiah's reign before the roll was found in the Temple. Zephaniah was of royal blood, being the great-grandson of King Hezekiah. As soon as he began to preach, men knew he belonged among the true prophets. He called the nation to account for its sins and pictured the evils of Josiah's day which the young King later tried to remedy. His ideal was the high and holy religion of the prophets; but he had little hope that the nation would attain this level of life. He could see nothing ahead for his people but destruction and, when news of the Scythian invasions reached Jerusalem, he believed that this was the beginning of the end. The Scythians were a half-savage tribe whose warriors swept down from the country now known as South Russia, and overwhelmed the nations in their path. About 630 B.C., they advanced toward Palestine, which was a land bridge to the rich valley of the Nile. When Israel's homes and cities faced almost certain conquest, Zephaniah rose and thundered judgment upon a sinful world. He said the coming of the Scythian hordes was only a prelude to God's day of judgment. His picture of the terrifying day of wrath (Zephaniah 1:14-18) is the best known part of his surviving prophecies. Nearly two thousand years later, about A.D. 1250, Thomas of Celano used a Latin translation of Zephaniah's ancient words, *Dies irae, dies illa,* to open his great medieval hymn.

After the Scythians retreated and their menace was forgotten, new rumors began to fly in the market place at Jerusalem. Every caravan from the east brought news of a powerful empire arising in Babylonia. This was the Chaldean or Babylonian Empire which now threatened Assyria's long domination. For centuries Assyria, one of the most cruel nations of antiquity, had brought terror to all western Asia. In 722 B.C., just as Amos had foreseen, the Assyrians invaded Israel and deported its people. As Isaiah promised, Jerusalem escaped capture in 701 B.C., when Sennacherib's Assyrian army, encamped outside the walls, was stricken with pestilence. Though Judah retained her kings, they were constantly threatened by mighty Assyria. Now Assyria herself was threatened by the Chaldeans. Finally in 612 B.C. came the news that the proud Assyrian capital of Nineveh was about to fall to the Chaldean conquerors. Jerusalem went wild with joy. The priestly historians must have put down their pens and gone out to join in the rejoicing. Nahum, a poet of that time, celebrated the occasion in a triumphal ode which ranks with the Song of Deborah and the Elegy of David among the great Hebrew classical poems. Nahum pictures the furious onslaughts of cavalry, the headlong dash of chariots, the sharp orders of the officers, the heaps of dead. He ends with the joyful shout of the peoples whom Assyria had kept in subjection. Years later someone added an acrostic poem about Yahweh's wrath to the beginning of Nahum's ode. The ode itself can now be read in the second and third chapters of Nahum.

The rejoicing in Jerusalem soon turned to fear. Though Assyria's power was crushed, the new tyranny of the Chaldeans took its place. The prophet Habakkuk listened to reports of the new conquests and wrote a powerful description of the invincible Chaldean army approaching on horseback. He trembled for the fate of Judah and even dared question the ways of God. "Why," he asked, "does God who is powerful and righteous allow the wicked Chaldeans to destroy righteous nations?" Thus Habakkuk brought into sharp focus the baffling problem of evil. His answer was given in the pregnant sentence:

The just shall live by his faith.
HABAKKUK 2:4

St. Paul later filled this sentence with deeper meaning, and Martin Luther made it a spiritual battle cry.

Habakkuk's contribution to Hebrew prophecy was brief but pointed. His words occupy only the space of two chapters. It is believed that the song in the third chapter entitled: A Prayer of Habakkuk the Prophet, was written for a hymnbook and set to music long after Habakkuk's time.

Nothing could stay the approach of the Chaldeans, and men knew that soon they would be outside the walls of Jerusalem itself. Finally in 597 B.C. the Chaldeans captured Jerusalem and deported many of her citizens to Babylonia. Perhaps some of the writers of the historical series went into exile at this time, carrying their precious rolls with them and continuing their work in a foreign land. The Chaldeans appointed the vassal king Zedekiah to rule over conquered Judea, but Zedekiah plotted rebellion against them. In 586 B.C., the Chaldeans again laid seige to Jerusalem and captured the rebellious city once more. This time the Temple was burned and the city destroyed. Again a pitiful group of refugees started on the long road into exile. Among them was a poet who could not forget the sights he had seen. In exile he wrote two mournful songs for his dead city. These are now in chapters two and four of the Book of Lamentations. Years later, three other dirges were added and the little collection was recited once every year in the new Temple in memory of the day in 586 B.C. when Jerusalem was destroyed. In this anthology we hear, as it were, all the ruined cities of the world, from Jerusalem to Hiroshima, crying:

> How doth the city sit solitary, that was full of people!
>                                         LAMENTATIONS 1:1

Lamentations was once thought to be from the pen of Jeremiah, the only great prophet known to have been in the city when it fell. But it now seems impossible that Jeremiah was the author of Lamentations. Would a prophet have said as Lamentations does: "Her prophets also find no vision from the Lord" or "Thy prophets have seen vain and foolish things for thee"? Surely Jeremiah's were neither false nor foolish prophecies, and through the dark days before the city fell we shall learn how he spoke words of profound meaning to his despairing countrymen.

## 12

### The Prophet to a Doomed Nation

JEREMIAH

IT was just eighteen years before the destruction of Jerusalem which we have just mentioned. On a cold December day in 604 B.C., King Jehoiakim sat in his palace in Jerusalem warming himself before the glowing coals of his brazier. A group of government officials entered the royal chamber with news of a strange event. A scribe named Baruch had caused a sensation in the Temple that very day by reading a scroll of prophecy. He had stationed himself in an upper window overlooking the Temple gate and from there he had read in a loud voice to all the people. Next, Baruch had read the book to the officials themselves and when they questioned him closely about it he had declared that the prophecies were dictated by a prophet named Jeremiah.

King Jehoiakim knew the prophet Jeremiah well. "That fellow again!" he must have muttered to himself, "I thought he was under house arrest and forbidden to prophesy."

Seeing the agitation of his ministers, the King ordered the scroll to be brought and read to him. He would deal with the matter once and for all. For more than twenty years Jeremiah had been prophesying, always stirring up the people, criticizing the government, and predicting the downfall of the nation. He had even dared criticize King Jehoiakim himself for compelling his subjects to work as slaves on the new palace. All this was poison in the minds of the people. Jehoiakim knew he must act decisively to prevent the dangerous ideas from spreading. He could easily lose his kingdom if men were convinced that Jeremiah's prophecies were really the words of Yahweh.

The roll was brought and its solemn words were read. The King took a penknife and as each column was finished he slashed it from the roll and tossed it on the glowing coals of the brazier. There the papyrus curled, blackened, and was consumed. Three of his counselors advised the King not to burn the roll. They were more than half convinced the words were indeed from God. Burning God's words was an act of extreme impiety. But Jehoiakim contemptuously brushed aside their pleas and continued feeding pieces of the roll to the fire. Soon all that remained of it were a few filmy, ghostlike particles floating in the air and a fine dust covering the furniture in the room. Thus the first edition of the Book of Jeremiah was burned in the palace at Jerusalem.

A sharp command rang out: "Jerchmeel, Seraiah, Shelemiah!" It was the King ordering his officers to seize Baruch and Jeremiah. "But," says the Bible story, "the Lord hid them."

Book burning has never proved very effective. In this case it was merely the futile gesture of an unwise king. Though the book was ashes, its author was still alive. For seven years Jeremiah and Baruch remained in hiding, time and again, no doubt, eluding the royal police who searched for them everywhere. There must have been many clever stratagems and hairbreadth escapes, but Jeremiah did far more than outwit the police. He took a fresh roll and, with Baruch acting as his secretary, he dictated a new volume of prophecy. It contained the words burned on the brazier and many more besides. This second roll was more carefully guarded than the first, and it can be read today in chapters 1 to 25 of the Book of Jeremiah.

The years in hiding must have been a sore trial to Jeremiah. He had been born in the pleasant country village of Anathoth and he always longed for the sights and sounds of nature. But his call to prophecy: "To root out, and to pull down, and to destroy, and to throw down, to build, and to plant," was a call which must be obeyed. Often Jeremiah cursed the fate that doomed him to be always on the unpopular, losing side. He was shy and sensitive by nature. His soul was torn between loyalty to his prophetic call and a keen desire to escape from the dangers and turmoils of his day and lead a quiet country life. The divine message was like a fire burning in his bones and he had to speak out. In the midst of his inner struggles he learned to turn to God and find joy and peace in a sense of nearness to Him. His personal experience of God marks the beginning of a new epoch in religion. Jeremiah has been called the "father of true prayer." He blazed a spiritual trail which became a highway for all the saints.

Echoes of Jeremiah's inner struggles found their way into the book he dictated to Baruch. If these prayers and self-searchings were to be separated from his prophecies and printed by themselves they would form a volume of confessions. In these confessions we are permitted to look into the heart of an ancient prophet.

To the prophecies and the confessions Baruch added a biography of the prophet. He traces Jeremiah's life from its beginning in Anathoth about 645 B.C., to its end in Egypt soon after 586 B.C. As we have seen in the preceding chapter, those were years of political turmoil. With Zephaniah he trembled at the news of Scythian invasions. He rejoiced when Deuteronomy was found, but he soon realized that Josiah's reforms had not really changed the heart of the people. Jeremiah's messages were not popular. He appealed to people to leave their evil ways marked by superstition, sensuality, and ignorance, and to turn their hearts to the Lord. When people did not listen Jeremiah said:

> They have forsaken me the fountain of living waters, and hewed them out cisterns, broken cisterns, that can hold no water.
>
> JEREMIAH 2:13

A day of destruction approached, declared Jeremiah. Assyria

had crumbled, but the new empire of Babylonia would soon conquer Judah. Nearly all the political crises of his lifetime are reflected in his prophecies.

Jeremiah faced angry mobs. He was thrown into prison. He spent seven years in hiding. He was flogged. He was put in the stocks. A kindly negro rescued him after he had been lowered into a muddy cistern to die. Jeremiah lived through the horrible days of Jerusalem's siege by the Babylonian army under Nebuchadnezzar. He saw the city fall and its buildings destroyed. He and Baruch were forced to accompany a group of refugees to Egypt, where the story of his heroic life ends.

His influence on religion was undying. It is partly due to him that we take it for granted today that God is good. To Jeremiah wisdom, power, and riches were as nothing compared to the supreme joy of knowing God and understanding His loving kindness.

> Let not the wise man glory in his wisdom, neither let the mighty man glory in his might, let not the rich man glory in his riches: But let him that glorieth glory in this, that he understandeth and knoweth me, that I am the Lord which exercise loving kindness, judgment, and righteousness, in the earth: for in these things I delight, saith the Lord.
>
> JEREMIAH 9:23, 24

In his own experience he knew a personal relationship with God. This was to be the star shining through chaos and despair when Judah perished as a nation in 586 B.C. Yahweh's people were scattered. Yahweh's dwelling place in Jerusalem no longer stood on Mount Zion. Was Yahweh Himself dead? Jeremiah's experience provided the answer. Every man could know God *in his own heart*. Though the nation and the Temple were lost, Yahweh was still Lord and dwelt in each person's heart. Inspired by this new teaching, the Hebrews triumphantly carried their religion with them when they went as exiles to Babylon. God's promise through Jeremiah strengthened them:

> I will put my law in their inward parts, and write it in their hearts; and will be their God, and they shall be my people. . . . for they shall all know me, from the least of them unto the greatest of them, saith the Lord.
>
> JEREMIAH 31:33, 34

# 13

## Written in Exile

### EZEKIEL AND THE HOLINESS CODE

NEBUCHADNEZZAR'S Chaldean army twice appeared outside the walls of Jerusalem and as we have already noted, captured the city on two different occasions. The first time was in 597 B.C. when they plundered the Temple and deported King Jehoiakim and many prominent families. Among the exiles forced to go to Babylonia was a young priest named Ezekiel. The prophet Jeremiah was allowed to remain in Jerusalem where he witnessed the frightful siege of the city eleven years later, in 586 B.C. Nebuchadnezzar again captured the city, following up his victory by burning the Temple, melting down the sacred vessels of brass, silver, and gold, demolishing the city walls, and deporting the people. Again a crowd of displaced persons turned their backs on the smoking ruins of Jerusalem and began their seven-hundred-mile journey along the old trade route to Babylonia, the land of the Chaldean conquerors. Among the exiles were princes of the royal house and

> All the mighty men of valor, even ten thousand captives, and all the craftsmen and smiths.
>
> II KINGS 24:14

They left behind their holy city, the familiar outlines of the Judean hills, the little country towns, the stony upland pastures, the pleasant fertile valleys, the village wells, and all their accustomed ways of life.

In Babylonia they found a flat, treeless plain with patches of green fields crossed by irrigation ditches. When they reached the Chaldean capital at Babylon they were awestruck by its massive walls and fortifications, its vast temple, and its brilliantly decorated palaces. They saw Babylon's famous Hanging Gardens, which were a series of roof gardens rising tier above tier and crowning the imperial palace with luxuriant trees and flowers. As they stumbled wearily down Nebuchadnezzar's festival avenue they saw the sun shine upon the colored glazed tiles adorned with animal figures. Here was the most splendid city of the age, built with tribute from many conquered nations and by the labor of many a captive.

The exiles from Judah soon settled down in the new country, often perhaps among other Hebrews who had arrived in the earlier deportation of 597 B.C. Some of them joined the gangs of builders erecting new palaces for the king; others became diggers of the endless miles of irrigation ditches which brought fertility to Babylonian fields. In an expanding empire there was plenty of work for Hebrew "craftsmen and smiths." The government service offered posts to some of the capable administrators among the exiles. Business and trade flourished under the Chaldeans, and many a Hebrew must have found opportunity for advancement in the banking houses and commercial establishments of the day. Though far from their native land and their beloved Temple, the exiles of the sixth century were in the wealthiest and most active center of civilization. Though some of them may have discarded the religion of their fathers and adopted heathen ways, more of them settled down to live in little Hebrew colonies where the customs and beliefs of the homeland were carefully preserved.

While all this was going on and the Hebrews were being absorbed into the Chaldean Empire, Israel as a distinct nation might well have disappeared from history. But this did not happen. The peculiar genius of Israel was her religion. This was a hardy plant of great vitality, which neither died nor withered in the alien air but kept alive the national consciousness of the captives. In exile Israel's religion flourished and put forth some of its sturdiest branches. The old national epics which celebrated Yahweh's care for His people were read and studied. The long-dead prophets continued to teach what God required of men. The ways of life and worship laid down in Deuteronomy were carefully cherished. Men began to understand the truth of Jeremiah's teaching that every heart can be a temple to the Lord. When Israel had no Temple, no sacrifices, and no priesthood, her religious leaders turned to teaching and to editing her literary heritage. As we have seen, some of the historical series from Joshua through the Books of Kings were completed during this period.

There were some among the exiles whose mood was expressed by a later poet:

> By the rivers of Babylon,
> There we sat down, yea, we wept,
> When we remembered Zion.
>
> PSALM 137

In this period, some of the mournful songs of Lamentations were probably written. Their sadness, however, is not characteristic of the creative work of the Babylonian period. This was filled with hope, with a new understanding of God, and with plans for a renewed nation. The genius of Israel reached new heights in captivity. Beside the irrigation ditches that watered the treeless Babylonian plain, Hebrews sat in their flat-roofed houses and wrote words that saved Israel from extinction. Ezekiel penned his visions, the author of the Holiness Code gave Israel new standards and laws, and it is believed that Second Isaiah composed his matchless spiritual epic.

The catastrophe of 586 B.C. divided Ezekiel's career into two parts. He was born in Jerusalem and his early years must have been spent within sound of the Temple bells, for his father was a priest of the family of Zadok. In 597 B.C., when the Chaldeans first seized Jerusalem, Ezekiel, then only a young man, was de-

ported to Babylon by the river Chebar. There he received his
call to be a prophet in an overpowering vision. In the midst of
a storm cloud he saw weird beings, partly animal and partly
human. In Ezekiel's confused account there is a hint of the giant
winged monsters of Assyrian art. He saw wheels within wheels
and the brightness of fire, and in the midst sat God upon a sap-
phire throne. A voice spoke and Ezekiel fell upon his face.
The Lord said to him:

> Son of man, stand upon thy feet, and I will speak unto thee.
>
> EZEKIEL 2:1

When the Spirit entered into him and set him on his feet Ezekiel heard words commanding him to prophesy:

> Son of man, I send thee to the children of Israel, to a rebellious na-
> tion that hath rebelled against me . . . And thou shalt say unto them,
> Thus saith the Lord God. . . . And thou shalt speak my words unto
> them, whether they will hear, or whether they will forbear: for they
> are most rebellious.
>
> EZEKIEL 2:3, 4, 7

His first prophecies to his fellow countrymen were filled with
"lamentations, and mourning, and woe." He denounced the
nation, saying that people profaned God's name and practiced
idolatry in the Temple. He predicted that doom would over-
take Israel and he carried out strange, symbolic acts to drive
home his message. At length Ezekiel became dumb, his prophetic voice ceased, and there was a hush before the end.

On the fifth of January, 585 B.C., an exhausted fugitive
reached Babylonia. He had escaped from the burning city of
Jerusalem to bring a message to the exiles beside the river
Chebar. "The city is smitten," he gasped.

From that moment a change came over Ezekiel. His voice
returned to him and he entered upon a new period of his
career in which he preached of a nation reborn. He remained
at Tel-abib beside the banks of the Chebar, ministering to the
exiles of 597 B.C. and to the new exiles who began to arrive in
585 B.C. from stricken Jerusalem.

He told them his vision of a valley of dry bones. The bones
came together and flesh came upon them and they stood upon

their feet and formed an exceedingly great army. The bones represented the nation of Israel which the Lord had made to live again. The exiles were encouraged by this vision and others like it, and they received comfort from Ezekiel's picture of Yahweh as the Good Shepherd of His people. But they were puzzled by a new and strange idea in Ezekiel's preaching. He said that each person was responsible for his own deeds. Every man stood or fell by his own actions. This was a revolutionary doctrine to men who believed that the sins of the fathers would be visited upon the children. They thought that a son inherited his father's sins just as he inherited his father's house and lands and wealth. Men had even been punished for crimes their fathers had committed. No wonder they shook their heads when Ezekiel declared that God rewards each person according to *his own* merits.

Ezekiel was disappointed at the ineffectiveness of his sermons. "With their mouth they show much love," complained the prophet, "but their heart goeth after their covetousness." He knew that many who heard him preach were far more concerned with the price of wool in the Babylonian market than with the messages he brought them from Yahweh. He was not content to be merely a form of entertainment.

> Lo, thou art unto them as a very lovely song of one that hath a pleasant voice, and can play well on an instrument: for they hear thy words, but they do them not.
>
> EZEKIEL 33:32

Ezekiel found a new way to deliver his messages. He purchased scrolls, ink, and pens and began to write. In the space of about twelve years he wrote three books, all of which are now combined in the Book of Ezekiel. For the first volume Ezekiel wrote from memory his speeches predicting Jerusalem's doom. Its title might well have been Denunciations. It is now thought to comprise chapters 1 to 24 and 33 to 37. It is filled with strange visions and the record of symbolical acts.

The second volume extends from chapters 25 to 32 and might be entitled Oracles Against Foreign Nations, for it pours out denunciations against the foreign nations who rejoiced in

Judah's downfall. One of these oracles pictures Tyre as a ship and gives a remarkably colorful and accurate picture of ancient seafaring and commerce.

Ezekiel's chief legacy to Israel is contained in the third book, Israel Reborn, written about 573 B.C. In this he draws up a plan for the restoration of his people, describing the future Temple with its priesthood and ritual. In a trance he saw all this with great clarity and his pen raced to set down the elaborate vision. He described the new Temple with its altar, courts, sacristies, and even its kitchens. "And the glory of the Lord filled the house." He told how the sacredness of the Temple area was to be guarded from any pollution or defilement, for this heart of the new Israel was the holy dwelling of Yahweh. The priests and people must observe strict rules. Ezekiel lays down rules even about the materials and cut of the priestly vestments. He describes the correct manner of offering the sacrifices which were designed to remove all sin from the people. Behind all these ecclesiastical details was his belief in the awful holiness of Yahweh and the need of strict rules to ensure the holiness of the Lord's people. Ezekiel's vision of Israel Reborn was one of the many Utopias men have created in their dreams. To none of them was given so splendid a name as Ezekiel gave his city: "The Lord is there."

Such is Ezekiel's story, if the book that bears his name was actually written by him. New theories now being tested question Ezekiel's authorship of the entire volume. Though we eagerly await the results of modern scholarship on this important book, we shall, for the present at least, think of Ezekiel as the prophet who stood at a crossroads of history. In a time of calamity his message was a signpost pointing toward a new age. He saw the old Israel perish but refused to believe in the finality of her death. The bones would rise again. His blueprint of Israel as a holy congregation turned men's eyes toward the day when the rebuilt Temple would stand at the center of Israel's life and its sacrifices, ritual, and priesthood would bind the nation to its God.

Harsh words have been used to describe Ezekiel: exclusive, narrow, legalistic, dogmatic. He has been called a fanatical visionary. For all that, almost singlehanded he rescued Israel from extinction and his narrow, legalistic plans preserved her religion from the dangers of the next five hundred years and more. The great religion known as Judaism sprang largely from him and he has fittingly been honored with the title: Father of Judaism. Dreamer though he was, his vision of a restored Israel was based on sound spiritual insight. A better time will come for Israel, he said, when the Lord transforms men's hearts. Moral and spiritual rebirth is the only soil out of which a better world can grow.

> A new heart also will I give you, and a new spirit will I put within you: and I will take away the stony heart out of your flesh, and I will give you an heart of flesh. And I will put my spirit within you, and cause you to walk in my statutes . . . and ye shall be my people, and I will be your God.
>
> EZEKIEL 36:26, 27, 28

Ezekiel was not alone in his belief that a holy God demanded holiness of His people. Among the exiles there was a priest who was deeply concerned with holiness. Righteousness and love had seemed all-important to the prophets and to the priestly writers of Deuteronomy, but to the unknown priest in exile, holiness was at the very heart of religion. Perhaps he discussed this matter with his fellow exile Ezekiel. It is difficult to say which of the two men influenced the other, for we believe that both lived at about the same time, in the same place, and held similar views. In his house in Babylonia the priest no doubt kept his collection of scrolls. These were a veritable law library and included the ritual laws, the social customs, and the moral precepts of Israel. One day the priest decided to make a compilation of those laws which he thought would insure the holiness of the people. The compilation he wrote is known as the Holiness Code and it can now be read in chapters 17 through 26 of Leviticus. The unknown exiled priest, using Deuteronomy as a pattern, wrote the Holiness Code in the form of a sermon of Moses. It contained a variety of laws about such things as:

the eating of meat, religious duties, marriage, the priesthood, festivals, real estate, slaves. The idea that holds together these miscellaneous subjects echoes like a refrain throughout the Code:

> And ye shall be holy unto me: for I the Lord am holy, and have severed you from other people, that ye should be mine.
>
> LEVITICUS 20:26

If the Holiness Code seems like a hodgepodge of museum pieces, we have only to search among its curious old laws and strange customs until we come to this:

> Thou shalt love thy neighbour as thyself.
>
> LEVITICUS 19:18

Here is evidence that there are living precepts in this museum of law. In this verse the ethical requirements of the Old Testament reach their highest point. When Jesus was asked which was the greatest commandment, He combined this seven word sentence from the Holiness Code with the command to love God and declared:

> There is none other commandment greater than these.
>
> MARK 12:31

# 14

## The Greatest of the Hebrews

### SECOND ISAIAH

THE hearts of the Babylonian exiles were heavy with misgivings. They had seen too much "desolation, and destruction, and the famine, and the sword." Yahweh seemed to have abandoned them. Had He forgotten His people? He had allowed Nebuchadnezzar to burn the Temple. Was Yahweh helpless before Bel and Nebo, the war gods of the Chaldeans? Ezekiel's promise that Yahweh would restore His people to their own land was still only a promise. Perhaps it would never be fulfilled. The new Holiness Code declared God's holiness, but men longed for assurance of His power. And why, if they were indeed Yahweh's own people, had He afflicted them so grievously throughout these many centuries? It was for exiles tormented with doubts like these that an inspired Hebrew wrote a series of magnificent poems. Among his spiritual ancestors were J and E, the author of Deuteronomy, and all the prophets. He inherited their glowing faith. To this inheritance he brought a new radiance, born out of the despair of exile and destined to shine through the centuries.

Who this outstanding spiritual genius was, we do not know; his name has disappeared and his exact place in history is unknown. All we have are his epoch-making poems which now comprise chapters 40 to 55, and perhaps 34, 35, and 56 to 66 as well, in the Book of Isaiah. We usually speak of him as Second Isaiah for his work follows immediately after the prophecies of the eighth-century prophet, the first Isaiah.

In our Bibles only a chapter heading separates the thirty-ninth chapter of Isaiah from the fortieth, but more than a century and a half separated the writing of these two chapters. In the thirty-ninth chapter King Hezekiah and Isaiah, the princely prophet of Jerusalem, are talking together. The time must be about 700 B.C. Then, as we begin to read the fortieth chapter we find that Isaiah's world of old Judah has passed away. Instead of Hezekiah's royal court, the stately Temple, and the altars to false gods we read of "thy waste and thy desolate places, and the land of thy destruction." At the fortieth chapter the voice of the staunch old prophet Isaiah has long been silent and the new voice of Second Isaiah begins to sing on a different note:

> Comfort ye, comfort ye my people,
> Saith your God.
> Speak ye comfortably to Jerusalem,
> And cry unto her,
> That her warfare is accomplished,
> That her iniquity is pardoned:
> For she hath received of the Lord's hand
> Double for all her sins.
>
> ISAIAH 40:1, 2

Second Isaiah's poems were filled with an exultation that his predecessor did not know. They are rhapsodies, not prophetic denunciations. His words were a light shining in the darkness of exile. Deliverance, he told his fellow exiles, was at hand. Cyrus with his conquering Persian armies would free the Hebrews and end their Babylonian captivity.

The references to Cyrus must have been written about 540 B.C. and, if they are authentic, we may give Second Isaiah a date near this time. This would make him a contemporary of Gautama Buddha, who was born in far-off India about 563 B.C., and of Confucius, the Chinese sage born in 550 B.C. While Second Isaiah carried Israel's religion to its highest peaks, Buddha taught how a man might attain to Nirvana, the state of happiness, by eliminating all his selfish desires. Confucius planted his feet firmly on the ground and advised men to think clearly, exercise self-discipline, and "while respecting spiritual beings, to keep aloof from them."

Second Isaiah probably never heard of the two other great religious leaders of his era, for there was little contact between Babylonia, where he lived, and India and China. Even so his life was lived against broad horizons. In his heart he carried longings for the land of his fathers, which he may never have seen. If, as we believe, his days were spent in the flat country of Babylonia, he had a good vantage point from which to watch the struggle of the two empires of Chaldea and Persia, for the supremacy of the western world. This wide international background challenged Second Isaiah's faith in Yahweh, the national God of Israel. To have value for exiles caught in the clash of two empires, Second Isaiah's message must contain more than a return to the ancient faith. The idea of Yahweh as one god among many and as Israel's own, special deity no longer sufficed. What was there to take its place? And how, according to the old faith, could the exiles explain Israel's centuries of affliction and her present plight? Finally, Israel needed to enter into a new relationship with other nations. This was the challenge that faced Second Isaiah. It was the challenge he met so magnificently, buttressing his soaring vision with valid insights and solid ideas.

He said that Yahweh, the God of Israel, was far more than a tribal deity, speaking in the thunder and riding forth to battle for His people. Such ideas belonged to the childhood of their religion. To Second Isaiah God was Creator of heaven, of earth, and of man.

> I have made the earth, and created man upon it:
> I, even my hands, have stretched out the heavens,
> And all their host have I commanded.

> ISAIAH 45:12

In these words Second Isaiah describes the power and majesty
of God:

> Who hath measured the waters in the hollow of his hand,
> And meted out heaven with the span,
> And comprehended the dust of the earth in a measure,
> And weighed the mountains in scales,
> And the hills in a balance? . . .
> Behold, the nations are as a drop of a bucket,
> And are counted as the small dust of the balance:
> Behold, he taketh up the isles as a very little thing . . .
> It is he that sitteth upon the circle of the earth,
> And the inhabitants thereof are as grasshoppers;
> That stretcheth out the heavens as a curtain . . .
> That bringeth the princes to nothing;
> He maketh the judges of the earth as vanity.
>
> ISAIAH 40:12, 15, 22, 23

He does not argue with the exiles who had lost their faith
in God's power, he merely sweeps them along in his triumphant
affirmation:

> Hast thou not known?
> Hast thou not heard,
> That the everlasting God, the Lord,
> The Creator of the ends of the earth,
> Fainteth not, neither is weary?
> There is no searching of his understanding.
> He giveth power to the faint;
> And to them that have no might he increaseth strength.
> Even the youths shall faint and be weary,
> And the young men shall utterly fall:
> But they that wait upon the Lord shall renew their strength;
> They shall mount up with wings as eagles;
> They shall run, and not be weary;
> And they shall walk, and not faint.
>
> ISAIAH 40:28-31

Israel had waged a long battle against belief in other gods.
From the days of Moses to the time of the Exile, there had been
altars to heathen deities. The gods of streams and mountains,
the gods of the harvests, the deities of the conquerors, all these
had tempted Israel. Indeed, the first commandment with its:
"Thou shalt have no other god, but me," assumes that there

may be other gods. For two hundred years the prophets had preached about one God, but it remained for Second Isaiah to be the first to deny in clear-cut words the existence of other gods:

> I am the Lord, and there is none else,
> There is no God beside me.
>
> ISAIAH 45:5

Today, in order to recapture the tremendous impact of these words on the exiles, we must in imagination stand with them by Babylon's sacred highway and watch the Chaldean conquerors bow low as their sacred idols are carried by in solemn procession. How did Yahweh and Yahweh's defeated people compare with Bel and Nebo and the mighty Chaldeans? As the exiles watched the splendid religious processions of Babylon the daring words of Second Isaiah strengthened their faith:

> Before me there was no God formed,
> Neither shall there be after me.
> I, even I, am the Lord;
> And beside me there is no saviour.
>
> ISAIAH 43:10, 11

Israel had a special relation to God. He had chosen them, and though they had been disobedient, He would pardon them and protect them forever:

> But thou, Israel, art my servant,
> Jacob whom I have chosen,
> The seed of Abraham my friend . . .
> I have chosen thee, and not cast thee away.
> Fear thou not; for I am with thee:
> Be not dismayed; for I am thy God:
> I will strengthen thee;
> Yea, I will help thee;
> Yea, I will uphold thee with the right hand of my righteousness.
>
> ISAIAH 41:8-10

But why did God's people have to suffer so many centuries of oppression? In giving his answer to this question Second Isaiah wrote perhaps the most profound chapters of the Old Testament. Israel was God's servant with a mission to accomplish:

> Behold my servant, whom I uphold;
> Mine elect, in whom my soul delighteth;
> I have put my spirit upon him:
> He shall bring forth judgment to the Gentiles . . .
> A bruised reed shall he not break,
> And the smoking flax shall he not quench . . .
> He shall not fail nor be discouraged,
> Till he have set judgment in the earth:
> And the isles shall wait for his law.
>
> ISAIAH 42:1, 3, 4

The Servant would liberate the oppressed and lead the hungry and thirsty by springs of water. But oppression and affliction would be his lot. Finally, in the greatest religious poem ever written, the fifty-third chapter, the meaning of the Servant's sufferings became clear. God's servant Israel is suffering for all nations, and all the nations in chorus sing:

> Surely he hath borne our griefs,
> And carried our sorrows . . .
> He was wounded for our transgressions,
> He was bruised for our iniquities:
> The chastisement of our peace was upon him;
> And with his stripes we are healed.
> All we like sheep have gone astray;
> We have turned every one to his own way;
> And the Lord hath laid on him the iniquity of us all.
>
> ISAIAH 53:4-6

Israel lost her national life in captivity, but Second Isaiah restored it to her again on a higher spiritual level. Not for her was there to be an Assyrian triumph or Babylonian prosperity or Persian power. Second Isaiah wrote that Israel's glory was to be in her suffering service for all nations. The fact that Israel rejected that vision does not make it any less remarkable.

> I will also give thee for a light to the Gentiles,
> That thou mayest be my salvation unto the end of the earth.
>
> ISAIAH 49:6

With Second Isaiah the old national religion burst its narrow bonds and for a brief moment offered its God to all men. In a vision that still, after twenty-four centuries, moves on ahead of us Second Isaiah sings that:

> Every valley shall be exalted,
> And every mountain and hill shall be made low:
> And the crooked shall be made straight,
> And the rough places plain:
> And the glory of the Lord shall be revealed,
> And all flesh shall see it together.
>
> ISAIAH 40:4, 5

These were tremendous ideas to come from the pen of any man. His inspired words rekindled Israel's faith. Though the message was written for sixth-century exiles it continues to stir men's hearts. Of all the Old Testament writings these spiritual masterpieces of Second Isaiah have had the greatest influence on mankind. Here, at the summit of Old Testament religion, we are not far from Christianity.

Who wrote the final chapters, 55 to 66, of the Book of Isaiah no one knows. Possibly Second Isaiah himself was their author. Or there may have been a Third Isaiah who in these chapters tried to interpret to a later generation the supreme message of his master.

After five hundred years had passed, on a certain Sabbath day a young teacher stood up to read the Scriptures in the synagogue at Nazareth. He chose the Isaiah scroll and read from its third section:

> The Spirit of the Lord is upon me,
> Because he hath anointed me to preach the gospel to the poor;
> He hath sent me to heal the brokenhearted,
> To preach deliverance to the captives,
> And recovering of sight to the blind,
> To set at liberty them that are bruised,
> To preach the acceptable year of the Lord.
>
> LUKE 4:18, 19

Rolling up the book, Jesus sat down and began to preach. "This day," He said "is this scripture fulfilled in your ears." Second Isaiah's ancient dreams of God's Servant, so faithfully echoed in the words of Third Isaiah, had at last found their embodiment.

## 15

# The Last of the Prophets

HAGGAI, ZECHARIAH, OBADIAH, MALACHI

IN the rise and fall of ancient empires we find clues to the meaning of many Old Testament passages. Palestine has always been a pawn in international politics and her changing fortunes are reflected on many a Bible page. On the pages of Amos, Hosea, Isaiah, and Micah we saw the shadows cast by Assyrian armies. Nahum's shout of triumph announces the end of Assyria's power and the rise of the new Chaldean Empire. The tramp of Chaldean soldiers echoes through the Books of Habakkuk, Lamentations, Jeremiah, and Ezekiel. Second Isaiah saw a new power arising in the east to overthrow the Chaldeans, and he hailed the coming of Cyrus with his invincible Persian army. Cyrus entered Babylon in triumph and freed the Hebrew exiles living there, allowing as many of them as desired to do so to return to their native land. A Persian governor was appointed to rule over them, Palestine being now only one of the provinces within the Persian Empire. The Hebrews were given freedom in religious matters. The moment so joyfully anticipated by Ezekiel and the other exiles had at last arrived, and the glorious return was now taking place.

There was little joy, however, when the exiles reached their ancient homeland. They found many of their countrymen who had never gone into exile still living amid the ruins of Jerusalem and suffering from misery and poverty. The light of religion had almost gone out. The four prophets of this period ministered to a discouraged people who had all but lost faith in Yahweh. It was a day, as Zechariah described it, "of small things." In the four short books written by these men their picture of a dying religion is only occasionally illuminated by flashes of the old prophetic splendor. Israel returned was not Israel reborn.

The first of Haggai's four sermons was preached in Jerusalem on August 29, 520 B.C. Eighteen years before, many exiles returning from Babylon under a safe-conduct from Cyrus had immediately built houses for themselves and set up businesses, but they had not rebuilt the Temple. Pointing to the heap of stones marking the site where Solomon's Temple had stood, Haggai asked:

> Is it time for you, O ye, to dwell in your ceiled houses, and this house lie waste?
>
> HAGGAI 1:4

Haggai has been called a prophet of "stones and timber," for the main burden of his message was: Rebuild the Lord's House. His words stirred Zerubbabel, the governor whom the Persians had appointed to rule Judea, and Joshua, the high priest, to action. They engaged masons and carpenters to work on the Temple. Haggai made a speech when the cornerstone was laid, declaring that Yahweh would bless his people from that day forward.

Two months after Haggai's first sermon, the prophet Zechariah raised his voice in support of the rebuilding program. Zechariah was more than a prophet of "stones and timber." He reminds us of Ezekiel, for his book contains visions of such things as a rider on a bay horse, a man with a measuring line in his hand, a scroll inscribed with curses, and a heavenly patrol riding in four chariots. At his best Zechariah echoes the teaching of the great prophets. Sacred rites are less important than right living, he declared.

These are the things that ye shall do; Speak ye every man the truth to his neighbour; execute the judgment of truth and peace in your gates: And let none of you imagine evil in your hearts against his neighbour; and love no false oath: for all these are things that I hate, saith the Lord.

ZECHARIAH 8:16, 17

Zechariah looked forward to a time when Yahweh would dwell in the midst of Jerusalem and it should be called the city of truth and in that happier day "the city shall be full of boys and girls playing in the streets thereof." Zechariah's prophecies are in the first eight chapters of the book bearing his name. A later editor added six chapters of miscellaneous prophecies about Jerusalem to the end of Zechariah's scroll.

Even after the Temple was rebuilt, the spiritual life of the Hebrews remained at a low ebb. They seemed to have forgotten the teachings of Second Isaiah. The idea of Israel's self-sacrifice and affliction for the benefit of all mankind was far from the mind of Obadiah. In 460 B.C. he wrote the shortest book in the Bible. Originally it consisted of only fourteen verses which cried for vengeance on Edom. The Edomites living in the mountain country south of the Dead Sea were traditional enemies of the Hebrews. When Obadiah described them as dwelling "in the clefts of the rock," he may have had in mind that "rose-red city, half as old as Time," the strange and incredibly beautiful rock-cut city of Petra. Hatred of Edom darkens some of the pages of Amos, Isaiah, and Jeremiah. When Jerusalem fell to the Babylonians in 586 B.C., Edom had profited by Judah's downfall and now Obadiah rejoiced, for he saw Edom herself falling a prey to marauding Arabs from the southern desert.

Malachi, the last of the prophets, was a contemporary of Obadiah's and lived in Jerusalem about 460 B.C. His real name is unknown and we call him by the title of his book, Malachi, though this is not a proper name and means "my messenger." We can picture this anonymous prophet preaching in the market place not far from the new Temple. Persian soldiers patrol the streets. A curious throng of citizens gathers about Malachi as he rebukes them for their religious indifference. He charges them with being lax in observing the Temple ritual. They offer blemished sacrifices and fail to pay the tithe. Even the priests come under Malachi's condemnation for their failure to teach and to observe the law. He goes on to denounce those who divorce their wives and marry non-Jewish women. The glimpse Malachi gives us of conditions in his day is the picture of a dying church.

Perhaps as Malachi preached, a cry rang out. Someone in that indifferent, disillusioned, and sceptical crowd was bold enough to heckle the prophet.

"Where is the God of judgment?" asked the heckler, and the crowd laughed when Malachi tried to reply. Another voice taunted him: "It is vain to serve God: and what profit is it that we have kept his ordinance?" The rude interruptions remained vivid in Malachi's mind and when he wrote his sermons he incorporated the questions in his book where we can read them today.

Malachi did his best to strengthen men's faith in a day of disillusionment. Some of his lines are unforgettable:

> From the rising of the sun even unto the going down of the same my name shall be great among the Gentiles; and in every place incense shall be offered unto my name, and a pure offering: for my name shall be great among the heathen, saith the Lord of hosts.
>
> MALACHI 1:11

> Have we not all one father? hath not one God created us?
>
> MALACHI 2:10

Malachi leaves us with the impression that all is not well with Israel. Her sickness is moral and spiritual, and she seems to have relinquished her claim to be God's chosen people. Was religion to die in Israel or would it be reborn?

# 16

## The Constitution of a Spiritual Commonwealth

### THE PRIESTLY CODE

WITH a storm of arrows shot at long range the Persians overwhelmed the armies in their path. Though the Greeks halted their advance into Europe in the battles of Marathon and Salamis in 490 and 480 B.C., the Persians with their new and terrifying method of warfare carved out the largest empire of antiquity. It extended from the Persian plateau southward through Mesopotamia, Syria, Palestine, and Egypt to Ethiopia, and from India westward to the Aegean Sea. This vast empire was divided into provinces which enjoyed a large measure of independence in local affairs.

The Persian kings did not interfere with the various religions found in their empire. When they affixed their signatures to edicts allowing subject people to worship as they chose, they little dreamed of the far-reaching effects of this policy. Under it, as we have seen, many Jews returned to Palestine and rebuilt the Temple. It is not hard to imagine what might have happened if the Persians had decreed otherwise. It was usually the fate of ancient peoples to mingle with their conquerors and to lose their distinctive qualities. This was not so with Israel. There was a return from exile. The heritage of law and prophecy was preserved. And it was given to a new group of writers to draw up a document which had a significant part in the rebirth of Israel.

The Hebrews who returned from exile to rebuild Jerusalem faced the realities of their situation. Persian power dominated the world. There was no hope for a restoration of their old Hebrew kingdom. Perhaps it was this despair which made the years of Haggai, Zechariah, and Malachi seem like a time "of small things." In spite of appearances there was far too much vitality in their ancient religion for them to forget their proud descent from Abraham, Isaac, and Jacob. Nor did they cease to believe that Yahweh had chosen them to be His people. Though the nation as an independent political state was dead beyond hope of reviving, a religious nucleus still survived. The vision of a new Israel within the Persian Empire began to take shape. The Hebrews began to see it as a holy nation, a spiritual commonwealth, with a high priest in place of a king. The supreme ruler was Yahweh Himself. Such a holy nation had never been seen before. It did not constitute a defiance of Persia, for it was essentially a church or a congregation of God-worshipers and its laws were ritual laws. In fact, the Persian authorities were well content to see the old Hebrew kingdom transformed into the new Church of Israel.

The dream of a new Israel had been Ezekiel's. Haggai's insistence in 520 B.C. that the Temple at Jerusalem be rebuilt was one of the first acts in the founding of the new Hebrew state. As we shall see in the next chapter, Nehemiah's rebuilding of the walls of Jerusalem in 444 B.C. protected the new spiritual commonwealth from its predatory neighbors. But its real builders were a group of priests who worked in the Temple library sometime between 520 and 470 B.C. Theirs was a silent kind of building. Instead of the ringing blows of the mason's hammer or the scrape of the carpenter's saw, only the noise of a scratching pen or the murmur of voices broke the stillness of the library where the new Israel began to take shape. Surrounded by old documents and the new rolls containing prophecies of Ezekiel, the Holiness Code, and poems of Second Isaiah, a group of priests were at work writing a constitution for the new commonwealth. They were writing laws, genealogies, and stories showing the origins of religious institutions. The document they composed is known as the Priestly Code. So well are its ideas summed up in the following lines that they might well have been used as the introduction to the whole Code:

> Now therefore, if ye will obey my voice indeed, and keep my cove-
> nant, then ye shall be a peculiar treasure unto me above all people:
> for all the earth is mine: And ye shall be unto me a kingdom of
> priests, and an holy nation.
>
> EXODUS 19:5, 6

Perhaps the priestly writers divided themselves into four committees, each specializing in one of the four aspects of their Code: the Sovereign, the people, the land, and the laws. A difficult task faced the group who wrote about their supreme Ruler. Since the time of Moses and Deborah the Hebrew ideas about God had grown from a tribal, warlike deity to Second Isaiah's one God, the Creator of the world. The priestly writers inherited these many conceptions and succeeded in combining them. It was granted to them to present the noblest idea of God in the Old Testament. The stately first chapter of Genesis with its marvelous account of God and His acts of creation is their work.

> In the beginning God created the heaven and the earth.
> And the earth was without form, and void;
> And darkness was upon the face of the deep.
> And the Spirit of God moved upon the face of the waters.
> And God said, Let there be light:
> And there was light.
>
> GENESIS 1:1-3

About five hundred years of theological development separate this majestic chapter written by the priestly writers from the second and third chapters of Genesis, which come down from the beginnings of Hebrew literature. In the ancient second and third chapters of Genesis God walks in a garden in the cool of the day and carries on conversations with Adam and Eve. All this reflects an early period in man's development. when his god is little more than a human being like himself. Years later, when the first chapter of Genesis was written, there had been an immense advance over the old ideas. The writers show us God as a spiritual being who exists beyond earthly limitations. He is the Creator of the universe and at His word the world is formed. He is not like an artisan fashioning man out of dust and woman out of man's rib, instead He creates man and woman by divine command. These conceptions of God on which the Priestly Code is founded were not the invention of the priestly writers. They were, rather, the crystallized essence of centuries of spiritual experience, and embodied the teachings of Amos and the other prophets, of Deuteronomy, Ezekiel, and Second Isaiah.

The two groups of priests who wrote the sections of the constitution dealing with the people and the lands of the new commonwealth were painstaking scholars, but not inspired writers. Laboriously they deciphered torn and faded documents for genealogies and old covenants and boundary descriptions. Their purpose was to trace the descent of God's people from Adam and Eve and to define the boundaries of the land the Lord had given them. Many of the sections they wrote make as dreary reading today as a real estate deed or a family tree. The citizens of fifth-century Jerusalem, whose real estate deeds these actually were and whose ancestors these genealogies traced, did not share our boredom when they read the pages written after so much careful research by the priests.

The laws of the Priestly Code form its longest section and are found scattered through Genesis, Exodus, Leviticus, and Numbers. They deal with the priesthood, festivals, sacrifices, purifications, the Day of Atonement, and various ritual matters. The origin of certain laws is often told in stories, but these cannot compete for drama, characterization, and vividness with those in the old J and E epics.

The Priestly Code begins on the first page of the Bible. It continues throughout the first six books, being embedded there among other writings. It forms the framework of Genesis, some chapters of Exodus, most of Leviticus and Numbers, and parts of Joshua. Usually dates, measurements, catalogues, and genealogies belong to the Priestly Code. Its style is prosaic, methodical, precise, abounding in stereotype phrases. The priests, however, were not incapable of writing literary masterpieces, for, as we have seen, the first chapter of Genesis is their work, as is the priestly blessing:

> The Lord bless thee, and keep thee:
> The Lord make his face to shine upon thee, and be gracious unto thee:
> The Lord lift up his countenance upon thee, and give thee peace.
>
> NUMBERS 6:24-26

The priestly writers were primarily men with legal minds. They were not trying to produce an entertaining book, but to write a body of sacred laws which would preserve the Jews intact as God's own holy people. In this they succeeded. On the day when they put down their pens and wound up the rolls containing the first edition of the Priestly Code there was little to show how effective their constitution would become. Outside in the streets of Jerusalem Malachi, the last of the prophets, was preaching to irreligious crowds. As we shall see in the next chapter, Jerusalem's walls still lay in ruins and the city was scorned among the nations. It needed the energy and vision of a statesman like Nehemiah to rally the people and put the Priestly Code into effect and to establish Judaism. Long after the downfall of the Persian Empire and other empires as well, the religion of the Jews still flourished. It is alive today, due in large measure to the fact that among its foundation stones is the Priestly Code.

## ⁓ 17 ⁓

## *The Memoirs of a Statesman*

### NEHEMIAH

NEAR the head of the Persian Gulf stood the city of Susa, or Shushan, from which Darius and his successors ruled their vast Persian Empire. There, about 430 B.C., in a room of the magnificent imperial palace a man sat writing his autobiography. He was an important official at the Persian court where his position as royal cupbearer brought him constantly into the presence of King Artaxerxes, the successor of Darius and Xerxes. The room in which he worked reflected his wealth and influence, for it was decorated with enameled bricks and its windows commanded a view of the Zagros mountains. A slave was in attendance, filling the inkwell and bringing new reed pens and fresh sheets of specially imported papyrus. For his book the writer was not using Persian cuneiform pressed into soft clay tablets, but he was writing with pen and ink on papyrus in the Hebrew language and alphabet, after the manner of his ancestors. The writer was Nehemiah, a Jew descended from one of the families of the Exile. Though his successful career lay in Susa, his heart was in Palestine, the land of his people. When he sat down to write his autobiography, he wrote not of his life at the imperial court but of his years as a Persian governor of Judah.

Nehemiah could hardly have realized what a unique achievement his book was to be. With the exception of certain Egyptian tomb inscriptions, his is the oldest autobiography we have of a person other than a king. Here, perhaps for the first time in history, a man set down in writing the story of his life. His autobiography sweeps away the barrier of twenty-four centuries and brings us face to face with a fifth-century statesman who did more than anyone else to restore self-respect and hope to the little Hebrew community at Jerusalem.

His autobiography opens with the year 444 B.C., when news reached Nehemiah in Susa of the pitiful condition of the Jews in Palestine. The dreams of Ezekiel and Second Isaiah of a glorious return from exile had not materialized. Even the new Temple, built about 516 B.C. through the influence of the prophets Haggai and Zechariah, had not revived the nation. Writing in 460 B.C., Malachi painted a picture of a dying church. The news that came to Nehemiah was disturbing. People were poor; fields were heavily mortgaged. Many wealthy and influential Jews had chosen to remain in Babylon. The walls of Jerusalem lay in ruins. City walls were a necessary protection against marauding bands of robbers and Yahweh's city was defenseless without them.

As Nehemiah carried the wine cup to Artaxerxes, the news from Jerusalem depressed him. The King asked why he was sad and Nehemiah replied:

> The city, the place of my fathers' sepulchres, lieth waste, and the gates thereof are consumed with fire.
>
> NEHEMIAH 2:3

His own personal success at the Persian court had not dimmed his patriotism nor extinguished his religion. Courageously he asked Artaxerxes to appoint him governor of the Province of Judah. Before long he was on his way to Jerusalem with a retinue of "captains of the army and horsemen." In his traveling pouch were clay documents stamped with the royal seal. One was a letter to the Persian "governors beyond the River" through whose lands he must travel. This safe-conduct assured him of fresh horses and comfortable lodgings on the long journey. Nehemiah also carried a letter to Asaph, the keeper of the royal forests, authorizing him to provide timber for Nehemiah's rebuilding operations. No doubt Nehemiah went armed with his credentials as a duly appointed Persian governor. We may be sure that he kept a sharp eye upon the heavy leather pouches containing his money: gold and silver bars stamped with Persian insignia and also some of the newer Persian coins.

When he reached Jerusalem, Nehemiah went out secretly by night to see for himself the real condition of the walls. In the morning he drew up plans for their rebuilding. He summoned the people together and urged:

Let us build up the wall of Jerusalem, that we be no more a reproach.

NEHEMIAH 2:17

His energy and enthusiasm inspired them and they gave their united reply:

Let us rise up and build.

NEHEMIAH 2:18

The builders worked with their swords girded on, for the Jews had enemies who did not want them to become strong. Sanballat, the ruler of Samaria, Tobiah the Ammonite, and Geshem the Arabian, heaped scorn on the workers and tried to halt the building. Trumpeters were stationed to sound an alarm should danger threaten the workers.

Everyone labored on the walls: priests, district rulers, merchants, perfumers, goldsmiths, and peasant farmers from outlying districts as far away as Jericho. As Nehemiah expressed it, "the people had a mind to work" and within fifty-two days the task was accomplished. For the first time in almost a century and a half Jerusalem was no longer a city to be scorned and despised. Her strong encircling walls restored self-respect to the entire nation.

A later writer, Ben Sirach, in his book, Ecclesiasticus, ended his "Praise of Famous Men" with Nehemiah who "raised up for us the walls that were fallen, and set up the gates and the bars, and raised up our ruins again." The walls and all they symbolized were his memorial. In his autobiography we read of other measures he carried through to make Jerusalem the religious center of Israel. Like the great prophets he sympathized with the misery of the poor and took action to help them. In his zeal to preserve racial purity he excluded from the city people of surrounding districts who were not of Jewish blood and he sternly forbade marriage with foreigners. He reformed Temple worship and ordered people to observe the Sabbath. His policies were all directed toward preserving the Jewish community in Palestine and fencing it off from contamination with foreign blood, foreign ideas, and foreign gods. Nehemiah crystallized Judaism. No longer was Israel's heritage of laws, ethics, and worship in danger of being absorbed and lost in other civilizations. Closing his eyes upon Second Isaiah's vision of Israel's world mission, Nehemiah labored for a nation and a religion as strong and exclusive as the very walls he had built around Jerusalem.

After a second visit to Jerusalem, Nehemiah returned to Susa. No doubt Artaxerxes summoned him into the royal presence to report on his governorship and give an account of his expenditures. Nehemiah may have felt there was something lacking in his report submitted to the Persian king. The work he had done in Jerusalem he had done primarily for his fellow countrymen and for his God. Perhaps that was the reason he sat down in his room in the palace at Susa and composed a second report. This was his autobiography or memoirs. To Nehemiah these memoirs were in the nature of an account of his life offered to God. "Here is what I did for you," he seems to say to God. And at the end of his book he wrote the little prayer:

Remember me, O my God, for good.

NEHEMIAH 13:31

Many years later an historian, known to us as the Chronicler, found Nehemiah's roll. He rewrote and edited some of it, but he also copied long portions of it into his Book of Nehemiah. Chapters 1, 2, 4, 5, and 6 are probably copied from the roll Nehemiah wrote. In chapters 7, 11, 12, and 13 scholars find that the Chronicler has largely rewritten Nehemiah's work. The whole book as we now have it gives an excellent picture of the man whose practical statesmanship and contagious energy played a decisive part in a crucial moment of Hebrew history. He transformed the discouraged Jews living in the Palestine of his day into a proud community conscious of a high destiny and purpose.

## *18*

## *Breaking Down Religious Exclusiveness*

### JOEL, JONAH, RUTH

THE three little books of Joel, Jonah, and Ruth have more in common than their miniature size. Scholars believe that they were all written at about the same time. The books themselves contain no dates, but the ideas they express and other internal evidence reflect the years around 400 B.C. when the Jewish church-state was becoming powerful and the Pentateuch was declared the sacred Law of Israel. It was a time of smug exclusiveness. Israel had her Law from Yahweh and believed herself secure in the divine favor if she were careful to observe every small detail of that Law. Foreign nations did not possess the Law, nor were they Yahweh's people. The strict party of Judaism actually believed foreigners could by their very presence in Jerusalem's Temple contaminate Israel. Joel belonged to the strict Jews. But there was room in Israel for a difference of opinion. Religious exclusiveness must have been hotly debated, for the two stories of Jonah and Ruth reflect the protests of those who opposed Joel's intense nationalism.

A terrible plague of locusts moved Joel to prophecy. Just as Zephaniah, years before, saw in the coming of savage Scythian warriors a herald of the day of wrath, so Joel saw in the coming of an army of locusts a warning of the Day of Judgment. He paints a vivid picture of the locusts swarming over houses, entering the windows, and darkening the sun. Crops were ruined: cattle had no pastures; famine threatened the land. In the Temple the sacrifices stopped for lack of offerings. Joel's message during this calamity begins on a stirring note:

> Blow ye the trumpet in Zion,
> And sound an alarm in my holy mountain:
> Let all the inhabitants of the land tremble:
> For the day of the Lord cometh, for it is nigh at hand.
>
> JOEL 2:1

He urges the people to repent and turn to the Lord with all their heart. All this rings with the spirit of the great prophets, until we discover what Joel means by repenting. To him it consists in performing those external ritual acts of his day: fasting, weeping, girding oneself with sackcloth, and attending a solemn assembly.

In immortal words Joel encourages the people, promising them that a happier time is to come when God will pour out His Spirit:

> And your sons and your daughters shall prophesy,
> Your old men shall dream dreams,
> Your young men shall see visions.
>
> JOEL 2:28

Joel was steeped in the literature of his race. He must have read and memorized many a ringing phrase from earlier prophets, for we discover a score of familiar quotations in his book. But for all his study of his predecessors, he missed Second Isaiah's great doctrine of Yahweh's concern for all nations and he repudiated the idea that Israel's mission was to lead the nations to her God. Joel was intensely nationalistic. He pictured the coming Day of Judgment when Yahweh would gather all nations in the Valley of Jehoshaphat, the valley of decision. A golden age would descend upon Yahweh's people, he said, but punishment awaited heathen nations:

> Egypt shall be a desolation,
> And Edom shall be a desolate wilderness,
> For the violence against the children of Judah . . .

But Judah shall dwell forever,
And Jerusalem from generation to generation.

JOEL 3:19, 20

His picture of Jerusalem, the holy city where the Lord dwells, ends:

Then shall Jerusalem be holy,
And there shall no strangers pass through her any more.

JOEL 3:17

Joel's idea that the mere presence of strangers in Jerusalem could contaminate her holiness was a popular idea of the time. But there were men to whom this narrow view was distasteful. The author of Jonah was one of them. He did not desire to build exclusive walls about his religion, but to tear the walls down. Much of the sublime vision of Second Isaiah was in this unknown author. Instead of arguing about exclusiveness in religion he wrote a tale about it which has become possibly the best-known story of the Old Testament. He spun it out of his own inventive mind, and like storytellers of the East he used marvelous and supernatural events to capture his reader's attention.

It is true that about 780 B.C., in the days of King Jeroboam II, there had been an actual prophet named Jonah. He is mentioned in II Kings 14:25, and no doubt our author found the name for his fictitious hero there. In much the same way, modern novelists find names for their characters on old tombstones or in the telephone book.

The story of Jonah is fascinating. It includes a journey by sea, a storm, a whale, a gourd, a worm, and a repentant city. Its wonders never cease. A man called to be a prophet runs away. A missionary preaches repentance to a city, hoping all the while that the people will *not* repent and that Yahweh will destroy them! A successful missionary, with a whole repentant city to his credit, simply sits down in the shade of his vine and sulks! Our credulity is strained on every page. A modern editor would doubtless reject the story with the comment "Impossible." It is, nevertheless, a masterpiece beloved by young and old, and half its charm consists in its very atmosphere of impossibility. It seems incredible that anyone ever thought the story was actual history. There is, however, an account of how Queen Victoria was so troubled by the story that she asked the Dean of Windsor if it really was necessary for her, as a Christian, to believe that Jonah remained alive three days inside the whale.

When we accept Jonah as an ancient tale, we find that its chief glory rests in its inspired teaching. The author implied that the narrow-minded members of the Jewish Church were like Jonah. Like him they wanted to keep Yahweh for themselves, not share Him with all nations. At the end of the story God Himself sharply rebuked Jonah and declared that He deeply cared for a heathen city. The Book of Jonah was an antidote against Joel's idea that God would soon wipe out other nations. It stood as a protest against the pride and exclusiveness of Judaism.

Like Jonah, the Book of Ruth is also fiction, but it, too, is more than a simple story. On the surface it is a charming idyll of a girl who lived long ago in the time of the "Judges." Between the lines one seems to read a protest against the stern legalism of the fifth century and a plea for tolerance toward people of other races. Nehemiah believed Jewish blood must be kept pure in order that the nation might be holy, and in his day there was a decree that Jewish men must divorce their foreign wives.

The author of Ruth took issue with this harsh and narrow decree. He selected for his heroine a girl from the foreign country of Moab on the eastern side of the Dead Sea. Ruth was a person of gentleness, loyalty, and devotion. The author gave her unforgettably beautiful words to say:

> Entreat me not to leave thee,
> Or to return from following after thee:
> For whither thou goest, I will go;
> And where thou lodgest, I will lodge:
> Thy people shall be my people,
> And thy God my God.
>
> RUTH 1:16

Behind these words we seem to hear the pleading and the tears of foreign wives who were separated by the law from those they loved.

Without arguing his point, the author skillfully closed his tale with the record of Ruth's descendants. This gentle foreigner became the mother of Obed, and Obed's most illustrious grandson was King David. Could anything show more clearly that the character of David's great-grandmother was as pleasing to God as pure Jewish blood? If the children of foreign wives were not true Jews, as the law stated, then what about David? The whole book is a plea for tolerance. The author asks us to believe that a foreigner like Ruth was worthy of being a mother in Israel.

## 19

# First Editions of the Bible

### The Law and the Prophets

O N the day when Nehemiah watched his masons fit the last stone into the walls of Jerusalem, a large part of the Old Testament had already been written. In the library of the Second Temple there were chests filled with rolls of law, legend, history, and prophecy. Some were very old, like the J epic of the tenth or ninth century. Others, like the Priestly Code, were so new that their authors were still alive. Here were the materials out of which the Old Testament would be constructed. They awaited the pens of compilers and editors who would combine the varied documents of Israel's literary and spiritual heritage and publish them in one book. If that had not been done many of these priceless writings would undoubtedly have been lost. We are indebted to the compilers, editors, and scribes who, as it were, packed up the old writings and prepared the volumes in which they were to journey down the centuries. We are also indebted to the unknown people who discerned the spiritual riches in the books and declared them sacred writings.

Perhaps the group of priests who wrote the Priestly Code never disbanded but organized themselves into a corps of editors and compilers. Although we do not know who actually compiled the first edition of the Bible, we believe the work was done in the library of the Second Temple within the new walls of Jerusalem. There, for many years, could be seen scribes bending over their papyrus or parchment rolls copying and editing the ancient texts. If our theories are correct, they did a great amount of sheer copying. Israel's religious experience had been deepened and ripened by the messages of the prophets. The scribes were not content to be mere copyists, nor were they antiquarians eager to preserve old documents simply because they were old. The scribes were primarily teachers of religion filled with the spirit of the prophets and as they copied they remodeled the old documents in the new prophetic spirit. The prophets speak to us primarily from the great books of prophecy, but we can also hear their voices on almost every page of the Pentateuch, which is the superb series of books compiled by the scribes in the Second Temple.

Some of the work of compiling had already been done. The old J epic of 950-850 B.C. with its stories of the patriarchs had long been joined with the E history of 750 B.C. and the resulting J E Document had replaced the separate rolls. Not long after Deuteronomy was found in the old Temple the J E Document had been added to it. In this J E D roll was the nucleus of the Bible. It contained Israel's early history together with her religious and civil laws. To this document of triple origin were to be added the Holiness Code brought from Babylonia, the Priestly Code written for the new Hebrew commonwealth, and other miscellaneous writings. The Priestly Code formed the framework. On the basis of this the editors succeeded in organizing the whole sweep of human history, law, religion, and institutions as recorded in their various documents. They wove this extensive body of materials, written over a period of five hundred years, into one great literary and spiritual masterpiece. This was the first Bible.

About 400 B.C. this first edition of the Bible was finished. For all its vast range it was a much shorter book than our Old Testament, for it comprised only Genesis, Exodus, Leviticus, Numbers, and Deuteronomy. The name given to this compilation was the Law or Torah. In addition to law, it also contains legends, stories, theology, and history. For centuries it was called the Law of Moses from a mistaken idea that Moses was its author. In the Greek period it was named the Pentateuch from "penta" meaning five and "teuch" meaning roll or book. Because of its length it was a work which had to be divided into five rolls. The Greeks gave to each of the five rolls the names now used for them:

> Genesis — The Beginning
> Exodus — The Going Out
> Leviticus — The Law Book of the Levites or Priests
> Numbers — The Numbering or Census of the Israelites
> Deuteronomy — The Second Giving of the Law

The period when the first Bible was in preparation was a time when there were no copyrights, no quotation marks, and no footnotes. Whatever the compilers wished to borrow from the old documents they were perfectly free to use. Much of their material they copied word for word from the old sources, leaving intact long sections from J, E, and D.

One clue scholars use in discovering the various original documents in the Pentateuch is the clue of style. J is the master storyteller. His style is vivid and concrete. His people seem to be real people. His plots move swiftly. E writes in a more conscious style. He is detailed and less direct than J. Deuteronomy preaches and is persuasive. It employs a distinguished vocabulary and its well-formed sentences have a pleasing rhythm. The authors of the Priestly Code were stiff, precise, legalistic, loading their text with lists, statistics, genealogies, and endless repetitions.

The points of view of the various authors also help to separate their work. J saw the world through the eyes of an ancient Hebrew who found nothing incredible in the idea that God walks and talks with men. A hundred years later E's ideas of God are more advanced. He tells how God reveals himself to men through dreams or by means of angels. The men who wrote Deuteronomy were reformers, and almost every line they wrote is stamped with this purpose. As we have seen, the priestly writers wrote the laws for a spiritual commonwealth. They interpreted Israel's past in the light of fifth-century Judaism. These are some of the clues by which scholars discover the various strata of writings in the Pentateuch.

Thanks to their painstaking labors we are now able to understand many conflicting ideas in these books. From the time of J to that of the priestly writers, men's ideas about God advanced steadily from a crude, materialistic stage to ever more spiritual conceptions. In this advance the prophets were the chief leaders. Many stages in Hebrew religious progress are reflected on the pages of the Pentateuch. We shall misunderstand it if we read it as the work of Moses in the thirteenth century B.C., for it contains the spiritual experiences of many Hebrews. It is a record of God's revelation of Himself, not merely to one man at one moment in history, but to many men throughout five hundred years.

The first edition of the Bible became the charter of Judaism, replacing and superseding the Priestly Code. It embodied Jewish religion, history, philosophy, and laws. It taught men how to worship. It became a handbook of ritual and morals. The Jews consulted it constantly, for they believed that it contained the Law of God. The Greek word for a measuring rod or a standard was "canon." The Jews felt that the Pentateuch measured up to the standards for divinely inspired writing and they declared it to be canonical. From the moment the Pentateuch was set apart from all other books as a special, sacred, canonical body of writing its contents became crystallized. Before 400 B.C. its documents had been freely changed. From about 400 B.C. when it was canonized, its text was carefully guarded from changes or errors. Our Pentateuch is substantially the same book declared to be canonical in 400 B.C.

The Samaritan sect or church which split off from orthodox Judaism about this time took to their new Temple on Mount Gerizim a copy of the Bible of that city. The Samaritan Bible even now contains only the Pentateuch. But the Jewish Church did not close its Bible of 400 B.C. against later additions. The historical books from Joshua through Kings contained, as we know, far more than bare history. They were basically religious. Israel believed that God controlled history. The historical series had been compiled from older sources in order to illustrate the great prophetic teaching that God stands behind history and requires righteousness and obedience of Israel. The books were both patriotic and religious. They were also very popular. By 200 B.C. the whole series was declared canonical and given an honored place beside the Pentateuch which for two hundred years had been a holy book. The historical series was classified as the Former Prophets and issued in four volumes: Joshua, Judges, Samuel, Kings.

Meanwhile the writings of the prophets from Amos through Malachi were being collected and edited. About 200 B.C. they also, like the Former Prophets, were declared canonical and issued in four volumes: Isaiah (including Second Isaiah), Jeremiah, Ezekiel, and the Twelve. This last was a collection of the twelve books in our Old Testament from Hosea through Malachi. Unfortunately, the books were not arranged in chronological order beginning with Amos and ending with Joel. We would have arranged them thus: first, the great eighth-century pioneers, Amos, Hosea, Micah; next, the voices of triumph and despair, Nahum, Habakkuk, Zephaniah; then, the post-Exilic prophets, Haggai, Zechariah, Obadiah, Malachi; and finally, the prophet of the locust plague and the Day of Judgment, Joel. There would have been only eleven prophets in our collection, for Jonah, being merely a story of a prophet, we would have put in another group.

Later the Jewish Church added to the Law and the Prophets a third collection of books known as the Writings. They formed a varied and fascinating group whose origins we shall now explore. It was not until the beginning of the Christian era that the Writings were given a place among the sacred Scriptures. When Jesus attended the synagogue school in Nazareth, the Bible was called the Law and the Prophets, and on more than one occasion He refers to it as such. Though the Psalms were not at that time included in the Bible, they were so well known from their use in Temple worship that they were almost in the same class with the sacred Writings. It was not until A.D. 90, however, that the Psalms together with the other Writings were formally declared to be canonical. With the Writings the Old Testament canon closed.

## ❧ 20 ❧

### *An Old Testament Masterpiece*

#### JOB

MANY people think that the most beautiful and brilliant book of the Old Testament is Job. Critics place it among the world's supreme literary achievements. There is nothing quite like it in the Bible. It is a story, a poem, a drama, a volume of philosophy, a description of nature, a guide to morals, and a religious masterpiece all in one. No wonder the book is difficult to classify and seems to belong on a shelf by itself.

Job's place in the lineage of the Bible is also hard to discover, for there is almost nothing in its pages to show who its author was nor when he lived. It has even been suggested that Moses wrote it about 1200 B.C.! But of course this is highly improbable. The various dates modern scholars give it differ by as much as five hundred years. The author's nationality has been questioned, for the background of the story seems to lack definite Jewish features and to be characteristic of the country of Edom. For this and other reasons some think the author may not have been a Jew at all but an Edomite sage. Perhaps as reasonable a guess as any among all these conflicting opinions is that Job was written by an unknown Jew about 400 B.C. This would make it a contemporary of the completed Pentateuch and of Ruth and Joel and Jonah.

Like Jonah and Ruth, Job also voices a protest. As we have seen, there was room for a variety of opinions, and orthodox Judaism, with its Temple, its priesthood, and its holy Book, did not stifle original thinking. Job contains some of the most original and profound thinking in the Old Testament. The theme of the book is the ageless problem of suffering. Its author dared to challenge the orthodox view which said that misery, wretchedness, and sorrow were God's way of punishing sin. The author of Job rebelled against this theory. He found it untrue to the facts, for many blind, crippled, hungry, and bereaved people led blameless lives, while the prosperous, the well-fed, and the healthy were often sinners. He could find no reward for goodness and no just punishment for wrongdoing here on earth. Accordingly he set out to explain his ideas.

Instead of writing a dull treatise, the author, like the writers of Jonah and Ruth, chose an original method of presenting his ideas. There was an ancient folk tale circulating in his day about a man named Job who, though innocent, endured terrible afflictions. In order to bring life and action to his deep subject, the author borrowed the old tale and used it as the framework of his book. It provided a prologue and epilogue and it introduced the chief character Job. The prologue and epilogue are in prose; the rest of the book in poetry.

Job was a wealthy patriarch of Edom, "perfect and upright, and one that feared God" and turned away from evil. In one day he lost all his oxen and asses, his sheep and camels. His servants were murdered and his ten sons and daughters were crushed to death when their house collapsed. Job himself fell ill with a terrible disease. No wonder his three friends Eliphaz, Bildad, and Zophar were speechless when they came to comfort him and "sat down with him upon the ground seven days and seven nights, and none spake a word unto him: for they saw that his grief was very great."

From here on the book is written in magnificent poetry. The seven days of silence are followed by a series of dialogues between Job and his three friends. Job opens the debate with a poem in which he curses the day he was born. The three friends speak, one after another, and Job replies to each one. This cycle of dialogue is repeated three times. A fourth man named Elihu suddenly appears in the thirty-second chapter, but the five chapters in which he harangues Job were probably not part of the original composition and must be considered as the additions of a later writer who was offended at Job's speeches and toned down the book so that it could be read by orthodox Jews.

The three friends, Eliphaz, Bildad, and Zophar, all try to comfort Job. They tell him that there is discipline in suffering. They advise him to seek forgiveness and they tell him there is still hope for him. But all three of his friends hold the conventional idea that Job's suffering must be the penalty for his sins.

> . . . Who ever perished, being innocent?
> Or where were the righteous cut off?
>
> JOB 4:7

Job bitterly denies their indirect accusation that he is guilty and deserves punishment. He calls them "miserable comforters." Everywhere he sees innocent people suffering and the wicked prospering. Surely calamity is no sign of the Lord's disapproval.

His friends are shocked as Job pours out his grief and accuses the Lord of cruelty and injustice. He believes that he is being punished unjustly and in an agony of spirit he cries out that God has abandoned him. Yet Job refuses to "curse God, and die." He still desires to find Him again and enter into fellowship with Him. In the midst of bitter suffering he cries out his faith in God "I know that my redeemer liveth" (Job 19:25). In a flash of insight Job sees that God Himself will be his ultimate champion and vindicator.

After the long debate between Job and his friends, we come to the twenty-eighth chapter with its matchless poem on wisdom.

> But where shall wisdom be found?
> And where is the place of understanding? . . .
> The depth saith, It is not in me:
> And the sea saith, It is not with me.

> It cannot be gotten for gold,
>> Neither shall silver be weighed for the price thereof.
>>>>> JOB 28:12, 14, 15

From here the book continues to its climax. In three superb chapters, 29, 30, 31, Job tells of his former happiness and his present misery. He concludes by describing his code of living. It is the code of a gentleman and its standards are in many respects higher than the requirements of the Pentateuch or the teachings of the prophets. When we read that he had not "made gold my hope," nor "rejoiced at the destruction of him that hateth me," we know that we are face to face with one of the noblest men of the Old Testament. With the challenge, "Behold, my desire is, that the Almighty would answer me," Job rests his case. Almost breathlessly we await God's reply.

By-passing the five chapters of Elihu's speeches, we come to the majestic poems of the final chapters, 38 to 40, where the Lord "answered Job out of the whirlwind." In a series of tremendous questions God showed Job the limits of his human knowledge.

> Where wast thou when I laid the foundations of the earth?
>> Declare, if thou hast understanding . . .
> Whereupon are the foundations thereof fastened?
>> Or who laid the corner stone thereof;
> When the morning stars sang together,
>> And all the sons of God shouted for joy?     JOB 38:4, 6, 7

Question after question piles up the evidence of God's infinite power and wisdom and makes Job see his own insignificance. How had he dared to question divine justice? Who was Job to declare that God should always reward the good and punish the evildoer? Job repented his rebellious word. His estrangement from God ended when he heard the voice from the whirlwind. He had been granted a deep, personal experience of God and that was enough for him.

> I have heard of thee by the hearing of the ear:
>> But now mine eyes seeth thee.
> Wherefore I abhor myself,
>> And repent in dust and ashes.     JOB 42:5, 6

In the mighty fact of God's nearness, Job's heart found the peace "which passeth all understanding." The problem of why the innocent suffer still remained a mystery, as it does to this day. Job was content to leave this problem unanswered, for his experience of God convinced him that divine justice was deeper than man could understand. Like Job, modern man has found in faith the only answer to the otherwise insoluble problem of suffering.

False ideas sometimes take centuries to die. Four hundred years after Job was written, the orthodox teaching about suffering as a punishment for sin still controlled men's minds. The disciples questioned Jesus about a blind man.

> Master, who did sin, this man, or his parents, that he was born blind?
> Jesus answered, Neither hath this man sinned, nor his parents.
>
> JOHN 9:2, 3

Though men were slow to accept Job's teaching about sin, punishment, and suffering, they were not blind to the sheer magnificence of the book. They were amazed at its large vocabulary, the most varied of any Old Testament book. Their minds were enriched by its wide learning. All who heard it read must have been spellbound by its superb poetry. Even though Job protested against some of the dogmas of Judaism, it was finally accepted into the canon of the sacred books of Israel where it has attained the immortality Job longed for.

> Oh that my words were now written!
> Oh that they were printed in a book!
> That they were graven with an iron pen and lead
>     In the rock for ever!
>
> JOB 19:23, 24

# *21*

## Wise Men of Israel

PROVERBS, ECCLESIASTES

A FAMILIAR figure in the ancient world was the sage or wise man with his store of pithy sayings and his reputation for wisdom. Egypt and Babylonia had their wise men; the sages of Edom and Greece were famous; and Israel, too, had her teachers of wisdom. They were quite different from the prophets who thundered: "Thus saith the Lord." Though they lacked the grandeur of such spiritual statesmen as Hosea or Isaiah, the wise men were highly regarded. They were professors of the art of living and addressed themselves to individuals rather than to the nation. They taught young men the rules of good conduct and how to live successfully. In any age their lectures would have been popular, for they spoke on such subjects as: How To Be Happy, How To Succeed In Business, The Value of Wisdom, The Ideal Wife, What Life Is About. From their store of worldly wisdom the sages taught the virtues of honesty, thrift, industry, chastity, truthfulness, and regard for others. Unlike the author of Job, most of the wise men taught that God would reward these virtues with long life, happiness, and prosperity.

In their day the sages were considered to be very learned men. They were able to read Hebrew as well as other languages, and their teaching material was drawn not only from their own observation and experience but also from an international fund of traditional wisdom. They were, moreover, literary craftsmen, clever with words, possessed of a keen sense of form and rhythm, and skilled in the writing of proverbs, sayings, and maxims. Each wise man must have taken pride in his own collection of proverbs, improving and polishing them until his young men students exclaimed over their brevity, imagination, and beauty. The wise men would have found much in common with Confucius, the great Chinese sage of the sixth century B.C., and had they been able to understand his language they would doubtless have borrowed many of his wise sayings.

About 400 B.C. someone decided to publish an anthology of wisdom. He chose eight collections of proverbs and sayings and published them in a single volume. This is the Book of Proverbs. Its title is the longest one in the Bible, occupying six verses and serving as an introduction. Many sages contributed to this little library of wisdom, and its title might well have been: Proverbs Ancient and Modern, From Eight Famous Collections. The actual title of the anthology itself as well as of three of its collections contain the words: The Proverbs of Solomon. Though Solomon's biographers claimed that "he spake three thousand proverbs," modern scholars think that the Book of Proverbs contains little if anything that he wrote. No doubt some of the ideas go back to Solomon's time, but their expression seems to belong to a period much later than the tenth century. By the fifth century, however, Solomon had become a sort of patron saint of the wise men and they named their anthology in his honor.

The first collection, comprising the first nine chapters, opens with its main theme:

> The fear of the Lord is the beginning of knowledge:
> But fools despise wisdom and instruction.
>
> PROVERBS 1:7

It is a long speech and, after the custom of the sages, it is addressed to an individual pupil called "my son" by an unknown teacher who calls himself "thy father." It advises the youth to search for wisdom which is "better than rubies" and it warns him against wicked men and evil women.

The second collection is entitled: The Proverbs of Solomon. It extends from chapter 10 to 22:16 and among its miscellaneous teachings are such well-known sayings as these:

> A soft answer turneth away wrath:
> But grievous words stir up anger.
>
> PROVERBS 15:1

> He that is slow to anger is better than the mighty;
> And he that ruleth his spirit than he that taketh a city.
>
> PROVERBS 16:32

> A merry heart doeth good like a medicine:
> But a broken spirit drieth the bones.
>
> PROVERBS 17:22

> A good name is rather to be chosen than great riches,
> And loving favour rather than silver and gold.
>
> PROVERBS 22.1

The next two collections are entitled: The Words of the Wise, 22:17—24:22, and the Sayings of the Wise, 24:23-34. They illustrate the international character of wisdom literature, for they are not Hebrew in origin but are adaptations from the ancient Egyptian book, The Wisdom of Amen-em-ope, of about 1000 B.C. An Egyptian papyrus copy of this book can now be seen in the British Museum. The compiler of Proverbs must have used a Hebrew translation of this as his source. In the Sayings of the Wise occurs the oldest known form of the Golden Rule. Here it is little more than a restraining hand upon a man who wants to "get even" with another.

> Say not, I will do so to him as he hath done to me.
>
> PROVERBS 24:29

In this we see the Egyptian ancestry of what was to develop into a high ethical teaching. Confucius, around 500 B.C., expressed the teaching negatively: "What you do not like when done to yourself do not do to others."

With Jesus the teaching reached its full stature:

> Whatsoever ye would that men should do to you, do ye even so to them.
>
> MATTHEW 7:12

The fifth collection is named for Solomon and the proverbs are said to be those "which the men of Hezekiah king of Judah copied out." These native Hebrew sayings are followed by two foreign collections: The Words of Agur the son of Jakeh, 30, and The Words of King Lemuel, the oracle which his mother taught him, 31:1-9. Finally, the Book of Proverbs closes with a matchless poem describing a worthy woman.

From Proverbs, with its practical help in living a good life, we come to the cynical volume entitled Ecclesiastes. It is a strange book to find in the Bible, for its teaching that human life is futile runs counter to almost everything else in the Old Testament. Like Proverbs, Ecclesiastes belongs to the wisdom literature and it seems to be the notebook from which a third-century teacher instructed the youth of Jerusalem. In Hebrew he is called "Qoheleth," which means "one who addresses an assembly." The Greek translation of "Qoheleth" is "Ecclesiastes" and its English equivalent is "The Preacher," but with all these names we still do not know who the author was. In the opening of the book the author speaks as though he were Solomon, son of David, but he soon throws off this disguise and becomes a typical third-century wise man who "still taught the people knowledge; yea, he gave good heed, and sought out, and set in order many proverbs. The preacher sought to find out acceptable words: and that which was written was upright, even words of truth" (Ecclesiastes 12:9, 10).

Qoheleth opened his book with the disheartening statement that "vanity of vanities, all is vanity" (1:2). He taught the young men of Jerusalem that "all things are full of weariness" (1:8) and that life has no meaning. Wherever he looked he seemed to see blind chance ruling the world and he said that:

> The race is not to the swift, nor the battle to the strong, neither yet bread to the wise, nor yet riches to men of understanding, nor yet favour to men of skill; but time and chance happeneth to them all.
>
> ECCLESIASTES 9:11

He "commended mirth, because a man hath no better thing under the sun, than to eat, and to drink, and to be merry" (8:15). In spite of its unrelieved despair Qoheleth's book was charmingly written and its description of old age and death in chapters 11:9 to 12:7 is a masterpiece:

> Or ever the silver cord be loosed, or the golden bowl be broken, or the pitcher be broken at the fountain, or the wheel broken at the cistern. Then shall the dust return to the earth as it was: and the spirit shall return unto God who gave it.
>
> ECCLESIASTES 12:6, 7

No doubt some of his students attempted to tone down the book's pessimism by inserting a few pious statements like:

> Remember now thy Creator in the days of thy youth.
>
> ECCLESIASTES 12:1

One editor actually warned readers against taking its teachings too seriously:

> Of making many books there is no end; and much study is a weariness of the flesh.
>
> ECCLESIASTES 12:12

Perhaps the sentence added by a pious editor at the end of the roll finally won for this strange and unorthodox book a place in the canon:

> Fear God, and keep his commandments: for this is the whole duty of man.
>
> ECCLESIASTES 12:13

Besides Job, Proverbs, and Ecclesiastes the Jews had other volumes of wisdom literature. Among these were Ecclesiasticus and The Wisdom of Solomon, which, as we shall see in another chapter, were not to become part of the Old Testament canon, but were preserved in the Apocrypha.

## 22

# Israel's Golden Treasury

## PSALMS

**M**ANY Bibles have a worn section exactly in the middle of the volume where the book tends to open of its own accord and the edges of the pages are no longer crisp. This is not surprising, for here is found the best-loved of all Old Testament books, the Book of Psalms. From about 100 B.C., when this anthology of religious poetry was finally completed, it has remained one of the most popular of books. On its pages people like ourselves left the record of their joys and sorrows, their faith and despair, their longing for God and their praises to Him. As Martin Luther said in his second Preface to the Psalter, here we "can look into the hearts of all the saints." Israel's prophets, lawmakers, historians, and sages often appear to us as strange and remote men of a vanished civilization. But with her psalmists we feel at home, for they seem to be like our own brothers.

Though we do not know the names of the psalmists nor exactly where and when they lived, some of their songs show us what sort of men they were. A few of them may have been shepherds guarding their flocks on the Judean hillsides. At night wrapped in their cloaks they looked up at the stars and tried to find words for the beauty of the heavens and their faith in God. Perhaps a shepherd poet composed the first version of such lines as:

> When I consider thy heavens, the work of thy fingers,
> The moon and the stars, which thou hast ordained;
> What is man, that thou art mindful of him?
> And the son of man, that thou visitest him?
>
> PSALM 8:3, 4

And who but one to whom the shepherd's life was familiar could have written the psalm beginning: "The Lord is my shepherd"?

Other psalms beat out the rhythm of marching feet and may have been composed by people on their way up to Jerusalem for the Passover.

> I was glad when they said unto me,
> Let us go into the house of the Lord.
>
> PSALM 122:1

Singing a song like this would surely help the pilgrims forget the dust and heat and weariness of the long road up to the Holy City. Year after year bands of pilgrims would sing the song, improving it from time to time, until at length so many had worked on it that no one could be called its author. It became as anonymous as a traditional folk song.

Some idea of the impressiveness of the Temple services which the pilgrims attended when they reached Jerusalem is given in this description from Ecclesiasticus:

> Then shouted the sons of Aaron, and sounded the silver trumpets, and . . . all the people together hasted, and fell down to the earth upon their faces to worship their Lord God Almighty, the most High. The singers also sang praises with their voices, with great variety of sounds was there made sweet melody.
>
> ECCLESIASTICUS 50:16-18

The silver trumpets no longer sound and the sweet melody has perished together with the guilds of singers who sang praises with their voices, but in many a psalm we hear an echo of the words in which the priests and people praised the Lord. Perhaps one of these is Psalm 95 which may have belonged in one of the Temple hymnbooks.

O come, let us sing unto the Lord:
Let us make a joyful noise to the rock of our salvation.
Let us come before His presence with thanksgiving,
And make a joyful noise unto Him with psalms.

Though all the tunes to which the psalms were once sung have perished, we know that the ancient Temple music was elaborate. In the last psalm, the 150th, there is a catalogue of musical instruments: trumpets, psalteries, harps, timbrels, stringed instruments, pipes, loud cymbals, and high-sounding cymbals.

Some of the obscure words which puzzle translators may be musical directions to the singers or to the musicians who played upon these various instruments. The word "selah," which occurs seventy-one times, may be a musical relic which once meant: Pause here for an instrumental interlude.

The group of psalms from 113 to 118 are known as the great *Hallel* and were part of the liturgy at the Passover and other festivals. Perhaps the "hymn" which Mark says Jesus and His disciples sang after the Last Supper before they went out to the Mount of Olives included Psalms 115 to 118, traditionally sung after the Passover meal.

The Book of Psalms contains a selection of the hymns used in public worship as well as many personal prayers and meditations. Among the psalmists were pious Jews who wrote, not so much for the guilds of singers nor for the multitudes worshiping in the Temple, as for those who carried on their devotions in the privacy of their own homes. Psalm 51 with its cry of "a broken and a contrite heart" belongs in the treasury of personal devotion. We shall be only partially correct if we describe Psalms as the Hymnbook of the Second Temple. It contains so many psalms of a personal nature that it may well have been used by the faithful Jew as a prayer book for his own devotions.

Among the psalmists of Israel, the shepherds, pilgrims, priests, singers, and devout men, there is not one whose name we know. Many a psalm has an introductory note which seems to tell the author and the occasion for which it was written, but these notes are thought to be late additions and unreliable. Various collections of psalms once bore the title: Psalms of David. When an individual psalm was taken from one of these collections it was labeled: "A Psalm of David." The word "David" in connection with a psalm cannot be taken as a statement of its authorship but as a gesture of dedication. Probably none of the psalms were composed by David, for the words in which they are written and the ideas they express belong to a period six hundred years and more after Israel's royal poet died. Just as the Pentateuch was attributed to Moses and Proverbs to Solomon, so, many psalms bear David's name, reminding us that to the Jews David was the symbol of poetry and song.

The Book of Psalms was in the making for three hundred years, from about 400 B.C. when the Pentateuch was canonized, to about 100 B.C. when the psalms were finally published. There are, however, a few psalms which possibly come from an earlier period. Psalm 104 seems to come from a period long before Moses and to be an echo of an Egyptian hymn written about 1370 B.C. by Ikhnaton to the Sun-god Aton. It is inscribed on the walls of a tomb in Tel el-Amarna, where it may still be read. Did some Jewish traveler see it there and use its monotheism and its imagery in a hymn of praise to Yahweh? For the most part the psalms were written when Israel's kings had long been dead, when the Exile was only a memory, and when the teachings of the prophets had at last been accepted by the average Jew and incorporated into his religion. The psalms reflect the period when Israel was a church-state, when her law was the Pentateuch, and her ruler was the high priest, and when the Temple was the heart of the nation.

Monotheism is the rock on which the psalms are founded. The long struggle against the "other gods" was all but won, and the faith of the prophets in one God, Yahweh, is the faith of the psalmists. They praise Him and offer Him thanks for His loving-kindness and righteousness. His majesty and His mystery inspire them to write some of the noblest lines in all poetry. In such a large collection we inevitably find different points of view, some cruder and less spiritual than others. Some of the psalmists glorify the Temple sacrifices, while others join the prophets in protesting against these rites. Some are satisfied with God's justice, while others, like Job, are perplexed to see innocent people suffering. Rampant nationalism that curses Israel's enemies is side by side with a belief like that of Second Isaiah's that God is Lord of all mankind. Here and there we find moods that are unworthy of Israel at her best: self-satisfaction, complaint, revenge. But from first to last the dominant note of the psalms is praise and thanksgiving to God and confidence in the Lord of Israel.

> He that dwelleth in the secret place of the most High
>> Shall abide under the shadow of the Almighty.
> I will say of the Lord, He is my refuge and my fortress:
>> My God; in Him will I trust.
>
> PSALM 91:1, 2

Many collections were available to the compiler of the Book of Psalms when he assembled his anthology about 100 B.C. From abundant stores he chose poems which would feed the heart and soul of the devout man of his day, the man described in the first psalm, which is actually a prose introduction to the entire collection. The age seems to have known a flowering of private worship and to this the Book of Psalms contributed in no small measure, as it continues to contribute to personal devotion today.

In imitation of the five books of the Law, the compiler divided the one hundred and fifty psalms he had chosen into five books, each ending with a doxology. The five books are: 2 to 41, 42 to 72, 73 to 89, 90 to 106, 107 to 150. This division was an artificial one. Within the books are evidences of older collections, such as the Psalms of David; the Pilgrim Songs of Ascents, 120 to 134; and the Liturgical Hymns sung at the Passover, 111 to 118.

One fascinating little collection of psalms are those now numbered 42 to 49, 84, 85, 87, 88. All these, with the exception of

43 which was once part of 42, contain in their title the words "A Psalm of the sons of Korah." Tracing the name Korah through the Old Testament, we find that Korah was an Edomite family or clan that settled down in Hebron and eventually became part of the Hebrew tribe of Judah. When the Korahites first entered the Temple service, they held the lowly position of servants. They acted as cooks and "had the set office over the things that were made in the pans" (I Chronicles 9:31). Some of the Korahites were Temple gatekeepers and "were over the work of the service, keepers of the gates of the tabernacle" (I Chronicles 9:19). This was a humble position, but, looking back upon it, the Korahites did not despise it. Later they were to sing in one of their anthems:

> I had rather be a doorkeeper in the house of my God.
> Than to dwell in the tents of wickedness.
>
> PSALM 84:10

Eventually their foreign origin was forgotten and they rose to become a guild of Temple singers who "stood up to praise the Lord God of Israel with a loud voice on high" (II Chronicles 20:19). No doubt the twelve psalms enumerated above were selected from the ancient hymnbook used by the Korahite guild of Temple singers.

The poetry of Psalms lends itself remarkably well to translation into English. Fortunately rhyme, which can seldom be carried over into another language, was not used by Hebrew poets. They achieved their beautiful effects by repeating the thought of one line in the second line, or by using the second line to contrast with or to complete the idea in the first line. Hebrew poetry flies, as it were, upon two wings.

> The heavens declare the glory of God;
> And the firmament sheweth his handywork.
>
> PSALM 19:1

Even when the parallel construction is more complicated, we can still hear the double beat of repetition or contrast or completion which carries the verse forward.

> The Lord is my light and my salvation;
>   Whom shall I fear?
> The Lord is the strength of my life;
>   Of whom shall I be afraid?
>
> PSALM 27:1

There is a further reason for the successful translation of the Hebrew psalms into English. Abstract ideas are difficult to translate, but the Hebrew poets did not use these. Instead, they expressed their ideas in concrete, vivid pictures. The psalms are not a museum of religious emotions with the exhibits carefully labeled and kept lifelessly under glass. They are, rather, a living collection where everything moves and breathes and cries and sings. Hebrew poets were incapable of smothering an idea with abstract words. They could not have written this: "In connection with the Divine Being it is fairly reasonable to assume that men can rely upon such a Being for leadership, for protection, and for provision for human subsistence." They said the same thing briefly, clearly, unforgettably:

> The Lord is my Shepherd;
>   I shall not want.
>
> PSALM 23:1

The word Shepherd "springs our imagination." The picture it paints is alive with many meanings, and our minds leap to understand all the psalmist packed into one common word. The psalmists were masters of the quickening phrase which has the power to kindle men's minds.

The psalms abound in vivid pictures of things we see and hear and handle. There are stars, rocks, mountains, storms, fortresses, cities, fields, grass, harps, cups, the shadow of wings, the cattle upon a thousand hills. And all the pictures move. There is sleeping and waking, building and teaching, leaping and running, casting down and lifting up. Each image flashes upon the screen of our imagination, setting in motion an endless series of thoughts and feelings. It is not so much what the psalms actually say as it is the thoughts they awaken in our minds that really matter. They act upon us in much the same fashion as a motion picture. As we all know, a motion picture is a series of shadows moving on a screen. Our imagination clothes these shadows with reality and we enter into the experiences of the people who first set the shadows moving. In a similar way the word pictures of the psalms are "carried alive into the heart" where they recreate afresh in us the spiritual experience of long-dead psalmists. As long as the psalms are able to effect this miracle they will remain what they have been to multitudes of devout people throughout the ages, an inexhaustible source of comfort, inspiration, and spiritual power.

## 23

### The Literary Harvest of a Century

CHRONICLES, EZRA, NEHEMIAH, SONG OF SOLOMON,
DANIEL, ESTHER

THE final books of the Old Testament were written in a little more than a century from 250 B.C. to 125 B.C., the same century that produced Ecclesiastes from its cynicism and many of the psalms with their triumphant faith. To this century belong the four-volume history comprising I and II Chronicles, Ezra, and Nehemiah; the anthology of love poetry known as the Song of Solomon; the stirring apocalypse of Daniel; and the historical romance of Esther. In addition, a number of the books of the Apocrypha were written during these years. Surely all these were a rich harvest to spring from the worship, the human joys, and the political turmoils of Jewish life in the third and second centuries B.C.

Modern scholars think it is probable that one man wrote the books of I and II Chronicles, Ezra, and Nehemiah (exclusive of the chapters from Nehemiah's Memoirs). No one contributed more pages to the Old Testament than this author and no one attempted to cover such a vast sweep of history as he did. His work extends from Adam to the Persian period in the fourth century B.C. The writer of this ambitious history is known to us simply as the Chronicler, a name suggesting ink and pens and a scholar poring over old rolls. In his own day, however, the Chronicler may have been famous not so much for his literary gifts as for his beautiful voice. It is almost certain that he was a Levite belonging to one of the guilds of singers who sang the psalms in the Temple. The glory of the Temple filled his mind and he seems to have written his four-volume book as an historical background to the laws, the ritual, and the music of Jerusalem's Second Temple.

Few readers have patience to follow the Chronicler through his endless genealogies and they find his statistics incredible. We are staggered by his assertion that David's army numbered a million and a half men (I Chronicles 21:5) and that the equivalent of three billion gold dollars (I Chronicles 22:14) were contributed to the Temple building fund. Can these huge statistics really be about David's reign? His portrait of David is so highly colored that David's biographer would hardly recognize his friend who rose from a shepherd boy to be a king of Israel. This is not the David we know, but a stained glass figure of the founder of an elaborate ecclesiastical organization. According to the Chronicler, David did little during his reign but capture Jerusalem, transport the Ark there, and collect materials for the building of the Temple. On every page we find anachronisms. The account of music and worship in David's reign is really a picture of the Jewish Church of the Chronicler's day, nearly seven hundred years after David. He magnifies the function of the Levites and singers to such an extent that at one point they overcome two armies merely by singing hymns (II Chronicles 20:20-31)! Indeed, there is so much singing in the Chronicler's books that we wonder at times whether this is history or opera.

For all his exaggerations and distortions the Chronicler left a valuable story. Though it is far from being history, it does preserve many an old record and it gives us an idea of Temple worship. For the two Books of Chronicles the author found material in the Pentateuch and in the old histories of Joshua, Samuel, and Kings. He also used books, genealogies, and official records now lost. All this material he selected, arranged, rewrote or edited, stamping the entire work with his own language and point of view.

His twin books of Ezra and Nehemiah are a continuation of Chronicles and carry the history of Israel down into the Persian period when the Temple was restored, the walls of Jerusalem rebuilt, and the Law became central in Judaism. To carry forward the story of this period, the Chronicler used long excerpts from Nehemiah's autobiography, probably written at Susa. In the Book of Ezra and in some chapters of Nehemiah he introduced the intriguing figure of a priest and scribe named Ezra. Today Ezra puzzles the scholars. Some think he was only an imaginary character invented by the Chronicler to embody the importance and prominence of the Law in this period. Other scholars believe Ezra actually lived, but came after Nehemiah rather than before. Even if we cannot rely on the Chronicler's story of Ezra for actual history, we do gain from it a picture of the scribes of this period. The scribes, a group who studied and taught the Law, were destined to become leaders in Israel, and it is in no small measure due to such men as Ezra and his followers that the Bible became a cornerstone of Judaism. The Chronicler served us well in preserving or creating the story of Ezra, who typifies one stage in the lineage of the Bible.

In the Song of Solomon there is singing also, but it is of a different kind from that of the Chronicler. Here are no choirs nor trumpets nor praises to Yahweh. This book is a collection of love songs, and religion has no place in it. Against a background of Palestine in the springtime these poems celebrate the love of a man and a woman and were perhaps written to be sung at wedding festivities. The songs in this anthology seem to come from several poets whose vocabulary and style of writing indicate that they lived about 250 B.C. Solomon's name in the title does not, of course, indicate that he is the author and this book can no more be attributed to him than can Proverbs or Ecclesiastes. These poems contain beautiful Oriental imagery, but they are definitely love songs and one wonders why they were included among the sacred Writings. Perhaps this came about when Jewish religious leaders went beyond the actual meaning of the words and interpreted them allegorically. According to their interpretation, Yahweh was the bridegroom and the Congregation of Israel was the bride. These allegorical interpretations raised the Songs into the class of religious works and Rabbi Akiba rebuked the young men of his day who sang them as love ditties in the wine shops. The Christian Church also looked beyond the literal meaning of the words and, as the headings in the English translation of 1611 show, interpreted the poems in terms of Christ and the Church. Today we take the same view of the poems as did the young men who sang them in the wine shops. To most of us they are valuable, not as religious meditations, but as examples of Hebrew secular poetry. We are fortunate to have inherited from the past such lovely poems as this one about spring:

> For, lo, the winter is past,
> The rain is over and gone;
> The flowers appear on the earth;
> The time of the singing of birds is come,
> And the voice of the turtle is heard in our land;
> The fig tree putteth forth her green figs,
> And the vines with the tender grape give a good smell.
> Arise, my love, my fair one, and come away.
>
> SONG OF SOLOMON 2:11-13

The last religious book of the Old Testament was written nearly a hundred years after the Chronicler's four volumes. This is Daniel, which appeared in 165 B.C. during the bitter Maccabean revolt. At this time the Syrian king, Antiochus Epiphanes, tried to force Greek culture and religion upon Palestine and to stamp out all traces of Judaism. He plundered the Temple of its golden treasures and desecrated it by offering heathen sacrifices to Zeus upon its altar. The author of Daniel writes of this as "the abomination that maketh desolate." Antiochus Epiphanes ordered loyal Jews to be executed and he burned the books of the Law. The Jews met this first religious persecution in their history with courage and steadfastness. Some

deserted to the Greek side, but many joined the desperate uprising of Judas Maccabeus, whose story is told in the Apocrypha
in I and II Maccabees. The author of Daniel belonged to a group
of loyal Jews, the Hasidim, who resisted persecution. His book
was a trumpet call to the Jews to stand fast in their faith and
trust in God's unfailing power. The first six chapters contain
the story of a Jewish hero, Daniel, who successfully resisted the
older tyranny of Persia, and withstood every test of his faith.
Though Daniel is supposed to have lived at the court of
Nebuchadnezzar, the trials he met were really those of the
author's own day when the Jews were suffering under Antiochus
Epiphanes. The Hasidim must have read with keen interest
the stories of the burning fiery furnace and the lion's den, and
of the handwriting on the wall at Belshazzar's feast when a king
of old who persecuted the Jews was condemned. These stories
quickened their hope and faith that God would protect and
reward their loyalty as he had Daniel's.

Chapters 7 through 12 contain a series of visions in which the
author comments on the terrible persecutions of the Jews of
his day. He predicts the end of foreign rule and the triumph of
God's faithful people. This type of writing is called an apocalypse. It is different from prophecy out of which it grew. Prophecy summons people to righteous living; an apocalypse encourages people to endure their present suffering by showing them
that their reward and deliverance is at hand.    Prophecy has
its feet on the ground. An apocalypse is in the clouds. The
prophets stood up and spoke their own message. The authors
of the apocalypses wrote anonymously and attributed their work
to the distant past. An apocalypse is visionary, unreal, fantastic,
abounding in symbols. Daniel is the Old Testament apocalypse
as Revelation is the New Testament apocalypse. There are, in
addition, shorter apocalypses written in Daniel's period and
inserted in Isaiah, Ezekiel, Joel, and Zechariah.

With such visions as this Daniel tried to show the righteous
Jew of his day that his sufferings would be rewarded in a glorious future:

> I saw in the night visions, and, behold, one like the Son of man
> came with the clouds of heaven, and came to the Ancient of days . . .
> And there was given him dominion, and glory, and a kingdom, that
> all people, nations, and languages, should serve him:  his dominion
> is an everlasting dominion, which shall not pass away, and his kingdom
> that which shall not be destroyed.
>
> DANIEL 7:13, 14

In Daniel occurs the first clear statement in the Old Testament of man's hope of a resurrection after death.

> And many of them that sleep in the dust of the earth shall awake,
> some to everlasting life, and some to shame and everlasting contempt.
> And they that be wise shall shine as the brightness of the firmament;
> and they that turn many to righteousness as the stars for ever and ever.
>
> DANIEL 12:2, 3

In both language and thought Daniel looks beyond the boundaries of the Old Testament and reminds us of the world of the New. Part of Daniel was written in the classical Hebrew of the Old Testament, a language which had become antiquated by the Maccabean period when it was spoken only by scholars and religious men. At this time the common people of Palestine spoke Aramaic, and it is in this new language that chapters 2 through 7 were written. Aramaic was to be the language spoken a century and a half later by Jesus and the disciples.

The apocalyptic chapters of Daniel exercised a profound influence in New Testament days. Jesus himself must have studied this book, for He found in Daniel's vision of the Son of Man coming with the clouds of heaven a picture which partly explained His own Being. When the High Priest asked Him if He were the Christ: He replied:

> I am:  and ye shall see the Son of man sitting on the right hand of
> power, and coming in the clouds of heaven.
>
> MARK 14:62

Written in the heat of a desperate struggle, the Book of Daniel matched the flaming zeal and courage of the Maccabean patriots. Even if they died they could hope that in the end God's cause would gloriously triumph. Daniel painted a background for the violent acts of the Maccabean revolt and this background is the "scenery of eternity."

Esther, the last Old Testament book to be written, is not a religious book but an historical romance that at times reminds us of the *Arabian Nights*. As soon as it was written by an un- known author in Jerusalem about 125 B.C. it became popular. Its heroine is a beautiful Jewish girl who became Queen of Persia and risked her life to save her people. It contains royal banquets, a beauty contest, an assassination plot, trickery, and revenge. Though the story opens with a feast lasting the in- credible number of 180 days and continues with other exag- gerations, it holds the reader's attention with its well-drawn characters, its lively dialogue, and its dramatic suspense. This book must have captured the imagination of its many readers in the second century B.C.

It is surprising to find such a book in the Bible. Search as we will through its ten chapters, we shall nowhere find in it the name of God. Esther is the only book in the Bible which does not mention the name of God. Patriotism, not religion, is its theme. It is a patriotism which at the end degenerates into revenge and exults when seventy-five thousand helpless enemies are slaughtered. Possibly this book was written to introduce a new patriotic holiday, the Feast of Purim. Every year on the fourteenth and fifteenth of Adar (March), the festival of Purim was celebrated and the roll of Esther read. What was at first merely a popular novel became so closely associated with the Feast of Purim that it was at last declared sacred Scripture. Certain additions were made to the Greek version of Esther and these included a long prayer of the Jewish Queen. Perhaps this prayer helped to win a place for Esther in the canon. Today these Greek editions are to be found in the Apocrypha under the title: The Rest of the Chapters of the Book of Esther.

Of course the story of Esther is fiction, not fact, for history knows nothing of a Jewish Queen of Persia, and Esther herself must be placed among the imaginary heroines of literature. Though King Ahasuerus probably represents Xerxes and the details of Persian life and customs are authentic, the book does not belong among the histories but with such other works of fiction as Ruth, Jonah, and Daniel. Though there were many who opposed including Esther in the Bible, it now stands there as a fascinating example of the ancient short story and as a reflection of the age in which its author lived. Its low level of nationalism, descending at times to revenge, matches the spirit of the period when the Jews under John Hyrcanus were fighting for survival. Lest we judge the period that produced Esther too harshly, we must remember that while this story represents its popular fiction many of the psalms represent its religion.

## 24

# The Books that Were Left Out

## THE APOCRYPHA

IN 200 B.C. the Hebrew Bible consisted of the thirteen books of the Law and the Prophets. Before long other books began to associate with these sacred Scriptures. In 132 B.C. Ben Sira's grandson wrote a preface to his Greek translation of his grandfather's book, Ecclesiasticus. In this he spoke of "the law and the prophets and other books of our fathers." Again he said "the law itself, and the prophets, and the rest of the books." Though these remarks do not tell us exactly what the "rest of the books" were, they do provide us with our earliest clue to the fact that the Hebrew Bible of the second century B.C. had a third section. This shadowy "rest of the books" was to become known as the Writings. Unlike the books of the other two divisions which seem to have been canonized as an entire group, the books of the Writings attained their sacred status one by one. The whole group was not clearly defined until A.D. 90 when the Council of Jamnia drew up a definitive list of the sacred Scriptures. Writing about the time of the Council of Jamnia the author of II Esdras speaks of ninety-four books. Of these, he said, the Lord commanded that the first twenty-four be published openly, but that the other seventy be kept hidden. The twenty-four books were the canonical books of Hebrew Scripture and consisted of the five books of the Law (Genesis, Exodus, Leviticus, Numbers, Deuteronomy), the four former Prophets (Joshua, Judges, Samuel, Kings), the four Latter Prophets (Isaiah, Jeremiah, Ezekiel and the Twelve, among whom were numbered Joel and Jonah), and finally, the eleven books of the Writings (Psalms, Proverbs, Job, Song of Solomon, Ruth, Lamentations, Ecclesiastes, Esther, Daniel, Chronicles, and Ezra-Nehemiah). These twenty-four books of the Hebrew canon, when we count each double book as two books, and each of the Twelve as one book, become the thirty-nine volume library of our Old Testament.

What, then, of the seventy volumes Esdras was commanded to keep hidden? Many of them have naturally been lost in the course of centuries. A surprising number still exist and a few have been discovered in recent years. This entire group of books is referred to as the Pseudepigrapha and it contains such books as: *Jubilees, The Martyrdom of Isaiah, Enoch,* and *Testaments of the Twelve Patriarchs.* These books are chiefly of interest to scholars. Though they must all have been popular in their own day, they were not considered sacred books.

There is, however, a curious little group of books lying between the twenty-four books of Hebrew Scripture and the large collection of the Pseudepigrapha. This collection is the Apocrypha. Throughout the years it has been tossed back and forth like a ball between the Scriptures on one side and the Pseudepigrapha on the other. Even today the game of the Apocrypha is still being played and not everyone agrees just where it belongs.

The story of the Apocrypha is a fascinating one. We have already mentioned several of its books: Esdras, the Rest of the Book of Esther, Ecclesiasticus (not to be confused with Ecclesiastes), the Wisdom of Solomon, and Maccabees. The contents of the Apocrypha differ from one list to another, but the books traditionally contained in the English versions number fourteen:

I Esdras

II Esdras

Tobit

Judith

Rest of the Book of Esther

Wisdom of Solomon

Ecclesiasticus

I Maccabees

II Maccabees

Baruch, including the Epistle of Jeremy

Additions to the Book of Daniel:

Song of the Three Children

Susanna

Bel and the Dragon

Prayer of Manasses

These books were written in the last period of Hebrew literature, from about 300 B.C. to A.D. 100. Early ones like I Esdras, Tobit, Ecclesiasticus, and Judith are contemporaries of such works as Chronicles, Daniel, Esther, and many of the psalms. The latest books like Wisdom, Baruch, and II Esdras are contemporaries of the letters of Paul and the four Gospels. The books of the Apocrypha form a sort of bridge between the Old and the New Testaments.

In these books we see Jewish literary genius in all its many-sidedness. Here are the romances of Tobit, Judith, and Susanna. I Esdras is a rewriting of history similar to Chronicles, while Maccabees is history itself. It tells the story of the heroic struggle led by Judas Maccabeus to win religious freedom for the Jews. Wisdom literature is represented in Ecclesiasticus and the Wisdom of Solomon. Baruch is prophecy; Bel and the Dragon is myth. II Esdras is a collection of apocalypses. The Prayer of Manasses is liturgy and was at one time used in the Christian Church.

The four hundred years from 300 B.C. to A.D. 100 when these books were written was marked by violence and war. The Jews often divided into hostile parties and fought among themselves. They resisted the efforts of their Greek conquerors to make them adopt Hellenistic civilization. They suffered under and rebelled against Roman misrule. Many a time they heard in their streets the tramp of foreign soldiers. They knew the bitterness of paying unjust taxes to a foreign power. Throughout these four unruly centuries there were, however, moments of calm when men had a chance to write their message. Most of the Writings and all of the Apocrypha and the Pseudepigrapha were written during this period. In these years there must have been a large reading public, not only in Palestine, but among the Jews of the Dispersion, who eagerly seized upon each new book as it came out. The literature produced was more varied and extensive than that of any other period.

Throughout the western world from Persia to Spain lived colonies of the Jews of the Dispersion, who far outnumbered their kindred in the homeland. Many were descendants of sixth-century exiles who had never returned to Palestine. In Egypt about one in every eight people was a Jew and there were many synagogues in the beautiful Greek city of Alexandria built by the Ptolemies at the mouth of the Nile. The chief synagogue was a stately basilica adorned with double rows of pillars. Not to have seen this building, one rabbi declared, was never to have seen the glory achieved by Israel. A human voice was lost in the vastness of this synagogue and a flag had to be waved when the congregation was expected to say "Amen." Alexandria in those days was a Greek-speaking city and many Alexandrian Jews understood no other language. When the Law and the Prophets were read in the synagogue, they had to be followed by a translation or explanation in Greek. A Greek translation of the Bible became a necessity.

There is a charming legend about how the Pentateuch was first translated into Greek. In Alexandria the Ptolemies collected a library containing more than half a million rolls. It was Callimachus, the librarian at Alexandria, who declared: "A big book is a big nuisance," and introduced the custom of dividing a long bulky roll into "books" or "parts," each of which could be written on a shorter, handier roll. Between 285 and 246 B.C., King Ptolemy Philadelphus of Egypt became active in enlarging his vast library. At that time there was no Greek translation of the Hebrew Law in existence. So much is history. Ptolemy sent to the High Priest in Jerusalem asking for six Hebrew scholars from each of the twelve tribes of Israel to be'sent to Egypt to translate the Scriptures. When seventy scholars arrived in Egypt each one was given a separate cell where he might work alone. For seventy days not a word was heard from the seventy scholars. Then all at once arose from all the cells a mighty shout. Seventy voices in chorus shouted, "Amen!" and the seventy translations were completed. Wonderful to relate, when all the manuscripts were compared all were found to be identical! This story, told perhaps to invest the Greek version with the same aura of sacredness its Hebrew parent text possessed, gave a name to the new Greek version. It was called the Septuagint, meaning "of seventy" and its name, as well as its modern designation, LXX, honors the seventy legendary scholars. The great library at Alexandria was burned by the mob that attacked Julius Caesar's forces in that city in 47 B.C. No doubt that fire destroyed documents which could have told us the true story of the Septuagint.

The Law of Moses could now be read in the language of Homer and Plato. Soon the Prophets and the Writings also were translated into Greek. The Bible existed in its first translation. Any Old Testament in a language other than Hebrew is technically known as a version. The Septuagint was the first version of the Old Testament and it was followed by other versions: Coptic, Ethiopian, Gothic, Slavic, and Armenian.

In its early years the Septuagint was not a single volume bound between covers, but a collection of rolls kept in boxes. The contents of the Law box were definitely fixed as well as the boxes containing the Prophets. But it was an easy matter to store another roll in the boxes containing the Writings, for this was a fluid collection. In this way the books of the Apocrypha probably found their way into the Septuagint.

From the very beginning the Old Testament read in the Christian Church and quoted by Paul and the evangelists was usually the Septuagint Greek Bible containing, no doubt, the Law, the Prophets, the Writings, and the books of the Apocrypha as well. We have proof of this, for Bibles based on the Septuagint have come down to us and these usually contain the Apocrypha. Moreover, in controversies with their Jewish opponents, the Christians often quoted from the Apocrypha.

This was intolerable to the Jews. They realized, moreover, a danger to the Jewish faith in the new Christian books then being written. These might easily become part of the Scriptures, as indeed they have in the Christian Church. The Jews felt that something must be done to set limits to the holy books. Those that lived in Palestine believed that true inspiration ended with the prophetic age in the time of Ezra. No one writing after that, they decided, could be truly inspired. The Jews in Alexandria were more liberal in their interpretation of inspiration. They believed that the Divine Spirit was still active in the minds of living writers and that in moments of clear insight or high exaltation these writers could produce inspired writings. But it was the Palestine Jews with their narrower theory of inspiration who decreed what the canon of the Hebrew Scripture was to be. This was done under the leadership of Johanan ben Zakkai at the Council of Jamnia about A.D. 90. The Alexandrian Jews might continue to read their Septuagint containing the books of the Apocrypha, but for the Jews of Palestine the sacred canon included only twenty-four books. Anathema was pronounced on anyone who "brings together in his house more than twenty-four books" and a warning was issued that such a person would "have no part in the world to come."

Thus the Apocrypha was abandoned by the Jews. The Christians, meanwhile, continued to read it in their Septuagint version. In Rome the walls of the catacombs where the early Christians hid from persecution were often decorated with scenes from Tobit, Judith, and Maccabees.

When the great Latin translation of the Bible known as the Vulgate was made by Jerome about A.D. 400, he objected to the inclusion of the Apocrypha. He had visited Palestine and there Jewish scholars had taught him Hebrew and showed him that the Apocrypha was not part of the Hebrew canon. Jerome was impressed by their arguments, but he did not succeed in persuading the Roman Church to reject the Apocrypha. To this day the Apocrypha forms an integral part of the Bible of the Roman Catholic Church. In its English translation, known as the Douay Version, the Apocryphal books are scattered through The Old Testament wherever they seem to belong and they are specifically declared to be canonical.

In the sixteenth century Martin Luther brought up the Apocrypha controversy in his preface to his German Bible when he declared: "The books of the Apocrypha are not to be regarded as Holy Scripture, yet they are useful and good to be read." He printed these books in a section by themselves between the Old and New Testaments.

Coverdale was the first man to translate the Apocrypha into English. In his Bible of 1535 he followed Luther's example and put the Apocrypha between the Old and New Testaments and on its separate title page he wrote: "Apocripha. The bokes and treatises which amonge the fathers of olde are not rekened to be of like authorite with the other bokes of the byble, nether are they foude in the Canon of the Hebrue."

The Authorized or King James Version of 1611 contained the Apocrypha, but as early as 1629 editions were printed in which it was left out. The Puritan party in England was opposed to the Apocrypha, which they found troublesome in view of their doctrine that every word of Scripture was divinely inspired. Finally, in 1827 the British and Foreign Bible Society refused to appropriate their funds to print the Apocrypha. Some old family Bibles include the disputed collection, but few Bibles printed today contain it.

The Apocrypha controversy reappeared at the time of the coronation of Edward VII of England. The British and Foreign Bible Society presented him with a beautiful copy of the Bible on which to take his oath. This presentation copy lacked the Apocrypha. As an old statute declared that only a complete Bible could be used for this ceremony, Edward VII was obliged to take his oath on another copy.

Freed from the necessity of believing each of its words directly inspired by God, we find much of value in the Apocrypha. We can read it in the Authorized Version of 1611, the Revised Version of 1896, or the new translation made by Edgar J. Goodspeed and published by the University of Chicago Press in 1938. Whichever translation we read, we shall find in it passages that seem no less inspired than many portions of the Old Testament itself. Sometimes even the Jews overstepped the canonical boundaries and listed Ecclesiasticus among the Scriptures. The New Testament becomes clearer to us after we have studied the Apocrypha, for the writers of the two collections lived in the same mental atmosphere. The Apocrypha is historically important as a bridge between the Old and New Testaments. It is, finally, a collection of important documents of great literary charm, beauty, and excellence.

# 25

## The Portable Fatherland of the Jews

### THE HEBREW SCRIPTURES

THE day in 621 B.C. when King Josiah listened to the reading of Deuteronomy was a significant one for Israel. From that time on a book was enshrined at the heart of the Jewish religion. As we have seen, other books were soon attracted into the sacred orbit of Deuteronomy, and guilds of writers copied and edited a library of twenty-four books worthy to stand beside the Deuteronomy kernel of the Bible. Though Jerusalem with her Temple, priesthood, and sacrifices dominated Judaism, the sacred books began to exercise a profound influence. Scribes and interpreters of the Law became men of importance, for the average person wanted to hear what the Scriptures contained. Between 400 and 150 B.C. the synagogue originated as a place where people assembled to hear the Pentateuch read and explained. Only in the Temple at Jerusalem might sacrifices be offered, but every town and village in the land had its synagogue where people gathered to listen to the sacred Scriptures.

The story of the Samaritan Sect which broke off from orthodox Judaism about 400 B.C. shows how important the Bible was in the religion of that day. The Samaritan Sect was founded by a group of Jews who were excluded from the Temple at Jerusalem, probably because they had married foreign wives. Angered by this they went to Samaria where they built a rival temple on Mount Gerizim. To this temple they carefully brought from Jerusalem a copy of the Bible of their day which in 400 b.c. consisted only in the Pentateuch. The Samaritan Bible never grew beyond these five books. When Jesus visited the Samaritan town of Sychar, a woman He met at the well was surprised that He, a Jew, spoke to her a Samaritan, "for," adds the author of the Gospel of John in explanation, "the Jews have no dealings with the Samaritans." The Bible Jesus read included the Law, the Prophets, and some of the Writings. If the Samaritan woman knew about her Bible at all, she knew that it contained only the Pentateuch. In complete isolation from the main stream of development, the Samaritan Pentateuch was handed down from about 400 b.c. until today. The last surviving members of the Samaritan Sect now live in Nablus, the ancient city of Shechem in Palestine. There they show to visitors a thirteenth-century copy of the Pentateuch descended from the book their ancestors took from Jerusalem when they were driven out twenty-three hundred years ago.

Wherever the Jews went they took their Bible. In Egypt the Jews of the Dispersion continued to listen to the Scriptures read in Hebrew long after they had ceased to understand that language. Finally, as we know, between 280 and 150 b.c. the Septuagint Greek translation was available for use in the synagogues. Trivial though the legend of its translation is, there is nothing trivial about the Septuagint. It was the first extensive translation ever made of a national literature and it became one of the most influential books in the world. For Judaism the Septuagint became the strong bond uniting all Greek-speaking Jews of the Dispersion and transmitting to them the literary and religious heritage of their fathers. Through reading the Septuagint great numbers of Gentiles became converts to Judaism. They found in the Scriptures higher ideals and a better way of life than that taught by paganism and they learned to worship Israel's God. On his missionary journeys Paul found many Gentiles who already knew the Scriptures and were prepared for his Christian message. Finally, the Septuagint was the first Bible of the early Christian Church.

In the first century copies of the Septuagint were in great demand. Jews of Egypt numbering nearly a million, Greek-speaking Jews of the Dispersion living in colonies from Persia to Spain, Gentiles everywhere, and Christians—all of these read the Septuagint. No doubt the publishing houses of Alexandria found it difficult to supply the demand. Publishing was organized on a large scale in the houses of the rabbis in the Jewish quarter. Papyrus was bought in the Egyptian market where it had been sold for centuries. The chief scribe of the publishing house was usually a rabbi. He read slowly from an approved manuscript of the Septuagint while a battery of five to ten trained scribes seated at desks facing the reader wrote in concert. They used pens and ink and they wrote swiftly and accurately in a beautiful hand. After being carefully proofread the long strips of papyrus were rolled up, packed, and put aboard ships for export to the entire Greek-speaking world.

While the Septuagint flourished, its parent Hebrew Bible faced a crisis. In their homeland the Jews entered a life and death struggle threatening their church-state, their religion, and their Scriptures. In A.D. 67 the Jews of Palestine revolted against Rome. The Roman Emperor Nero sent Vespasian at the head of three legions to quell the uprising. Perhaps the words of a Galilean teacher put to death more than thirty years before troubled the citizens of Jerusalem: "There shall not be left here one stone upon another."

If Jerusalem fell, would the ancient religion of the Jews survive? It was a crisis similar to that of 586 B.C. when the Chaldeans destroyed Jerusalem. After that older calamity there had been a rebirth, and Judaism itself had emerged from the Exile. Now, with the Temple, the priesthood, and the sacrifices all at the mercy of the most powerful empire on earth, what would be the verdict?

At this crisis a teacher of Jerusalem, Johanan ben Zakkai, left the doomed city—some people said in a coffin—and had himself taken to Vespasian's military headquarters. There the wise and scholarly Jew asked a favor of the proud Roman general. The teacher wanted permission to establish a school for Jewish youths in the small town of Jamnia. To the Roman general the request for a school sounded harmless enough and he gave his consent. Thus Judaism was saved from complete destruction.

Vespasian was proclaimed Emperor shortly after this and returned to Rome, leaving his son Titus to capture and destroy Jerusalem. After bitter fighting and frightful massacres the Holy City was taken in A.D. 70 and burned, and the Tenth Legion encamped in the ruined Temple. Only thirty miles away in his school at Jamnia, Johanan ben Zakkai heard the news that the Temple was in ashes, the golden vessels stolen, and the Temple copy of the Bible on its way to Rome as the personal loot of Titus. As the author of the *Apocalypse of Baruch* wrote at this time: "Zion has been taken from us and we have nothing now save the Mighty One and His Law." But Johanan did not despair. He had brought copies of the sacred books to his school and there he was training young men in all the lore of the sacred Scriptures. When Jerusalem lay in ruins Jamnia took her place as a Jewish religious center. Now there were teachers and scribes instead of priests. The sacrifices ceased but the Scriptures survived. Henceforth the Hebrew Bible became the "portable fatherland" of the Jews.

It was at Jamnia in the famous school of Johanan ben Zakkai that the council met about A.D. 90 to decide which books belonged to the canon. Pointing, no doubt, to the actual rolls brought from the Temple, the scribes and learned men of the council argued the merits of the various books. At length, they established the Hebrew canon in which the Writings were included, but the Apocrypha was left out. Having escaped a thousand dangers the Hebrew Scriptures now emerged to take their place at the very heart of Judaism. Famous schools were established in Babylonia and in Palestine where scholars were trained to preserve and guard the sacred text.

The copying of the Bible was done with extreme care, for every syllable was thought to be sacred. One rabbi warned a copyist not to drop a single letter nor to add one, lest he destroy the Law. The copyists wrote on parchment specially prepared from the skins of "clean" animals. Their ink was compounded of soot, charcoal, and honey. They were trained not to depend upon their memories for a single word, but to read and pronounce aloud each word of the original before writing it in the copy. The copyist washed his pen before writing the four sacred letters of God's name: Y H W H. If the proofreaders discovered more than two errors on a page they destroyed it. With elaborate rules like these to guide them the Jewish copyists produced Bibles of marvelous accuracy.

The ancient Hebrew alphabet contained only consonants. This had been true of its parent alphabets, the Canaanite-Phoenician and the Sinaitic, found at the turquoise mines of Serabit el-Khadim. About 400 B.C. the shapes of the Hebrew letters were changed into the "square" or Aramaic script which resembles the Hebrew characters of today. But even the Aramaic script contained no vowels and usually no mark to show the division of the text into words. A line of the Bible was similar to this:

N D T H R T H W S W T H T F R M N D V D

Reading a continuous stream of consonants was like decoding a cipher, or at best reading abbreviations and shorthand notes. Only after years of training and memorizing were scholars able to attach the right sounds to the letters to form words and sentences. A great body of tradition grew up about the correct pronunciation of the text. The Hebrew word for "tradition" is *masora*. From this word came the name of the guild of scholars who guarded the accuracy of the text and preserved the traditions of its pronunciation. They were called the Masoretes. With deep reverence for the Scriptures these patient Masoretes labored to check, compare, annotate, and count the letters of the text. They introduced a much-needed improvement about A.D. 500 when they invented a system of vowel "points." These were dots and strokes placed beneath the consonants to indicate vowel sounds. They also used accents to show the relation of words in a sentence. With the Masoretic vowel points and accents the line of consonants above would become as easy to read as this:

ND.  TH.  RTH.  WS.  WTHT.  FRM.  ND.  VD.
 a    e    ea    a    i ou    o    a    oi

Thanks to the Masoretes the oral traditions governing the sound of the text which had been handed down from time immemorial were now reduced to writing and incorporated in the text itself. The Masoretic text stood complete about A.D. 700.

Curiously enough, no early manuscripts of the Masoretic text survive. While we have manuscripts of the Greek Bible from the second, third, and fourth centuries, the four oldest Hebrew manuscripts, with the exception of a few fragments, date from the ninth, tenth, and eleventh centuries. In the British Museum there is an old Hebrew manuscript of the Pentateuch written in strong and beautiful letters, pointed and accented, three columns to a page. This was probably written about A.D. 850. There are two manuscript copies of the Prophets: one in Cairo dated A.D. 895, the other in Leningrad dated A.D. 916. The oldest complete manuscript of the Hebrew Bible is dated A.D. 1008 and is in Leningrad. Why have older manuscripts not survived?

The Jews had an interesting custom with regard to their old Bibles. When the synagogue roll was worn out a new copy was made and carefully tested for accuracy against the old manuscript. An aura of sacredness still clung to the old roll whose words had so often been read in the synagogue as the very words of God. In order that the old roll might not be profaned it was stored in the Geniza or storeroom attached to the synagogue. From time to time the contents of the Geniza were taken out and ceremonially burned. So perished the old manuscripts, though not until they had transmitted their accuracy to the new copies.

The first part of the Hebrew Bible to be printed was the

Book of Psalms. This was a small folio volume issued in an edition of three hundred copies in Italy at Bologna in 1477. Eleven years later, in 1488, the first edition of the complete Hebrew Bible was printed at Soncino. At that time Christian scholars became keenly interested in the Hebrew Bible. When Daniel Bomberg printed an edition of it in Venice in 1517 he dedicated it to Pope Leo X. For this he was granted a papal copyright which forbade any other publisher, under penalty of excommunication, to reprint this Hebrew book for ten years.

From the first songs sung by Hebrew nomads around their campfires to the first printed Hebrew Bible, the story of the Old Testament has been one of astonishing adventures. The writing, preservation, and canonization of the books has been amazing enough. To that we must add their survival in the catastrophe of A.D. 70 and their long history as the "portable fatherland" of the Jews. But for Christians the story of the Old Testament is merely a prelude to an even more remarkable one, and it is to that story we must now turn.

# PART II

## *The New Testament*

## 26

# The Dawn of a New Era

## CHRISTIANITY EMERGES

TO all who stood watching on Golgotha beneath three crosses it seemed like the end. Between two thieves Jesus of Nazareth was dying upon a cross. It was a Friday afternoon in early spring, and here and there on the barren hillsides around Jerusalem there were patches of green. Since noon the sun had been clouded and in the strange darkness which covered the land Jesus' life was drawing to its close. The days of His teaching and healing were now over. No more of the gracious and wonderful words which had stirred men so profoundly would come from His lips. No longer would He travel along the dusty roads of Galilee and Judea with His little group of disciples. His mission, which some had hoped was to be that of the Messiah, was now ending.

Only a short time before, a glorious idea had stirred in Peter's mind. Trained as he was in the faith of Israel, Peter knew that God had spoken to his fathers in times past through the prophets. But as Peter and the others accompanied Jesus they had become aware of something even more wonderful. They saw the meaning and purpose of God breaking through into the world in the words and deeds of Jesus. "What manner of man is this?" they wondered. And then in a moment of inspired insight Peter cried out: "Thou art the Christ, the Son of the living God."

But now in the darkness of that Friday afternoon the disciples felt mocked by their once shining hope. Surely the Son of God would not be condemned by their religious leaders and crucified by the Romans. It was not possible that the fulfillment of the promises written in their ancient Scriptures was a man dying upon a cross. Sick with disappointment and the wreckage of a vision that now seemed false, Peter and the disciples fled. At the foot of the Cross there remained only the disciple Jesus loved and Mary the mother of Jesus.

As the end approached, a dark curtain seemed to fall. Jesus had left no written record of His life. Only in the hearts and minds of those who knew Him were there stored memories of His deeds and words. The lame who walked because of Him, the blind who could now see, the hungry who had been fed, the children who had been blessed, the possessed who were now sane men, the ordinary men and women who had found new hope in Him, the disciples who had seen a glorious vision—all these would perhaps remember Him a few years longer. But after that, what? At their best, human minds are frail storehouses. The record of all that Jesus did and said was stored in no other place. Would the record survive?

That seemed unlikely. The shock of His execution was enough to wipe out even these memories. There was so much shame and fear and blasted hope for them in Jesus' death that there was little chance the disciples would want to remember their brief years with Him.

After three hours of darkness there came a cry from the Cross: "It is finished," and as Jesus died the bystanders heard Him say: "Father, into thy hands I commend my spirit."

Surely this was the end.

Heavy with sorrow, the disciple Jesus loved led Mary back to his house in Jerusalem. The priests and elders and scribes pointed to the dead figure on the central cross and said: "He can never stir up the people against us again." In the crowd streaming back toward the city there was perhaps not one who understood the meaning of what he had just seen. At this supreme moment in human history the citizens of Jerusalem were intent upon returning to their shops and synagogues and homes. The priests and scribes went back to their scrolls of the Law and the Prophets, little realizing that He who had died was the fulfillment of all the promises. They would continue to read of the Founder of the Kingdom, the Redeemer, the Restorer of Israel, the Light of the Gentiles, and the Judge of the World. And they would continue to sigh and wonder when this great Messiah would come.

Back in Jerusalem in Herod's Palace the Roman procurator of Judea, Pontius Pilate, signed the official report of the execution and sent it by imperial courier to Emperor Tiberius in Rome. The whole affair was now practically ended and forgotten. There might be a few lines about it in the official histories of the period. The Roman historian Tacitus briefly mentioned "one Christus, who in the reign of Tiberius had been condemned to death by the procurator Pontius Pilate . . ." History has little space to devote to hopes that die and movements that fail.

For the space of one Sabbath day there was silence, sorrow, and despair. The world waited. Then very early in the morning on the "first day of the week" the dark curtain blinding men's eyes was drawn aside and they saw the radiance of the Resurrection. The events of that first day and the others that followed were told again and again.

With heavy hearts the women came to the rock-cut tomb where Jesus had been laid. They carried spices to prepare His body for burial. When they found the heavy stone guarding the tomb entrance had been rolled away, they looked in and saw that the tomb itself was empty. An angel spoke to them saying that Christ had risen from the dead. Mary Magdelene in the garden near the tomb saw and spoke to the living, risen Master. She ran and told Peter and John and they, looking in the empty tomb, saw and believed.

At first the stories that Jesus had risen from the dead were not believed. Some of the disciples regarded them as "idle tales," but for forty days the evidence of the Resurrection grew. The eleven disciples saw Him. Two men walking along the road toward Emmaus met Him and ate supper with Him. Doubting Thomas touched the spear wound in His side. Five hundred brethren at one time saw him. The chief priests and the Roman officials in an effort to discredit the news bribed the soldiers who had guarded the tomb and instructed them to say that the disciples had stolen the body. All this was to no avail. The testimony of the resurrection of Jesus was overwhelming. It has been called one of the best-authenticated facts in history. Without the Resurrection there would be no explanation for the change in the followers of Jesus. On the day of the Crucifixion they were terrified, sorrowful, despairing. Within a few weeks they had become men of unshakable courage. No longer did they meet in secret behind closed doors "for fear of the Jews." Joyfully they came out of hiding and proclaimed their faith in Christ crucified and risen again. They spoke to great crowds in Jerusalem and as time went on they preached their triumphant message "in all Judaea, and in Samaria, and unto the uttermost part of the earth."

The mission of Jesus did not end, as it seemed to on Golgotha, in suffering and shame. His words and deeds were not to be forgotten. After that "first day of the week" the disciples began to understand their Master. All their recollections of Him came flooding back, transformed in the light of the Resurrection. His words took on fresh meaning. His acts became charged with new significance. Out of full hearts and richly stored memories the Apostles preached and taught, imparting to crowds of people their new faith in the risen, victorious Christ. Individual men and women caught fire from the Apostles and the Holy Spirit came upon them and they were made new. Thus the Church was born. And out of the life of the Church and in answer to her needs and her eager questions sprang those tremendous and immortal writings which we call the New Testament.

# 27

## Spreading the Good News

### FORTY YEARS OF THE ORAL GOSPEL

IN its simplest aspect the New Testament is a collection of twenty-seven documents written within the space of a hundred years. Four of these are gospels, one is a history, twenty-one are letters, and the last is an apocalypse. The oldest document is Paul's First Epistle to the Thessalonians, written in Corinth about A.D. 50, twenty years after the Crucifixion. The oldest Gospel is that of Mark, written in Rome about A.D. 70, forty years or so after the events it records.

These facts immediately raise a problem. If our earliest Christian documents were written many years after Jesus lived, how can we be sure they contain authentic records about Him? Our problem is beset with other difficulties. Not only were the Gospels and Epistles written many years after Jesus lived, but none of them, so far as we know, was written by one of the original disciples. Paul never actually saw Jesus, though he had an overpowering vision of Him on the Damascus road. Mark may have seen Jesus, but if he did it was for little more than a brief moment in the darkness at Gethsemane. How, then, can we put our trust in the New Testament documents? These books have been called the "title-deeds of our faith." For this reason it is necessary for us to discover whether these title-deeds are valid documents or whether our faith rests upon a worthless collection of myths, speculations, and the fanciful dreams of men who never knew Christ.

Facing our problem squarely, we can see that the heart of it is this: What connection is there between the actual facts of Jesus and the written record in the New Testament? How fully and how accurately were the memories of the men and women who had known Him reproduced in the New Testament documents? Today we have stenographic reports, newsreel pictures, phonograph recordings, and newspaper accounts. Television and radio enable us to see and hear history in the making, but in the first century there were only human voices and human memories to carry the burden of historical fact. The records of Jesus were entrusted to the men and women who had known Him. How did they fulfill their trust? In the events of the years between the Crucifixion and the publication of the first Gospel there must be clues that will provide answers to these questions. We shall, then, search through the known facts of the forty years for evidence that our Gospel records are authentic and rest on solid facts.

If these forty years had been years of silence about Jesus, if all the Apostles and eyewitnesses had died without ever mentioning His name, there would surely have been no Christianity. Then all that we find written in the New Testament would be merely a dream created by a group of clever writers and sadly we would have to admit that the facts on which Christianity rests are not facts at all but a shimmering literary mirage. But those forty crucial years were not years of silence: they were years of the most enthusiastic witnessing and missionary activity the world has ever seen. They were years in which the Apostles and the hundreds of people who had seen and heard Jesus proclaimed their belief in Him and offered eyewitness testimony to buttress their faith. Something of the tremendous surge and power of early Christianity is reflected in the pages of Acts and the Epistles of Paul. By A.D. 70, there were Christians and Christian Churches not only in Palestine, Syria, and Asia Minor, but in Egypt, Greece, Italy, and possibly in far-off Spain. All this implies a vast amount of preaching, teaching, and witnessing. The earliest followers of Jesus opened their storehouses of memories and broadcast the seed of Christianity so that it became a rapidly expanding movement taking root and flourishing in all parts of the ancient world. Its basic message rested on a fact, on genuine historical records supplied by those who had seen and heard. "The Word was made flesh, and dwelt among us, and *we beheld his glory.*" So great a chorus of living witness filled the early years that we can be sure Christianity is not a literary creation nor an idle dream.

In Acts the first voice we hear is that of Peter, Jesus' first disciple. All his fears and uncertainty have fallen from him like a worn-out garment and he stands up boldly in Jerusalem facing the very people who a few weeks before clamored for Jesus' death. The city is alive with rumors. There is talk that Jesus is not dead. His disciples and followers seem possessed with a strange joy. Can it be that they are drunk? In the manner of the prophets Peter demands a hearing from the crowd.

> Ye men of Judaea, and all ye that dwell at Jerusalem, be this known unto you, and hearken to my words.
>
> ACTS 2:14

The murmur and mockery of hundreds of voices becomes stilled and in the hush Peter preaches his first sermon. He quickly disposes of the accusation of drunkenness. This radiance of spirit is not from wine but from the outpouring of the Holy Spirit. Peter goes on to his main point.

> Jesus of Nazareth, a man approved of God among you by miracles and wonders and signs, which God did by him in the midst of you, as ye yourselves also know: Him . . . ye have taken, and by wicked hands have crucified and slain . . .
>
> ACTS 2:22, 23

So far Peter is only stating facts everyone in Jerusalem knows. The crowd stirs at the term "wicked hands," but something in Peter's fearless manner keeps them silent, waiting for his climax. Peter hurries on to the heart of his message.

> Whom God hath raised up, having loosed the pains of death: because it was not possible that he should be holden of it.
>
> ACTS 2:24

There it is: the first open proclamation of the Resurrection. In case they have not understood his first statement Peter repeats it: "This Jesus hath God raised up," he declares and stretching out his arm toward the eleven stalwart figures standing up beside him he adds, "whereof we all are witnesses."

Peter was on fire with a spiritual radiance which kindled the faith of "three thousand souls" who that day became believers. The Resurrection had convinced Peter that Jesus was indeed the Son of God. He felt compelled to share his new faith and the solid facts on which it rested with all who would listen. This was the first wave of an incoming tide which flooded the world with Christian witness. It was the beginning of a spiritual movement which in the space of a hundred years produced the New Testament.

We note that an Apostle was the first witness to the facts. He spoke out of his own knowledge and experience to people who were themselves not ignorant of all that had happened. Paul appealed to their own firsthand knowledge of events: "as ye yourselves also know." Christianity was first expressed and its message developed, not after all those who had known Jesus were dead, but while the events on which it rested were still capable of being checked and verified.

Time and again the question: "How can you prove it?" must have been hurled at the first Christians. Their faith was constantly on trial in that skeptical and argumentative first century. We find evidences of this throughout the New Testament. Everywhere Christian writers and teachers fell back upon the testimony of eyewitnesses. There was Peter's gesture toward the eleven and his phrase: "whereof we all are witnesses." In writing of Jesus' Resurrection appearance, Paul said:

> He was seen of above five hundred brethren at once; of whom the greater part remain unto this present, but some are fallen asleep.
>
> I Corinthians 15:6

Luke in his preface mentions those who "from the beginning were eyewitnesses and ministers of the word." The author of

the Gospel of John asserts: "we beheld his glory." Again in the
First Epistle of John he wrote:

> That which was from the beginning, which we have heard, which
> we have seen with our eyes, which we have looked upon, and our
> hands have handled, of the Word of life . . . declare we unto you.
>
> I JOHN 1:1, 3

As the message grew, its spokesmen kept their eyes firmly
fixed on reliable fact. There was, to be sure, a whole crop of
fantastic stories about Jesus, a "wild" growth that troubled the
great Christian leaders, but the authentic traditions were carefully guarded. Writing the latest book of the New Testament
about A.D. 150, the author of II Peter said:

> For we have not followed cunningly devised fables, when we made
> known unto you the power and coming of our Lord Jesus Christ, but
> were eyewitnesses of his majesty.
>
> II PETER 1:16

Thus even the latest writing in the New Testament bases its
claims upon facts as they had been handed down to the author
from the very beginning by those who actually knew.

The old habit of checking the facts and seeking authentic information from those who had been close to Jesus lingered on
long after there were four Gospels in which to read the record.
Some men, like Papais, seem to have preferred the oral Gospel
to the written word. When he wrote the following fragment
about A.D. 140, he was the Bishop of Hierapolis, but he is
evidently speaking of an earlier period in his youth when followers of the original disciples still lived and preached.

> If anyone happened to come my way who had been a follower of the
> Elders, I would enquire about the sayings of the Elders — what An-
> drew said, or Peter, or Philip, or Thomas, or James, or John, or
> Matthew, or any other of the Lord's disciples; also what Aristion or
> the Elder John, the disciples of the Lord, say. For I did not think I
> got so much profit from the contents of books as from the words of a
> living and abiding voice.

We can be sure that the first forty years echoed with abundant
testimony and freely-shared memories and that the Gospel materials rest on a broad base. The hundreds of people who had

heard and seen Jesus no less than His own disciples became careful "stewards of the mysteries of God." With plenty of material available, their problem was not to create but to select the truest and most useful parts. They developed the message against opposition and in the presence of those who could check the facts and when the "good news" was finally written down its authors acknowledged the importance of firsthand sources.

Without doubt the first connected story the Church developed was the story of Christ's death and Resurrection. The spark that kindled Christianity was the Resurrection. That stupendous fact was its first good news. Everything grew out of it. From the teaching of the Resurrection came the message that conquered the world. It was the Gospel during the months following the Ascension, as Peter's three great speeches show.[1] It is the starting point of Paul's message: "And if Christ be not risen, then is our preaching vain" (I Corinthians 15:14).

Perhaps the first questions new converts asked were, "How did it happen that Jesus was crucified?" "What events led up to the death of the Son of God?" In meeting such questions the Passion narrative grew. It began with the triumphal entry into Jerusalem and continued through the events of the final week, the Last Supper, the arrest, the various trials, the Crucifixion, and finally the Resurrection and Ascension. It was a long story packed with dialogue and action. The Apostles could supply many of its details, but some, at least, of those three thousand new converts in Jerusalem must have made contributions to it also. The story was an edifice built by many hands. Far from becoming more vague and unreliable, the story gathered strength, firmness, and sharper outlines with each retelling. Its early audiences checked its accuracy and insisted upon uniformity in its telling. It is not surprising that when the Gospels were written, this one story, which is the record of a single week in Jesus' life, occupies at least a third of each of the books of Matthew, Mark, and Luke.

---

[1] Acts 2:14-36; 3:12-26; 4:8-12.

Churches began to spring up everywhere, for Apostles and teachers traveled far and wide with the new message. It would be interesting to know how many miles of travel were implied in the narratives of Acts alone; it must be many thousands. Almost everywhere the first Christian missionaries went they found a welcome. Hospitality became one of the characteristics of the new religion. Scores of eager converts crowded about those who had known Jesus and besieged them with questions.

"What did He teach about obeying the Law?"

"What did He say about money and taxes?"

"How did He answer the Pharisees?"

"Did He really cause the blind to see?"

"In our church we have this problem: What did He say about it?"

In answering such questions as these the Apostles and missionaries drew upon their store of remembered words and actions of their Lord. They recited His sayings and retold His stories. Earnest questions served to bring the Christian message into focus and to develop a series of answers. The Gospels were later to be built out of such materials. They were not spun out of pale theories, nor composed in an ivory tower of contemplation, nor written for artistic effect. Instead, they sprang vigorously to life in answer to the questions of people who needed help in living Christian lives in the actual world.

Some of the material now in our Gospels must have been originally selected and shaped for the purpose of training new leaders and outlining the message they were to preach. As early as A.D. 34 or 35, when Paul was led blinded into Damascus after his vision on the road, there was a definite body of facts for each new leader to learn. Paul indicates that his training in Damascus was definite and thorough, and that it rested mainly on the historical record.

> For I delivered unto you first of all that which I also received, how that Christ died for our sins according to the scriptures; and that he was buried, and that he rose again the third day.
>
> I Corinthians 15:3, 4

Not only the facts about Jesus' life but the words He had spoken were important in the early Church. In those days it was not unusual for the followers of a teacher or rabbi to commit his teachings to memory. No doubt the sayings of Jesus were stored in the memories of His Apostles and many of His other followers. Paul, in this quotation, seems to be referring to the custom of memorizing the Lord's sayings:

> Ye ought . . . to remember the words of the Lord Jesus, how he said, It is more blessed to give than to receive.
>
> ACTS 20:35

Memorizing was certainly necessary in the years before there was a book in every church and in every home. The burden of transmitting to new converts the sayings and stories of the Lord fell upon the early Christian teacher. There was less for him to do after the Gospels were written, but up to A.D. 70, at least, he shaped and taught the Gospel materials word by word to his eager students.

We are often struck with the fact that the written Gospels seem to be built of short, disconnected bits. We find individual sayings, brief anecdotes, and parables. The Gospel authors skillfully grouped these short units and wove them together. Nevertheless, we can still see behind the Gospels a large stock of brief, miscellaneous materials. Were these the teaching units of the early Church? It is possible that teachers condensed the eyewitness accounts of Jesus and His sayings and parables into these easily memorized units. Small details were sometimes changed. In the interest of brevity the settings of time and place were often omitted, but the essential meaning of the incident was carefully guarded. The fact that the record was not embellished but compressed for easier memorizing gives us renewed confidence in it.

Before the period of the oral Gospel ended many a Christian must have put his pen to use in the service of Christianity. How we wish we had even fragments of this first literary activity! Perhaps Christian writing began when some early teacher made a written collection of his teaching material. Some scholars now believe that the Apostle Matthew aided his memory by writing down Christ's sayings in Aramaic, the language in which they were spoken, and that part of this collection can be found in Matthew, Mark, and Luke. Were there early Christian hymn-books, and did Luke borrow from them the four exquisite songs of his first chapter? In his preface Luke says that "many had taken in hand to set forth in order a declaration of those things which are surely believed among us." Possibly there were prim-itive gospels written in Aramaic which gathered up the testi-mony concerning Jesus and provided sources for later Gospel authors. Perhaps a converted Jewish scribe made a collection of Old Testament prophecies for the use of teachers and writers who wanted scriptural authority for the person and message of Christ.

Finally, we leave speculation behind with the year A.D. 50 when Paul, then living with Aquila and Priscilla in Corinth, pushed aside the materials out of which he was making tents and began to dictate our oldest New Testament document, the First Epistle to the Thessalonians.

When the time was ripe for the Gospels to be written, Chris-tian hands were full of treasures. During the forty years of oral tradition the Gospel had been tested in experience, per-fected, and deeply realized. Newspaper reporters running to the telephone with fresh news seldom transmit more than the bare bones of an event. Its meaning and significance come later as the event is related to its entire background. As we have seen, the facts concerning Jesus were checked and guarded during the oral years by eyewitnesses and by the Church to which the message was entrusted. Those years served, not to fade nor falsify the Gospel, but to focus it and develop its overwhelming significance. Sighing for the impossible, we sometimes wish we had a full stenographic report of all that Jesus said, or a moving picture record of a day in His life. But there were many who actually saw and heard Him and still did not understand nor believe. It was only as the Holy Spirit illumined their minds that Peter and the eleven, Paul, the early converts, and all the

New Testament writers began to understand the meaning of the facts. When the New Testament was written it was more than a stenographic record: it carried overtones of men's experience of Christ and their faith in Him. Christ is known both by the record of His life and by what He does in men's lives. The Gospels and the Epistles hold the mirror up to Christ and at the same time they reflect the life of the early Church. This double image, developed during the interval of the oral Gospel, is a heritage without which Christianity would be impoverished.

We need not be disappointed that none of the Gospels or Epistles comes to us in the handwriting of a disciple. As we shall presently discover, the Gospels stand very close to the men who accompanied Jesus. The words they heard Him say, the acts they saw Him perform, together with what these things meant to them are reliably reported in the Gospels. In all probability Peter himself preached in Rome and it was the same people who heard Peter's message who adopted Mark's Gospel as the official Gospel of the Church. We need no better proof than this, that Mark's Gospel coincides with the preaching of Peter.

Moreover, underlying the entire New Testament there is a fact that stamps the record as authentic. The first Christians believed that God revealed Himself to the world through Jesus. Their religion was founded upon an historical person. If the record of Him was a fabrication then it was useless to say that God had revealed Himself to men. But if Jesus truly lived and died, as they testified, then was the divine revelation true. Thus Christianity necessarily rested on historical fact. There is always a tendency to elaborate and magnify facts, and heretical groups were guilty in this respect. But the main stream of Christian witness remained loyal to the facts, realizing that these were Christianity's credentials. The facts planted in men's memories sprang up after the Resurrection and became an abundant harvest. When this was gathered together into the Epistles and Gospels, it was found to contain not the bare bones of dead facts but the seeds of an unfailing harvest.

# 28

## The Oldest Gospel

### THE GOSPEL OF MARK

IN the month of July, A.D. 64, a fire broke out among the wooden buildings around the Circus Maximus in Rome. It raged for a week before finally burning itself out and leaving a large part of the city a mass of charred and smoking ruins. Rumor had it that the Emperor Nero set the fire so that he could rebuild the city to his own glory. People said that Nero played his fiddle as he watched Rome burn. Nero himself blamed the Christians. A group of them had been living in the city for almost twenty years, quietly going about their own affairs. Nero decided to make them the scapegoats for the disastrous fire and he had many of them executed at night in his gardens on the Janiculum. Peter and Paul are said to have died in these terrible massacres and, according to tradition, the place where Peter died is now the site of St. Peter's in Rome.

In the imperial city Christianity faced a desperate situation. With its great leaders dead and its members terrified of renewed persecution, the Church needed strengthening. Men and women no longer heard the triumphant message of Christ preached with Paul's deep conviction. They lacked the assurance Peter's very presence had given them that Christianity rested firmly on actual historical facts. It was in this crisis that the author of the first Gospel undertook his great service to Christianity. He decided to give the Christians in Rome a written account of their Lord to take the place of Peter's now silent voice.

Tradition names Mark as the author of this earliest of the Gospels and there is every reason to believe that in this case tradition is true. John Mark, to give him his full name, was not an outstanding figure in the early days; if he had been, we might question the tradition of his authorship of the earliest Gospel. Antiquity loved to attribute a book to the most important personage it could find. But John Mark played only a minor role in the opening acts of Christianity, being always associated with someone more prominent than himself: first Barnabas, then Paul, and later Peter. No one, however, in the early Church, except perhaps the Apostles themselves, was in a better position to know the facts than Mark.

He is mentioned nine times in the New Testament, and from these references we can sketch the main outlines of his life. His mother Mary lived in Jerusalem and probably owned a large house there which became the meeting place, perhaps the headquarters, of Christ's followers after the Resurrection. It may have been in an upper room of this house that Jesus ate the Last Supper with His disciples. Mark's account of the arrangements for that meal are so detailed that it seems as though he were writing about an event that took place in his own house.

In the account of Jesus' arrest in the garden of Gethsemane there is a strange little incident that adds nothing to the story and apparently has no reason for being inserted in the midst of great events.

> And there followed him a certain young man, having a linen cloth cast about his naked body; and the young men [1] laid hold on him: and he left the linen cloth, and fled from them naked. And they led Jesus away to the high priest.
>
> MARK 14:51-53

This seems to be the story of a young man who was perhaps awakened in the night by someone bringing a warning that

---

[1] Part of the armed mob that came to seize Jesus.

Jesus was about to be seized. Such a warning might well have been brought to the house where Jesus had just eaten supper with His disciples, the house where John Mark probably lived. The young man evidently knew where Jesus had gone after the Last Supper, for without even pausing to dress he sped to Gethsemane, only to find that his warning was too late and that Jesus was already under arrest. Was this "certain young man" John Mark himself? Many people believe that it was and that Mark, writing years later, added this unessential fragment because it was his only personal connection with the Gospel story.

Barnabas was Mark's cousin and in A.D. 47 the two men, together with Paul, sailed to Cyprus on a missionary journey. Mark and Barnabas later returned to Cyprus on a second visit. Next we read of Mark in Asia Minor and in Rome with Paul. Paul speaks of Mark as "profitable to me for the ministry." Finally, Mark seems to have assisted Peter in Rome, for, in the tradition preserved in the First Epistle of Peter, Mark is described as "Marcus my son." Thus we have reliable evidence that for thirty-five years Mark labored with the great Christian leaders, helping them carry the Gospel from Jerusalem to the Gentile world.

Our chief authority for Mark's authorship of the earliest Gospel is Papias, Bishop of Hierapolis about A.D. 140. Papias bases his statements about Mark on what a certain Church elder had told him. This chain of evidence takes us back to a time fairly close to the date of Mark. Papias writes:

> The elder used to say the following: Mark, who became the interpreter of Peter, wrote accurately as much as he remembered of the Lord's sayings or doings, but he did not write these in their order. For he had not himself heard the Lord nor been his personal follower, but was later, as I said, a follower of Peter, who used to adapt his teaching to the occasion but not as though he were framing an ordered account of the Lord's sayings. So Mark made no error when he wrote some things as he remembered them. For he had only one purpose: — to leave out nothing and to falsify none of the things he had heard.

This valuable fragment from Papias sheds light not only on Mark's authorship of the Gospel, but on Peter's manner of teaching and also on the way the Gospel materials developed. Peter was far from being a professor of history, and the Roman Christians were not taking a course in the life of Christ. Instead, they were men and women attempting to live Christian lives in the chief city of the Roman Empire. They needed facts about Jesus on which to base their faith. They needed His sayings to guide them in everyday problems. Peter was in the habit of responding to their needs "as the occasion required." Peter, as we know, had originally been a Galilean fisherman and his Greek could not have been very good. No doubt he spoke it with such an Aramaic accent that Mark had to interpret for him. When Peter died no one was better fitted than Mark to preserve in writing all that Peter had taught. Papias, quoting very early Church traditions, stated that Mark's book was accurate, complete, and without false statements. This is high praise, indeed, for any historical record.

Sometime between A.D. 65 and 70 Mark completed his Gospel. To the Roman Christians who were its first readers the Gospel brought the very sound of Peter's voice. Here were his familiar stories of Jesus' baptism, of the calling of the disciples, of that amazing Sabbath day in Capernaum, and all the rest. Many phrases were Peter's own, for Mark had somehow managed to retain many little eyewitness details, like the unnecessary touches about the "Hired Servants" (Mark 1:20), and the "other little ships" (Mark 4:36), which Peter's vivid memory had treasured. all the years.

Mark's readers often heard an echo of Peter speaking in the very form of the sentences. "They went into Capernaum; and straightway on the sabbath day he entered into the synagogue, and taught." "When they were come from Bethany, he was hungry." "They came to a place which was named Gethsemane: and he saith . . ." A good writer tries to keep his story focused on one character, but here we have a rapidly shifting point of view alternating between Jesus and the disciples. It is as inartistic as certain other clumsy sentences: "But Simon's wife's mother lay sick of a fever, and anon they tell him of her." In any other writer such awkward sentences would be criticized, but we are glad to find them in Mark, for they bring us the very cadences of Peter's voice reminiscing about his years with Jesus and saying: "*We* went into Capernaum and straightway he entered into the synagogue." "When *we* came from Bethany he was hungry." "*We* came to Gethsemane and he said . . ." "But *my* wife's mother lay sick and *we* told him of her." All these touches are, we believe, Peter's signature in Mark's Gospel.

The Roman Christians needed more than the assurance of Peter's familiar words. Nero's massacres proved that it would be neither safe nor easy to be a Christian. They dreaded the knock that might come at their door and the summons that meant martyrdom. They needed a message of fortitude and the assurance of final triumph. In Mark's Gospel they found it. Here was the story of a Man who lived as dangerously as they. The Cross began to cast its shadow from the third chapter onward. Through mounting opposition Jesus moved with great power. He was a man of action. Again and again He appeared in the midst of a complex scene and transformed it with a mighty word or act. His words were like a ray of sunlight shining through a storm cloud and illuminating a world of fear, doubt, and despair.

> Come ye after me, and I will make you to become fishers of men.
>
> MARK 1:17

> Be of good cheer: it is I; be not afraid.
>
> MARK 6:50

> Whosoever shall lose his life for my sake and the gospel's, the same shall save it.
>
> MARK 8:35

To Roman Christians trembling under the threat of persecution, sayings like these must have brought assurance and power. If we read the Gospel with the eyes of a first-century Christian, we see how wisely Peter chose his message and how well Mark selected what he recorded.

The words of Jesus written in Mark are in sharp contrast to the fabric of the Gospel. They flash brightly. They are creative.

They ring down the centuries like the trumpets of victory. Knowing all too well Mark's matter-of-fact style, we realize that he was incapable of inventing sentences like these. Their very quality is a guarantee of their source. They come not from Peter nor Mark but from Jesus Himself.

No greater pages have ever been written than Mark's story of the death of Jesus. In their simplicity and restraint they convey stark tragedy. Mark was too deeply moved by this event to utter elaborate lamentations. He did not let his pen run freely, lest in the welter of his own emotions he obscure the profound significance of the Cross. He dared write the dying words of Jesus:

> Eloi, Eloi, lama sabachthani?
> My God, my God, why hast thou forsaken me?
>
> MARK 15:34

This was not the sort of thing anyone could possibly invent. One certainly does not expect to find it in a book which opens on the sublime note: "The gospel of Jesus Christ, the Son of God." But Mark, writing it just as he heard it from Peter, here added the supreme note of tragedy to the story and gave final proof of the manhood of Jesus.

Outside the Christian Church the publication of Mark's book did not arouse any enthusiasm. The Roman poets, orators, dramatists, and historians of this Silver Age of Latin literature were busy with another type of writing altogether. The fact that Mark's Gospel was written in Greek would not have been a barrier to its spread in Rome, for all educated Romans at this time knew Greek. Indeed, the poet Horace said that Rome, the conqueror, was herself conquered by Greek civilization. Such great masters of Latin prose as Caesar and Cicero spoke more Greek than Latin in their everyday lives, and the Christian Church in Rome remained a Greek-speaking Church for more than two hundred years. All the New Testament documents were written in Greek. The reading public of Mark's day could easily have understood his Greek, but they would surely have criticized his style which lacked polish and betrayed an Aramaic flavor. They would have found his sentences, which are loosely strung together with "and . . . and . . . and," monotonous and crude. Popular authors of the day wrote for wealthy patrons who enjoyed an elegant style and clever phrases more than originality and sincerity. But even the haughtiest of the Roman authors would have been forced to admit the vivid pictorial quality of Mark's Gospel. He would have seen that, even though it is built out of a mass of short, disconnected reports, the Gospel possesses dramatic structure and unity. Certainly a Roman writer would have felt, as we do, that here he was in the presence of something strange and immense which is only dimly seen and partially understood. Without any literary skill at all, but with sheer honesty and profound faith Mark succeeded in writing a book of surpassing vigor, heroism, challenge, and triumph. The cleverest literary craftsmen of the Silver Age never produced anything to equal it.

Mark's Gospel was copied, becoming the pattern for all the Gospels. From its opening words: "The beginning of the gospel of Jesus Christ, the Son of God," came the word "gospel" which served as the title of the three other books which followed it and the noncanonical gospels as well. Matthew and Luke both took over Mark's Gospel and rewrote it for different audiences. John, also, used parts of it.

So popular was it that it is difficult to see why its ending was lost. The most ancient manuscripts of Mark all end with "for they were afraid," and everything following this was added by later copyists or editors who realized that the original Gospel could not have ended on this note of fear. No one knows why Mark ended so abruptly. Did he die before he finished the book, or was the end of the roll torn off and destroyed in some persecution? The lost ending of Mark remains one of the unanswered problems of the New Testament.

Many of the Christians who knew Mark and read his Gospel must have stood in the crowd lining the Roman Forum on the day Titus returned with his legions from Jerusalem. It was A.D. 70 and the Emperor Vespasian had prepared a splendid public triumph for his son Titus. Rome rejoiced that the Jewish revolt had been crushed and Jerusalem destroyed. Hundreds of captured Jews marched in the procession. Plunder from the Temple was carried by and the sun flashed on the gold of the seven-branched candlestick borne on the shoulders of the legionnaires. All the pride and might of the Empire was on parade. The moment was later carved in marble to adorn the triumphal Arch of Titus which stands in Rome today. Mark's Gospel is a contemporary of the now crumbling Arch of Titus. It, too, celebrates a victory, not of armies but of a mightier power which came into the world through Christ.

## 29

# A Gospel for the Early Church

## THE GOSPEL OF MATTHEW

AFTER the fall of Jerusalem Titus had passed through Antioch on his triumphant way back to Rome. Antioch is in Syria, three hundred miles north of Jerusalem. In those days it was a magnificent city, and, after Rome and Alexandria, it was the third largest city of the Roman Empire. Few cities could boast of so many beautiful public buildings, market places, triumphal arches, and temples. There were statues and fountains everywhere. Antioch lavished its wealth on pleasures of all kinds: it had theaters, public baths, and race courses. There was an aqueduct and miles of marble-paved streets lined with shady colonnades. It may have been the splendor of sunlight reflected from the gilded statues and marble buildings that gave Antioch her title of "the golden." When Titus arrived here in A.D. 70 he brought with him the Cherubim from Jerusalem's ruined Temple. These were Antioch's share of the spoils and she proudly set them up as ornaments over her city gates. There is good reason to suppose that here in Antioch, not long after the Roman soldiers set the Jerusalem Cherubim above the gates, the Gospel of Matthew was written by a leader of the Antioch church. His real name was lost long ago, but we shall call him Matthew, the name by which his book is known.

The news about Christ had reached Antioch soon after the Resurrection. After Stephen was stoned the Jerusalem church experienced its first persecution and Christians fled in terror from the city.

> Now they which were scattered abroad upon the persecution that arose about Stephen travelled as far as Phenice [Phoenicia], and Cyprus, and Antioch, and preaching the word. Acts 11:19

The blood of the martyrs has ever been the seed of the Church. There is a direct connection between the death of Stephen and the arrival of Christianity in Antioch. Here in this Syrian city the followers of Christ were first called "Christians," and here Paul and Barnabas spent a year before setting out on their first missionary journey with Mark. The church in Antioch was the earliest one, so far as we know, to organize missionary work. It claimed Peter as its first bishop. There were many Jews of the Dispersion in Antioch, as well as Syrians, Greeks, and Romans who flocked to hear the new teaching and to become members of the new Church. Before A.D. 70 Antioch became the chief center of Gentile Christianity.

All this is so clearly reflected in the Gospel of Matthew that Antioch seems to be its most likely cradle. Here its author must have met Peter, who has a more important role in this than in the other Gospels. Like Antioch, this Gospel is Greek-speaking but it is, at the same time, the most Jewish of the Gospels. Matthew was doubtless a Jew by race, but it is interesting to note that the quotations he uses from the prophets are taken from the Septuagint Greek Version. The Gospel opens from a Jewish point of view by tracing Christ's ancestry back to Abraham. It closes with the command: "Go ye therefore, and teach all nations," reminding us that the conversion of the Gentile world was a deep concern of the Antioch church.

As a citizen of Antioch, Matthew lived at one of the busiest crossroads of the Roman Empire where he must have heard many languages spoken in the market place. In the midst of a crowd of Syrians, Greeks, Romans, and Jews he watched the chariot races or walked in the shade of the marble colonnades.

He felt the Church of which he was a member drawing its strength from both Jewish and Gentile sources. No wonder that the book he wrote stands first at the crossroads where the Old and New Testaments meet.

It may have been the fall of Jerusalem that gave Matthew his key to the meaning of Christianity. Perhaps he stood in the crowd at the city gate and watched the soldiers set up the Temple Cherubim which were a symbol that Jerusalem had perished. No longer was it possible for the Holy City to be the center of Christianity, for the very hammer blows of the soldiers sounded a death knell to the hopes of those Jews who had tried to make Christianity one of the sects of Judaism. Christianity and Judaism had moved apart forever. Matthew believed that Christ was indeed the Messiah of Hebrew prophecy, but he also believed that in rejecting Him the Jews had thrown aside their inheritance of the Kingdom of Heaven and had brought destruction upon themselves. As the Cherubim now belonged to Antioch, so the heritage of Israel now belonged to the Christian Church.

It was a priceless heritage and Matthew recognized its worth. Israel gave Christianity a holy Book and the idea of inspired writings which at length produced the New Testament. She taught Christianity how to pray and bequeathed her many of the forms of prayer. She endowed the Church with her passion for monotheism. Righteousness of life and the conception of universal brotherhood were two of Israel's best gifts to the new Church. Christianity caught fire from Judaism's hope in the future and from her missionary spirit. All this Matthew inherited as a Jew. His Christian possessions were boundless. He had no doubt known Peter, Barnabas, Mark, Paul, and other early leaders mentioned in Acts. His memory was filled with stories these leaders had told. He had learned many of the Lord's sayings and he was well acquainted with the entire oral Gospel. Moreover, his library shelves soon after A.D. 70 held some of the most valuable documents of the early Church. He had a copy of Mark's new Gospel. He also owned a collection of the Lord's Sayings written in Greek. Beside these volumes there was his copy of the Septuagint and perhaps a short roll containing selections from Old Testament prophecies that seemed to foreshadow Christ. Thus equipped Matthew began to write his Gospel.

He was a literary architect and he worked according to a carefully thought-out plan. In the back of his mind were all the ideas we have considered and many more besides. They would inevitably color his book, but his immediate plan was a very practical one. He wanted to issue a new edition of Mark's Gospel combined with the Sayings of the Lord. There was a demand in the Church for a handbook telling all Christ was and did, together with all He taught. The earliest Christians needed two things: faith in a Person and high standards of living. Mark's Gospel revealed Christ, who was the object of their faith. The Sayings gave them rules for Christian living. Matthew proposed to combine these two necessary elements of faith and practice in one Gospel. Matthew reminds us of many another nameless editor and copyist of his race who in preceding centuries, working with Old Testament documents, had selected, combined, rewritten, and edited the masterpieces of Hebrew literature according to new needs. As we know, the original documents out of which the Old Testament was made no longer survive as separate works, all having been cut and shaped and fitted into the books as we now have them. But fortunately with Matthew it is different. The framework of Matthew is Mark. Of the 661 verses of Mark's Gospel 600 reappear in Matthew. Mark is practically incorporated in Matthew. As we still have Mark intact, we can compare the two books and see how Matthew used Mark. He seldom copied word for word from the older Gospel, for Matthew was a better writer than Mark and he did not hesitate to rewrite Mark wherever he could improve the style and make the sentences flow more smoothly. He changed Mark's matter-of-fact, blunt statements and his portrait of Christ is less human than Mark's. We miss Mark's impressiveness, but in Matthew we gain a churchly conception of Christ.

In the scene where Jesus heals the man with the withered hand, Mark adds the vivid eyewitness detail of Jesus confronting the scribes and Pharisees:

> When he had looked round about on them with anger, being grieved for the hardness of their hearts.
>
> MARK 3:5

Thus human display of emotion seemed so unsuitable to Matthew that he left it out entirely and hurried on to the divine act of healing:

> Then saith he to the man, Stretch forth thine hand. And he stretched it forth; and it was restored whole, like as the other.
>
> MATTHEW 12:13

Mark wrote that in Nazareth Jesus "could there do no mighty work" and that he "marvelled because of their unbelief" (Mark 6:5,6). Will Matthew let this admission of lack of power and this evidence of surprise stand? In the parallel passage in Matthew we find exactly what we expect. Matthew has skillfully toned down Mark: "And he did not many mighty works there because of their unbelief" (Matthew 13:58). These are typical of the changes Matthew made in his rewriting of Mark.

To Mark's simple framework of the deeds of Christ, Matthew added a wealth of sayings. The original document from which Matthew took these has disappeared. Matthew's skill lay in his arrangement of the miscellaneous sayings. He was not content with a hit-and-miss collection, but grouped the sayings in five sections according to subject matter, and interrupted Mark's narrative at five points to insert these sayings. The first and most famous group is in chapters 5, 6, and 7 and is called the Sermon on the Mount. Each of the five groups of sayings ends with the formula: "And it came to pass, when Jesus had finished these words."[1] The entire collection of sayings might easily have been spoken in a couple of hours, for of all that Jesus must have said, Matthew preserved only what the Church had found most effective.

The five collections of sayings divide the ministry of Jesus

---

[1] Matt. 7:28; 11:1; 13:53; 19:1; 26:1.

into five parts. In planning the Gospel this way Matthew may have had in mind the so-called five books of Moses or the Pentateuch. First we read of Christ's early ministry; next, of his work throughout Galilee; third, of the beginning of opposition to him; fourth, of wider travels to spread the message; and fifth, of the last journey up to Jerusalem.

Though the bulk of Matthew's Gospel is built from Mark and the Sayings of Jesus, there are about four hundred verses which cannot be traced to either of these sources. These verses include the ancestry of Jesus, the Wise Men's visit, the flight into Egypt, Peter walking on the water, Judas' death, Pilate's wife's dream, Pilate washing his hands, and the earthquake at the Crucifixion. No doubt Matthew took this varied material from oral teachings and from a written collection of Jerusalem tradition. Scattered through the Gospel are many references to Hebrew prophecy, introduced by the familiar refrains: "That it might be fulfilled which was spoken by the prophets . . ." or "For thus it is written . . ." In Matthew's day there may have been a collection of Scripture texts used by teachers to prove that Jesus was the Messiah foretold by the prophets. Either from this collection or from his own copy of the Scriptures, Matthew chose quotations to show how Christ's life fulfilled the prophecies.

When Matthew's Gospel was published sometime between A.D. 80 and 90, it immediately became popular. Teachers found that its clear arrangement helped their students and that the grouping of the Sayings made them easy to memorize. In one volume were now combined the contents of the two chief Christian documents of the day: Mark and the Sayings of Jesus. It enlarged Mark's portrait of Jesus as a man of action and showed Him as a teacher also. In the Sermon on the Mount people were given Christian standards of life. This statement of ethical ideals has never been surpassed, except in Matthew 25:40 where ethical teaching reaches its climax in this: "Inasmuch as ye have done it unto one of the least of these my brethren, ye have done it unto me."

We would like to know who the man we have been calling "Matthew" really was. It is clear that he was not one of the twelve disciples, for in this Gospel there are none of the eyewitness stories and details that a disciple would surely have added. It is a book obviously copied from Mark and the Sayings. Would a disciple have depended on Mark's account? Surely not. Far from copying Mark, a disciple would have written an original narrative altogether. But our Matthew looked up to Mark as an authority. Furthermore, the Gospel was written fifty or sixty years after the events it describes, a long time for one of the original disciples to wait before writing down his memories.

How then did the name of St. Matthew, the disciple of Jesus, become attached to this Gospel? St. Matthew or Levi, as he is sometimes called, was the official whom Jesus saw "sitting at the receipt of custom: and he saith unto him, Follow me. And he arose, and followed him." Papias, about A.D. 140, wrote: "Matthew composed the Sayings in the Hebrew language and everyone translated them as he could." Such a collection of Christ's very words made by one of the original disciples would have been highly valued in the early Church. We do not know whether Matthew's Sayings were in oral or written form, nor do we know who translated them into Greek, but it is probable that the author of the Gospel incorporated these Sayings into his book. It was natural for the name of Matthew to become attached to the Gospel in which the Sayings formed so important a part. The name serves to remind us that this account of Jesus probably rests upon the testimony of at least two disciples: Matthew, the tax collector, who first assembled the Sayings, and Peter, the fisherman, whose stories are preserved in Mark.

The actual author of the Gospel of Matthew probably wrote his book after all the original disciples had died. After the fall of Jerusalem Christianity moved into a new period of her history, and Matthew's Gospel was designed to meet the new problems and the different needs of this period. Reading him today we remember that Matthew lived in a city over whose gates were the Jerusalem Cherubim. Any day he could walk through the beautiful streets and enter churches where both Jews and Gentiles worshiped together. Between the lines of this Gospel we hear echoes of the old controversies. We hear Jews asking: "How is this new Church joined to the old Israel of our fathers?" Matthew gives them Christ's words in reply:

> Think not that I am come to destroy the law, or the prophets: I am not come to destroy, but to fulfill.
>
> MATTHEW 5:17

The Gentiles have their question also: "Can we also have a share in Christianity?" For answer Matthew quotes Christ's words:

> Many shall come from the east and west, and shall sit down with Abraham, and Isaac, and Jacob, in the kingdom of heaven.
>
> MATTHEW 8:11

Matthew's final sentence shines above the stormy controversies of the first century:

> And, lo, I am with you alway, even unto the end of the world.
>
> MATTHEW 28:20

# 30

## Luke's Two-Volume History

### THE GOSPEL OF LUKE AND THE ACTS OF THE APOSTLES

SPEAKING Greek and traveling over Roman roads and along the shipping routes of the Mediterranean, the early Christians soon carried their faith far and wide throughout the western world. The enormous vitality of Christianity was the main reason for its rapid diffusion, but there were other factors which aided it. Alexander's conquests of the fourth century B.C. brought Greek civilization to his subject peoples and succeeded in breaking down the exclusive national groups of the earliest Old Testament days. Greek language, literature, and philosophy stormed the barriers separating peoples of different races, languages, and religions, and as the barriers were broken down, the world slowly became cosmopolitan. The various tribes or nations ceased to be of prime importance in this Greek-speaking, Greek-thinking world, and individual men assumed the center of the stage. It was into such a world that Christianity came. It was a time when paganism was slowly dying of weariness and despair. Christianity blew through this world like a fresh wind of joy and triumph, proclaiming its faith in One who had said: "Be of good cheer; I have overcome the world."

In the market places of all the cities of the Roman Empire

one encountered Christians eager to tell of their faith. Converts flocked in great numbers into the new churches which formed a mighty chain linking all the great centers of the Empire: Jerusalem, Antioch, Damascus, Ephesus, Philippi, Athens, Corinth, Alexandria, and Rome. Christian missionaries often paused for rest at roadside inns on their ceaseless journeys. They traveled by ship and sometimes they went in chains as prisoners escorted by Roman soldiers. Frequently they were the defendants in trials before Roman magistrates. All too often an uproar in one of the cities grew from an act of violence against a Christian. Sometimes they were locked in prisons. There were escapes and rescues, persecutions and martyrdoms. Christianity did not grow and spread and permeate all classes of society without coming into conflict with the Jews and with the state. Even so, many a Jew was converted and many a Roman official wanted to know more about a religion which gave its believers an incredible courage and joy. The pagan faiths had no such power.

One of the Roman officials attracted by Christianity was Theophilus. Exactly who he was or where he lived we do not know. His position is not stated, but his title was "most excellent." Today his great distinction lies not in his forgotten official position but in the fact that the Gospel of Luke and the Acts of the Apostles were dedicated to him. His name appears in the third verse of Luke and the first verse of Acts and thus serves as a kind of pin fastening these two books together. Without Theophilus we might not have realized that these two works belong together and form a two-volume history of the rise and spread of Christianity. The first tells "all that Jesus began both to do and teach" and is a record similar to those in the first two Gospels. When the Church included Luke in the earliest four-volume collection of Gospels, it became detached from its companion volume of Acts. Acts carries forward the history begun in the Gospel of Luke and tells what Christ through the Holy Spirit continued to do and to teach in His Church. This second volume is really a history of early Christianity.

Luke-Acts opens with a short preface containing a great deal of information. It answers the questions: In what situation was it written? What were the author's qualifications? What sources were used and how were these employed? Why was it written and for whom? In an earlier chapter we saw that there were abundant sources of information about Jesus in the early Church. Many "eyewitnesses and ministers of the word" had drawn up both oral and written statements of the facts upon which Christianity rested, and by A.D. 75 there were at least two written Gospels: Mark and Matthew. In the very multiplicity of witnesses there must have been confusion. Christ was known to men in different ways. It has always been so. He was the object of their faith, and faith is an individual matter. As Theophilus listened to the oral tradition and read the early documents, he may have wondered which was the authentic message. The accounts often conflicted. They lacked order. They did not show the development of Christianity. They did not explain why Christian missionaries so often appeared to be men who "turned the world upside down." Theophilus and his friends were educated people who read both the Greek and the Roman classics. They regretted the fact that Christianity did not speak to the educated world of their day through a well-written, authentic, historical account. Mark's Gospel was powerful but crude. It was a record. Matthew's was useful for church reading and instruction, but it was primarily a church book. The Greek-speaking world needed something different: something to appeal to a wide, reading public. It needed a book to show that Christianity was a religion of kindness, brotherhood, and joy rather than a conspiracy against the state. It was to meet these needs that Luke-Acts was written.

The author's name does not appear in either volume, but since the second century Church tradition has attributed these books to Luke. Like Mark, Luke was not one of the chief men of the Church, for he, too, was always associated with someone more important than himself. In Acts there are many repetitions of the pronoun "we." "We saw," "we arrived," and similar expressions are common. These "we-sections," as they are called, give us a clue to the author's identity. They occur frequently in the last part of Acts and they describe events in which Luke himself must have been present. He is mentioned by name three times in the New Testament: once as "the beloved physician," and again as Paul's "fellowlabourer." The last reference is in the fragment of a letter written by Paul from Rome in which he says:

> Only Luke is with me. Take Mark, and bring him with thee: for he is profitable to me for the ministry.
> II TIMOTHY 4:11

The idea of Paul, Luke, and Mark together in Rome stirs the imagination. What a meeting of New Testament writers that must have been! Between them these three men were destined to write more than half of the New Testament. When they met in Rome Paul had already written and sent his letters to the churches, but neither he nor anyone else had thought of collecting and publishing them. Doubtless Mark was already planning his Gospel, and Luke had written his travel diary.

Luke was a physician, which implies that he was a well-educated man. We know that Paul suffered from some bodily ailment and quite likely Luke first became associated with the missionary movement as Paul's doctor. Tradition says Luke, like Matthew, was a native of Antioch, but there is no certain information about which Greek city he came from nor where he wrote his books. He seems to have traveled extensively with Paul, and in addition to being Paul's physician and probably his secretary as well, Luke would have helped Paul with travel arrangements and plans for meetings. "From the very first," as Luke said in his preface, he had an excellent opportunity to learn the facts upon which Christianity rested and to watch the development of the Church. He made the best possible use of his opportunities.

It was probably in Philippi that the idea first came to Luke of keeping a diary. He arrived in this Macedonian city with Paul, Silas, and Timothy about A.D. 49. They preached to a group of women gathered for prayer at the river bank outside the city. In this little group was the successful businesswoman, Lydia,

who became Paul's first convert on the continent of Europe. As
a historian and a very careful observer, Luke realized the significance of the arrival of Christianity in Europe, and this may have
given him the idea of keeping a record of all he saw and all
that Paul did. Diaries were not unusual in Luke's day. Nearly
a hundred years before, Caesar had kept a diary of his campaigns
in Gaul. Luke may have written his diary on tablets of wood
coated with wax. His pen was a stylus and with this he scratched
his letters on the wax surface. In all likelihood the story beginning with Acts 16:9 is the opening of Luke's travel diary.

One could not travel ten or twelve years with Paul and avoid
recording in one's diary a history of the spread of Christianity
throughout the Roman Empire. But Luke's interest in preserving records did not end with his own travel diary. Wherever
he went he found brief documents about Jesus and the early
happenings in the Church. He met men and women who could
not write but were eager to tell him what they remembered of
the Master and His Apostles. Luke collected documents and
transcribed records. At Antioch he may have purchased a roll
of the Sayings of Jesus based on the collection of the Apostle
Matthew. Both Luke and Matthew are thought to have used
this collection in their Gospels. Luke's beautiful cycle of stories
about the birth and infancy of Jesus he probably learned while
he was in Jerusalem. From there also must have come the gene-
alogy which traces Jesus' ancestry and does not stop with Abraham, as Matthew was content to do, but goes back to Adam. We
do not know Luke's exact source, but it is likely that one of the
ministering women, "Joanna, the wife of Chuza, Herod's steward," or Susanna, or Mary Magdalene told these and other
stories to Luke when he visited Jerusalem with Paul about A.D.
56. Luke may have found an early hymnbook and copied from
it the four exquisite songs in his gospel:

> Mary's Magnificat:
>> My soul doth magnify the Lord,
>> And my spirit hath rejoiced in God my Saviour . . .
>>> LUKE 1:46-55

Zacharias' Benedictus:

> Blessed be the Lord God of Israel;
> For he hath visited and redeemed his people . . .
>
> LUKE 1:68-79

The Angel's Song:

> Glory to God in the highest,
> And on earth peace, good will toward men.
>
> LUKE 2:14

Simeon's Nunc Dimittis:

> Lord, now lettest thou thy servant depart in peace,
> According to thy word . . .
>
> LUKE 2:29-32

Luke spent the years A.D. 56-58 in the seaport of Caesarea because Paul was imprisoned in the fortress there awaiting trial. As Luke was free to come and go, he doubtless spent part of his time collecting new documents and listening to oral traditions. Philip, the deacon, and his four prophetess daughters lived in Caesarea and from them Luke might have heard of the stirring years following the Crucifixion when Philip's fellow deacon, Stephen, was stoned and became the first Christian martyr. In the midst of the busy city of Caesarea with its fine harbor on the Mediterranean and its new public buildings, Luke may have found a quiet room in which to work on his collection of documents. Possibly he arranged them in order, beginning with the stories of Christ's birth and ending with his own travel diary. He may even have made a rough draft of his Gospel and Acts during these years in Caesarea. But if he did, the first draft must have been a sketchy document, for we know that Luke eventually inserted large portions of Mark in his own Gospel, and Mark had not yet been written.

Fortunately he left his notes and records, his tablets and papyrus rolls behind in Caesarea when he embarked for Rome with Paul. On the voyage they were shipwrecked off Malta. Though everyone on board was saved, the cargo was tossed overboard and the ship broke up in the surf. If Luke's precious documents had not been safe in some cupboard in Caesarea they, too, would surely have been lost.

Luke seems to have remained in Rome with Paul until the

latter's death. No doubt he experienced the terror following Nero's persecutions. While in Rome he may have read Mark's Gospel from the original manuscript. He recognized at once its importance and probably had a copy of it made to add to his collection. The fact that in later years Luke used Mark as the basis of his Gospel is an additional proof of the reliability of Mark.

After this we do not know where Luke went nor what he did, except that sometime before A.D. 90 he wrote Luke-Acts. Some scholars think Luke completed his history by A.D. 65, before Paul died, for Acts does not tell of Paul's martyrdom. However, as Luke may have had a good reason for omitting this, other scholars date Luke-Acts about A.D. 75, for the Gospel clearly mentions the fall of Jerusalem. Still other scholars date the Gospel about A.D. 90.

If it is true that a man's character expresses itself in his writing, we have abundant evidence of the sort of person Luke was. In the first place he was a literary artist, for his books are still charming to read and rank among the most beautiful writings of the Bible. An old legend says that Luke was an artist and that he painted a portrait of the Virgin Mary. There is symbolical truth in this story, for even if Luke was not an artist of brushes and pigments, he painted word pictures which have inspired artists in all ages. His stories of the Nativity and of the boy Jesus' visit to the Temple are unforgettable. He alone of all the evangelists gives the parables of the Good Samaritan, the Lost Sheep, the Prodigal Son, and the Rich Man and Lazarus.

Only Luke records the passage Jesus chose from Isaiah when he stood up to read the Scripture in the synagogue one Sabbath day.

> The Spirit of the Lord is upon me, because he hath anointed me to preach the gospel to the poor; he hath sent me to heal the brokenhearted, to preach deliverance to the captives, and recovering of sight to the blind, to set at liberty them that are bruised, To preach the acceptable year of the Lord.
>
> LUKE 4:18, 19

"This day," Jesus declared, "is this scripture fulfilled in your ears." For Luke this quotation from Second or Third Isaiah summed up the ministry of Jesus.

Luke often shows us Jesus praying and he alone records the prayer on the Cross: "Father, forgive them; for they know not what they do." He also includes Christ's assurance to the penitent thief on the other cross: "Today shalt thou be with me in paradise." He enriches our understanding of Christ's sympathy and love for all humanity. He records the miracles of compassionate healing, the teachings about the danger of riches and the dignity of poverty. From Luke's stories the world gained new respect for womanhood. His entire Gospel is filled with an atmosphere of glad tidings, joy, and the new power of the Holy Spirit.

The colors with which Luke painted the portrait of Christ illuminated the Acts of the Apostles also and began to permeate the whole fabric of Christianity. The second volume, like the first, is radiant with prayer and rejoicing and brotherhood. The words "joy" and "rejoice" occur more often in Luke than in all the other evangelists put together. Acts, like the Gospel, contains a gallery of portraits of the men and women who launched Christianity. With all their varied traits and sharp individuality these people bear a striking family resemblance, for Luke shows them all bound together in the fellowship and power of the Holy Spirit. With great narrative skill, Luke writes of the clash of their personalities. Paul's figure dominates Acts and his controversies with the Jews are portrayed with dramatic power. In scene after scene, compressed sometimes to a few verses, he unfolds the heroic stature of the first Christians. The settings are varied. We are taken into temples and theaters, courts and prisons, homes and palaces. We live through one of the most thrilling accounts ever written of a storm at sea. The Gospel and Acts together form a continued story which moves swiftly, according to Luke's careful plan, from its opening scene in Jerusalem before the birth of John the Baptist, to its close with Paul in his own hired house in imperial Rome. Seldom has the march of history been so vividly or so powerfully recorded. Perhaps never has humanity been portrayed in such radiant colors.

## 31

# The Synoptic Problem

## THE GOSPELS OF
## MARK, MATTHEW, AND LUKE VIEWED TOGETHER

TO all who enjoy solving puzzles the New Testament offers a most fascinating one. This is the relationship of the first three Gospels and it is called the synoptic problem. In the three previous chapters we looked at Mark, Matthew, and Luke separately. In order to solve this puzzle we shall look at them together or synoptically. The word "synoptic" comes from *syn* meaning "together" and *optic* meaning "to view" or "to see." Viewing the first three Gospels together brings to light some extraordinary facts. All three are very often alike, agreeing sometimes word for word. That makes us think that somewhere there has been copying. Our problem is: who copied from whom? At other times the Gospels give different accounts of the same event, or one Gospel develops a story or group of sayings the others omit. Does all this shed any light on who wrote the Gospels and when and why?

Indeed it does. Much of what was said about the first three Gospels in preceding chapters is based on the answers scholars have found to the synoptic problem. It is a problem, however, that is not entirely solved. Our story of the origins, purposes, and authors of the Gospels must still be told with many a "possibly" and "perhaps" and it still offers scope for further study and fresh theories.

The best way to see the Gospels synoptically is to write their contents in three parallel columns, rearranging the material in such a way that similar accounts of the same incident appear on the same page. This laborious task has already been done by scholars who have prepared harmonies or synopses of the Gospels. These are printed to show at a glance the literary relationships of the Gospels. This is a typical example:

| Matthew 19:13-15 | Mark 10:13-16 | Luke 18:15-17 |
|---|---|---|
| Then were there brought unto him little children, that he should put his hands on them, and pray; and the disciples rebuked them. | And they brought young children to him, that he should touch them: and his disciples rebuked those that brought them. | And they brought unto him also infants, that he would touch them: but when his disciples saw it, they rebuked them. |
| But Jesus said, Suffer little children, and forbid them not, to come unto me: for of such is the kingdom of heaven. | But when Jesus saw it, he was much displeased, and said unto them, Suffer the little children to come unto me, and forbid them not; for of such is the kingdom of God. | But Jesus called them unto him, and said, Suffer little children to come unto me, and forbid them not: for of such is the kingdom of God. |
| | Verily I say unto you, Whosoever shall not receive the kingdom of God as a little child, he shall not enter therein. | Verily I say unto you, Whosoever shall not receive the kingdom of God as a little child shall in no wise enter therein. |
| And he laid his hands on them, and departed thence. | And he took them up in his arms, put his hands upon them, and blessed them. | |

When we count the verses which are alike in the three books we find that the kinship of the first three Gospels is very extensive. Mark contains 661 verses in all. Of these Matthew repeats or reproduces the substance of 600. Luke uses only 350 of Mark's verses, but some of these are different from those Matthew gives. There are, in fact, only 31 verses of Mark which do not reappear in some form in Matthew and Luke. This begins to look as though Mark were the oldest Gospel and the one copied by both Matthew and Luke.

Our theory of the dependence of Matthew and Luke on Mark is strengthened by the order of events in the three books. Matthew usually arranged his copied material in the same order he found it in Mark. In a few cases where Matthew rearranged Mark's order Luke preserved it. When Luke followed his own sequence of events independently from Mark, Matthew usually gave Mark's order. Clearly, Matthew and Luke were not copying each other. They must both have derived much of their material and sequence from Mark. This solution of the synoptic problem shows us that Mark is the primary Gospel, the original record on which later documents were based. The Gospel of John also used Mark and even the *Gospel of Peter,* an heretical book not included in the canon, was based on Mark. Mark is the rock on which written testimony concerning Jesus is based.

This theory of the primacy of Mark is confirmed by the way Matthew and Luke change and adapt the material they copy from Mark. Neither of the two later writers were slavish imitators. Naturally both Matthew and Luke had their own style of writing and each had a special purpose and a different audience. They wrote at a time when Jesus of Nazareth had become the object of Christian faith. They both wanted to portray Christ's divinity, and so they carefully toned down Mark's eyewitness details which convey so rich an impression of Christ's humanity. In Mark, Jesus is sometimes amazed or sorrowful, angered or grieved. In Matthew or Luke these details are usually left out.

In the scene where Jesus blesses the little children we note that Matthew omits Mark's: "when Jesus saw it he was much displeased," feeling perhaps that this picture of displeasure marred the portrait of Christ. Mark describes how Jesus "took them up in his arms, put his hands upon them, and blessed them." But Matthew leaves out the human gesture of taking the children in His arms and gives only the churchly gesture of blessing. "And he laid his hands on them." Luke, after the manner of Matthew, omits the picture of Jesus' displeasure and the act of taking the children in His arms.

This and many other similar examples support our theory that Mark was the first Gospel and very close to the eyewitness sources from which it was derived, while Matthew and Luke represent a later period and a more developed theology.

The synoptic problem has another fascinating angle. Mark is the shortest of the Gospels. Both Matthew and Luke have a great deal of material not taken from Mark. From what source or sources did they obtain this? Comparing this material in Matthew and Luke, we find that about two hundred verses of it are common to both Gospels. Again we propose a theory of copying to account for this large area of similarity. The two hundred verses consist mostly in the Sayings of Jesus. Surely there must have been either an oral or a written collection of the Sayings of so great a teacher as Jesus. Perhaps, according to the custom of those days, His disciples began to make this oral collection and commit it to memory while they still traveled with Him along the roads of Galilee and Judea. We do not know when the oral collection of Sayings was written down, but we remember that Papias said: "Matthew composed the Sayings in the Hebrew language and everyone translated them as he could." No doubt these Sayings of Jesus were one of the sources used by both Matthew and Luke and account for the similarity of the two hundred verses they have in common.

Modern scholars designate this common source of Matthew and Luke as Q from the German word *Quelle*, meaning "a source." The document itself has been lost, but ingenious attempts have been made to reconstruct Q. None are entirely successful. One is tempted to. see the symbol Q as standing for "Question," for it is still a question whether the Sayings were oral or written, whether they were in Aramaic or Greek, whether the disciple Matthew or some other person collected them, whether Matthew and Luke used the same version of Q. It has been suggested that Q was well known in Rome and that Mark derived some of the Sayings in his Gospel from some version of Q. Possibly Mark wrote his Gospel to supplement these collected Sayings. Paul gives evidence of knowing some, at least, of the Sayings.[1] But the source Q still abounds in questions.

In a harmony of the Gospels we find many places where Matthew or Luke stands alone. The material for these passages each writer must have taken from his own special sources. Matthew had one source for his birth stories, while Luke seems to have had a different one. In the chapters on Matthew and Luke we saw where these two writers might have obtained their unique material.

Such is a brief account of the synoptic problem. The theories help us to understand how the three Gospels were written, but they leave us with scope for further study. Perhaps in the future better theories will be proposed. It is unlikely, however, that newer theories will be able to shake our well-grounded confidence in these three books. The more we study them, the better we see that these are trustworthy records of the Founder of Christianity.

So far we have said little about the Fourth Gospel. When we compare it with the others we see at once that the Gospel of John stands alone. On very few pages of the Gospel harmony is there a fourth column containing the text of John. John is usually printed in solid blocks by itself rather than in a column parallel to the others. Clearly it does not belong with the synoptic Gospels. It is like them in that it traces the life of Jesus, but it does this in its own original way. It is not a compilation nor a rewriting of the oral or written record, but a fresh creation by a great spiritual genius. The synoptic problem thus points to the uniqueness of the Gospel of John and leads us to ask: Who wrote it and when and why and for whom?

---

[1] I Cor. 7:10, 9:14.

## ✒ 32 ✒

### *Christ's Interpreter to the Greek World*

#### THE GOSPEL AND EPISTLES OF JOHN

IN the entire Roman province of Asia no city was more important than Ephesus. It was the capital of the province and one of the wealthiest and most splendid cities of the Empire. From its crowded harbor on the Aegean Sea Greek and Phoenician merchantmen loaded with the products of Asia sailed to all the Mediterranean ports. Prosperous Ephesians had built their homes above the heart of the city on the slopes of Mount Prion. From its summit one could see the whole panorama of ancient Ephesus. It was surrounded by the broken forms of mountain ranges, while to the north rose the snow-capped peak of Tmolus. Toward the west were the sparkling blue waters of the Aegean and the dim outlines of the mountainous island of Samos. Through the plain below, the river Cayster wound toward the sail-filled harbor. In the midst of the plain stood one of the Seven Wonders of the ancient world: the magnificent Temple of Diana of Ephesus. Its marble columns were the highest in the world and rose sixty feet into the sky. Many people came to this great city on business, but multitudes arrived on the pilgrim ships to worship at Diana's shrine. For a few years Antony and Cleopatra lived here in great luxury. Paul knew the city well, having spent the years A.D. 54-57 in Ephesus.

He preached in the school of Tyrannus and wrote his First Epistle to the Corinthians here. Some people think that Paul was well acquainted with the prison at Ephesus and from there wrote Philemon, Colossians, and Philippians. Luke must have been here also, for his account of the riot in the theater is vivid with eyewitness detail.[1]

Today Ephesus is a desolate ruin. Its harbor is silted up, and the place where Diana's Temple stood has become a stagnant pool. Frogs now croak where once men cried: "Great is Diana of the Ephesians!" Broken fragments of the Temple's huge columns were found twenty feet below the present surface and some of these remarkable sculptured drums are now in the British Museum. The glory of Ephesus has long since vanished, but the greatest thing ever created there remains as a permanent possession of humanity. This is the Gospel of John.

Peter, Paul, and John are the three outstanding men of the early Church. Peter's courage and zeal helped to weld the first little band of Christ's followers into a Church. Paul crystallized the Christian message and carried it far beyond the limits of the Jewish world into the main stream of Greco-Roman life. John plumbed the depths of spiritual understanding and gave the Church its profoundest interpretation of the life and message of Christ. Peter was the "rock"; Paul was the statesman; John was the interpreter. Peter and Paul had their Luke, and thanks to him their personalities still live and their deeds are remembered. But John had no biographer. Though time has erased all certain knowledge of who he was and where and when he lived, we still have his matchless Gospel and the three Epistles attributed to him and from these we can gain some idea of John. It is thought that he lived in Ephesus, but even this is not a proved fact. Uncertainty surrounds John on every side, and we have to build his story on a foundation of probability, theory, and legend.

There was a disciple named John whom Jesus found one day fishing with his brother James from a boat on the Sea of

---

[1] Acts 19:23-41.

Galilee. Both these sons of Zebedee were called to become disciples and they followed Jesus to the end. Was this disciple John the same John who wrote the Gospel? Possibly he was, but the great bulk of evidence is against it. Mark says that Jesus named John and James "the sons of thunder." Luke tells how these impatient young disciples wanted to call down fire upon a village that refused to accept Jesus. This does not sound like the man who wrote the Fourth Gospel. Paul stated that John's ministry was only to the Jews,[2] but the Fourth Gospel is written for all the world. It is the most Greek in point of view of all the Gospels. Could John, a Jewish fisherman from Galilee, have written such a book? All the evidence points to a date around A.D. 100 for the appearance of this Gospel. By this date the disciple John would have been about ninety years old. Papias handed down the tradition that both James and John were martyred in Jerusalem by the Jews before A.D. 70, thirty years before the Fourth Gospel was written. This Gospel never mentions John the son of Zebedee by name, but it does speak of "the disciple whom Jesus loved." Many scholars believe that John Zebedee and the Beloved Disciple are the same man. If this is so, it throws further doubt on the authorship of this Gospel by the disciple John, for it is hard to believe that he would have described himself as the disciple Jesus loved. Perhaps the most telling argument against John's authorship of this Gospel lies in the fact that it depends largely upon Mark's Gospel. Would an actual disciple have based his work on the report of a man like Mark who had known Jesus only at second hand? Surely not.

Many people reading this wonderful Gospel and believing it to be the testimony of John, the disciple Jesus loved, are keenly disappointed when they realize that this John cannot be the author. At first this appears to undermine our confidence in the book itself. If it cannot claim apostolic authorship, by what authority does it speak to us? But then we remember that the other Gospels were not written by Apostles, either. This

---

[2] Gal. 2:9.

Gospel, like them, was tested in the crucible of early Christianity. Amid cries of heresy and the flames of persecution the Gospel of John won a place for itself and was accepted by the Church. Centuries of Christian experience endorse it. It is an inexhaustibly deep well of spiritual refreshment and from it men have always drunk the "living water" which Christ promised them. Who then dug this well?

Perhaps we can never be entirely sure. The author was careless of his own literary immortality in his profound concentration on the Person of Christ. It is possible, though, that we can find someone whose life fits the internal and external conditions of this book. We shall try to recreate the story of such a man, realizing that all of our details are possible but not one of them is absolutely certain. Without argument we shall sketch a tentative picture of the author, so that we may better understand his book.

The author's name was John. At the age of twelve his parents took him up to Jerusalem for the Passover. There, like the other Boy twenty years before, he eagerly watched the busy life around him. That year the city was in a turmoil. John listened wide eyed as Pilate shouted:

"Will ye therefore that I release unto you the King of the Jews?"

He trembled, not knowing why, when the crowd roared:

"Not this man, but Barabbas!"

The boy John trailed the mob out toward Golgotha, but it was not until afterward that he understood what he saw that Friday afternoon outside the walls of Jerusalem. In later years some people said: "This Jesus was not actually a man at all: He was really just a spirit." But John had stood on Golgotha and he knew. In his First Epistle he could write:

> That which was from the beginning, which we have heard, which we have seen with our eyes, which we have looked upon, and our hands have handled, of the Word of life . . . declare we unto you, that ye also may have fellowship with us.
>
> I JOHN 1:1, 3

The boy's keen observation of the villages he traveled through on the Passover journey stood him in good stead, for years later the geography of Palestine was still clear enough in his memory to give authority to his Gospel account.

Sometime John must have met his older namesake who was a disciple and one of the sons of Zebedee. Were the older and younger Johns related by blood or was the tie between them that of spiritual father and son? We do not surely know, but we believe that the younger man honored the elder as the disciple closest to Jesus.

If there had been Jewish influences in John's early life, these soon began to fade. From his early manhood he must have lived in cities where Greek was spoken. Perhaps Ephesus was always his home. On his tongue was the language of Homer and Euripides, more fluid and colloquial now, but still beautiful. John's eyes were accustomed to the half-circle shape of the Greek theater and the beauty of the marble columns gleaming in the sun. He attended the gymnasium and schools of philosophy where he argued with other young students about the doctrines of the Alexandrian philosopher Philo, who taught that God governs the world through the "Logos." To the Greeks, Logos was "reason" or the divine "word." Years later, meditating upon the meaning of Christ, John saw that Philo's Logos or word was a key to the mystery of His Person. As John read books like the dialogues of Plato, he was fascinated by the play of thought and the development of ideas this dialogue form made possible.

When John became a Christian we do not know. He left no hint of a sudden change like that of Paul's on the Damascus road. Perhaps from that Friday afternoon in Jerusalem he belonged to Christ. As the years went by he watched Christianity grow and he grew with it. Ships putting in at the harbor of Ephesus often brought teachers and missionaries with news from the churches springing up everywhere. As John listened to teachers reciting the oral tradition of Christ's life, he checked their stories of the Crucifixion with his own boyhood memories. After Paul's eventful years in Ephesus, John knew that Christ's message found more fertile soil in the Gentile world than in the Jewish community. When a ship arrived at Ephesus in A.D. 70 with news of the fall of Jerusalem, John, like Matthew, realized that a new era was beginning for Christianity. It was no longer a small sect within Judaism but a new and universal religion needing interpreters like himself to translate its message into Greek words and Greek ways of thinking.

Besides the missionaries and the news, the ships brought documents. First came Mark's Gospel from Rome and later possibly Matthew's Gospel and the two-volume Luke-Acts. Some of Paul's Epistles had been written here, and copies of these and his other letters may have been carefully preserved and read in the churches of Ephesus.

John became a leader among the Christians there. He was a well-known preacher and men flocked to hear his sermons about Christ. John called Him the Logos or the Word and the "true Light, which lighteth every man that cometh into the world." People listened spellbound to his tremendous phrases and sentences that conveyed so powerfully his own experience of the Lord.

> Whosoever believeth in him should not perish, but have eternal life.
>
> JOHN 3:15

> Jesus said . . . I am the bread of life: he that cometh to me shall never hunger; and he that believeth on me shall never thirst.
>
> JOHN 6:35

> I am come that they might have life, and that they might have it more abundantly.
>
> JOHN 10:10

Christianity was beset with difficulties in first-century Ephesus, but as John faced and met its problems, his influence grew and men accorded him the title given to the greatest of Church leaders, that of "Elder." Elder John saw opposition developing from four directions. The Jews of Ephesus said it was blasphemy for the man Jesus to be made equal to God. A curious little sect in Ephesus remained ignorant of Christ but continued to be

followers of John the Baptist. The Gnostics denied the humanity of Jesus and made Him a spiritual being altogether. Other
strange new doctrines began to divide the Church. John the
Elder combatted this opposition and these heresies with all the
resources of his keen mind and dedicated heart. He answered
the Jews of Ephesus with many an argument based on the words
and deeds of Jesus. "He that hath seen me hath seen the Father."
"I and my Father are one." He announced to the followers of
John the Baptist that Christ had indeed come and he reminded
them of John's own words:

> I said, I am not the Christ, but that I am sent before him . . . He
> must increase, but I must decrease.
>
> JOHN 3:28, 30

Gnostic teaching tended to evaporate the solid historical
foundation of Christianity into a spiritual dream. The Gnostics
told a strange story in one of their gospels which the Church
considered heretical. They said that Christ watched the Crucifixion from afar, for it was not He who died on the Cross. Christ
to them was only a spiritual Being, not an actual man. John
answered this Gnostic challenge to the manhood of Jesus by
declaring that: "The Word was made flesh, and dwelt among us,
and we beheld his glory." Throughout all John's teaching, no
matter how high his theology soared, he never lost sight of the
real Jesus who once lived as an actual person in Galilee and
Judea. There was a strong mystical strain in John similar to the
mysticism of his Gnostic opponents, but he wisely saw that if
they succeeded in chopping off the historical roots of Christianity it would die like a cut flower.

When strange new doctrines threatened the unity of the
Church, John preached of Christ as the "vine" and warned that
"as the branch cannot bear fruit of itself, except it abide in the
vine; no more can ye, except ye abide in me."

In all this we see John meeting the needs and problems of
those in the early Church who looked to him for leadership. Out
of the facts of history and from his own spiritual experience
John forged the materials he was later to use in his Gospel. His

teachings won men's respect and he became so popular that people from neighboring towns gladly walked many a hot and dusty mile under the blazing sun of Asia Minor to reach Ephesus and hear John preach.

As a young man Papias must have journeyed the hundred miles between his home in Hierapolis and Ephesus to sit at John's feet. He was always eager to question anyone arriving from Ephesus about what John was preaching. In his often-quoted fragment preserved by Eusebius, Papias said:

> If anyone happened to come my way who had been a follower of the Elders, I would enquire about the sayings of the Elders—what Andrew said, or Peter, or Philip, or Thomas, or James, or John, or Matthew, or any other of the Lord's disciples; also what Aristion or the *Elder John,* the disciples of the Lord, say. For I did not think that I got so much profit from the contents of books as from the words of a living and abiding voice.

This fragment shows us that for Papias the authority of the Elder John was nearly as important as that of the Apostles themselves. It also indicates that the oral Gospel remained popular even when there were written documents.

By the end of the first century the Elder John must have held the position of a bishop. This theory is strengthened by a tradition that the Bishop of Ephesus at this time was named John. But not everyone accepted the Elder's authority. In one of the outlying churches a leader named Diotrephes refused to receive men arriving with letters of introducton from John. This obscure church quarrel is the subject of the Third Epistle of John, which is a letter from the Elder to his loyal friend Gaius, a member of Diotrephes' church. It is a personal letter short enough to fit on a single sheet of papyrus, but its contents and signature provide one link in the chain of evidence pointing to John the Elder as the author of the Fourth Gospel.

Again in his role of Bishop of Ephesus, John wrote another brief letter. This is the Second Epistle of John, and it is addressed to a local church. He does not name the church but calls it "the elect lady and her children." He signs himself simply,

"The Elder." He warns this church against receiving Gnostic teachers who do not acknowledge that "Jesus Christ is come in the flesh." It is the sort of letter a bishop might have written to a church under his jurisdiction.

Both these short letters indicate that John traveled from church to church in his district, but he also probably sent out messengers to speak for him. These men often carried copies of John's sermons to read in the churches they visited. The First Epistle of John is probably such a sermon. John addressed those who would listen to it as "my little children." He gave them three tests by which they could distinguish between true Christian faith and the popular heresies. Good conduct is the first test:

> We do know that we know him, if we keep his commandments.
>
> I JOHN 2:3

The Gnostics would have failed his second test of right belief:

> Every spirit that confesseth that Jesus Christ is come in the flesh is of God.
>
> I JOHN 4:2

The final test is love:

> He that loveth not knoweth not God; for God is love . . . If we love one another, God dwelleth in us.
>
> I JOHN 4:8, 12

This sermon or Epistle took its hearers to the heart of Christianity and showed them the basic elements of the faith in their practical and everyday aspects.

We have watched the Elder as he sent messages to ever-widening circles: an individual, a church, and several churches in the neighborhood of Ephesus. Using perhaps the same pen with which he had written the Epistles he now began to write a book for all Christians, not only in first-century Ephesus, but everywhere and in all times: this is the Gospel of John. Its style, vocabulary, and ways of thought are almost identical with those of the Epistles, indicating that the man who wrote the Fourth Gospel is the same man who wrote the Epistles.

From the room in Ephesus where the Elder worked he could

perhaps see the sails of ships entering the harbor. He could hear the crowds at the temple chanting: "Great is Diana of the Ephesians!" When he went to the market place he met all kinds of people: sorcerers, silversmiths, writers of the books on magic, slaves working for the publishing houses, priestesses of Diana, pilgrims come to worship at her shrine, Roman officials, Greek merchants, Jews. The coins John used were probably stamped on one side with the image of the Asian goddess of fertility and on the other side with the head of the Roman Emperor Domitian, who claimed divine honors for himself.

All these sights and sounds of Ephesus receded from John's mind, when he sat down to write his Gospel. Asian superstition, Greek culture, and Roman power faded into a dim background as John found words to express what had never been expressed before. His thoughts did not bear the imprint of Diana nor of the Emperor, for they belonged to a new coinage and came freshly minted from Christ. John's mind and heart were centered in his Lord. Once he had seen Him face to face in the flesh. These many years he had known Him through his own deep experience. John believed that the power and abundant life he had found in knowing Christ was available to all men. He wrote his Gospel with the purpose:

> That ye might believe that Jesus is the Christ, the Son of God; and that believing ye might have life through his name.
>
> JOHN 20:31

John's purpose was to help recreate the Christian experience in the hearts of his readers. They had Mark's factual record; John gave them an interpretation of that record. He painted a portrait of Christ. Out of the thirty years of Jesus' human life John chose the events of only twenty days or so and he devoted his entire Gospel to these. He began with a phrase that echoed the opening of Genesis and he showed Christ before the creation of the world. This eternal and heavenly picture of the Lord was the shining reality behind all that followed. John developed his story by telling such events as the water changed into wine, the secret visit of Nicodemus, the woman at the well, the feeding of the five thousand—not merely to record the facts, but to help men understand Christ. He knew how easy it was for men to miss the full significance packed into Mark's matter-of-fact account and so he expanded the bare records of word and deed, weaving into them the colorful strands of dialogue and comment. John respected the facts, and it is even thought that at several points his Gospel corrected the Synoptic record and preserved a more reliable tradition. John started with facts, but his goal was faith. To John, the Jesus of history was the Christ of his faith. These formed the warp and woof of the rich fabric of his Gospel.

Again and again John used the great words of his Epistles and sermons as radiant points in his Gospel. He wrote of: love, light, life, truth, knowledge, belief. Out of the quarry of the Greek language he created new phrases, "the light that lighteth every man," "the Father's house," "eternal life." As a poet, philosopher, and theologian John endowed these words and phrases with deeper meanings so that they might convey his faith. He carved those superb portraits of Christ by which we know Him today. He was the Word of God, the Bread of Life, the Water of Life, the Light of the World, the Good Shepherd.

John's Gospel rises to a tremendous climax in chapters 14 to 17. These are the great discourses where we can almost hear Christ speaking to us and where we feel ourselves included in His prayer.

> Neither pray I for these alone, but for them also which shall believe on me through their word.
>
> JOHN 17:20

Here are perhaps the best-loved chapters of the Bible, and in all literature there are no greater devotional pages than these.

The very heart of this Gospel, and indeed of the Bible itself, is in the third chapter where John wrote his most inspired sentence:

> For God so loved the world, that he gave his only begotten Son, that whosoever believeth in him should not perish, but have everlasting life.
>
> JOHN 3:16

We can imagine that as John the Elder wrote the last word of his Gospel the afternoon sun shone low over Ephesus. The Temple of Diana cast long shadows and the blue, red, and gold painted on its white marble glowed with deeper tones. In the last hour of daylight John read his book from its first majestic sentence: Ἐν ἀρχῇ ἦν ὁ λόγος to its final story of doubting Thomas.

The words can be read in an hour, but so rich are they in meaning that they continue to satisfy us for a lifetime. To this author were given the twin gifts of understanding and expression. He was able to put his profound experience of Christ into words that kindle faith. In the end we see that this Gospel's authority lies not so much in who John really was, nor even in his closeness to the historical Jesus, as in this book's power to quicken, release, and refresh men's souls. As we read it we forget the author and, as John himself no doubt planned it, we seem to stand in the very presence of Christ. From this Gospel come those abundant materials out of which each Christian may create for himself his own fifth gospel to round out the canon of his faith.

John's Gospel is but one of four similar books, each with its own value and each contributing an essential element to the portrait of Christ. The early Church realized this and sometime in the second century decided to publish an edition of the four Gospels in order to preserve the fourfold record. Possibly the beautiful twenty-first chapter of John was written by the editors of the four-fold Gospel and added as the final message of the entire collection. It contained a story of the risen Christ and His charge to Peter: "Feed my sheep." They realized that John's Gospel was not widely enough known and so they added their endorsement of it in the twenty-fourth verse.

This is the disciple which testifieth of these things, and wrote these things: and we know that his testimony is true.

It is interesting to note that these men could hardly have believed the disciple John was the author. If they had they would surely have given his name, for that would have been all the authority the Fourth Gospel needed. Their final sentence with its understandable exaggeration fittingly closed the four-Gospel collection:

> And there are also many other things which Jesus did, the which, if they should be written everyone, I suppose that even the world itself could not contain the books that should be written. Amen.
>
> JOHN 21:25

Which Gospel would we choose if we could keep only one? That difficult choice would surely depend upon circumstances. If one lived with people who questioned the historical reality of Jesus one might well keep Mark. A teacher or missionary would need Matthew. A literary man would choose Luke. But if we were condemned to live alone on a desert island, would we not take John?

## *33*

## Paul's Legacy to Christianity

### Ten Epistles of Paul

THE four Gospels stand first in our New Testament, not because they were written first, but because they concern the first and central fact of Christianity, namely Jesus Christ. It is appropriate that the fourfold story of His life precedes everything else, though in point of time the Gospels are not the oldest Christian literature. When Mark began to write his Gospel in Rome about A.D. 65, there were already ten New Testament documents in existence, which neither Mark nor anyone else at that time considered Scripture. They form nearly one quarter of the New Testament and, as they were all written between A.D. 50 and 65, they are therefore our oldest Christian documents.

They are letters written by the greatest Christian of the first century, Paul of Tarsus. Though born in a Greek city, Paul was a Jew with Roman citizenship, but race, language, and citizenship do not completely explain Paul. To understand him we must travel with him down the road toward Damascus about three years after the Crucifixion. Paul, or Saul as he was then called, is a fiery young Jew zealous to stamp out what seems to him to be an alarming heresy claiming that Jesus who was crucified is the Messiah. It is midday. A brilliant "light out of heaven" appears and a voice speaks. The whole company of horsemen with whom Saul is journeying dismount and throw themselves on the ground, but only Saul sees Christ in glory and understands His Voice.

> Saul, Saul, why persecutest thou me? . . .
> Who art thou, Lord? . . .
> I am Jesus whom thou persecutest . . .
> Lord, what wilt thou have me to do? . . .
> Arise, and go into the city, and it shall be told thee what thou must do.
>
> ACTS 9:4-6

This vision on the road was the central event of Paul's life. From this moment until his martyrdom in Rome nearly thirty years later, Paul was possessed by Christ. As zealously as he had persecuted, he now spread the new Faith. His special field was the Gentile world and many of the Greek-speaking cities of the Roman Empire heard his voice and rapturously embraced faith in Christ.

In the year A.D. 50 Paul arrived in Corinth. Built on an isthmus, Corinth was a city facing two ways. From her western harbor of Lecheum on the Gulf of Corinth ships sailed to Italy, Gaul, and Spain. To her eastern harbor of Cenchreae on the Gulf of Aegina came Egyptian, Asiatic, and Phoenician galleys. The creaking wagons of Corinth shuttled back and forth between the two ports carrying the merchandise and provisions of the ancient world, for as yet no canal cut the Isthmus of Corinth. In this Greek city facing two ways Paul's life also began to face two ways, for here a second door of opportunity opened to him. Up to now he had preached and founded churches everywhere. His second door of opportunity faced the future, for here about A.D. 50 he was to write the first of that great series of Epistles which projected his message far beyond his own century and which form his chief legacy to Christianity.

At this time Paul was living in the house of Aquila and his wife Priscilla. During the day they employed him as a weaver in their tentmaking shop, but in the evening they and their friends sat around him listening spellbound as he retold his experience of Christ. Silas, Paul's able helper, had recently joined him and now both missionaries eagerly awaited the arrival of their companion Timothy who had remained behind in Thessalonica to strengthen the new church there.

One day a man stood in the doorway of Aquila's shop and looking up Paul saw that Timothy had come. The smile on his face told Paul that the news from Thessalonica was not as bad as he feared it might be. In spite of the riots which Paul's presence in that city had caused, and in spite of Paul's forced and hurried withdrawal, the little church was carrying on. Nevertheless there were difficulties and as Timothy recounted these Paul's brow wrinkled. The Thessalonians clearly needed help, but Paul could not go to them. What was to be done?

Paul may have thought of the plan himself, or it may have been suggested to him by any one of the little Christian group in Corinth: Aquila, Priscilla, Titus Justus, Crispus, Silas, Timothy, or some unnamed follower. Or perhaps Paul did now what he always did under such circumstances: he wrote a letter to the Thessalonians. It would not be surprising if Paul had written many letters before this one, for letter writing was very common at this time, but if earlier letters once existed they have now perished and his First Epistle to the Thessalonians is our oldest surviving Christian letter, as well as the oldest New Testament document.

He must have dictated it in the evening after he put aside his weaver's shuttle and the clatter of the looms was stilled. Outside in the two harbors of Corinth sails were furled and ships rode silently at anchor. The last rays of the sun faded from the heights of Acro-Corinth, the gigantic peak rising above the city. People passing in the dark streets must have seen a candle shining from Aquila and Priscilla's shop and exclaimed, "What are those Christians doing?" Inside, the entire little Christian company watched as a professional letter writer spread his papyrus on a table under the candlelight. He arranged his bottle of ink and his reed pens. The first New Testament document was about to be written. All was in readiness for Paul's opening words. They were a salutation in the usual Greek form which with admirable directness first announced the sender's name:

> Paul, and Silvanus, and Timotheus, unto the church of the Thessalonians which is in God the Father and in the Lord Jesus Christ: Grace be unto you, and peace, from God our Father, and the Lord Jesus Christ.
>
> I THESSALONIANS 1:1

Paul had given much thought to this letter and had possibly already made notes to guide him in dictating, for this Epistle would carry his message on several disputed points. The letter-writer was skilled and wrote swiftly the words that came tumbling from Paul's lips. Here and there Silas and Timothy interrupted with a suggestion. When the letter was done the scribe handed it to Paul for approval. In the space left at the bottom of the sheet Paul wrote in his own hand the last four verses of personal message and blessing. These verses took the place of a signature and were a guarantee of the letter's genuineness.

Folded, tied with a cord, and sealed with wax, the letter was now ready to be sent. The next morning Timothy entrusted Paul's letter to the captain of a vessel about to set sail, and the first New Testament Epistle was soon on its way over the Aegean Sea to its destination in Thessalonica, the Macedonian city named for the sister of Alexander the Great and today the Greek port of Salonika.

The entire Thessalonian church assembled to watch their leader break the seal and unfold Paul's letter. They must have listened with deep attention as the letter was read aloud, for every word in it applied to them. Unlike us, they did not puzzle over what Paul really meant by this and that. His meaning was perfectly clear to them, for the letter answered their uncertainties and commented on their difficulties. At the end they read a set of practical exhortations that went far beyond their own immediate problems and gave them standards to guide them in their church life. Here was a document to be kept and read again and again to the assembled church. Accordingly, they placed it in their church chest with the sacred vessels and their volume of the Septuagint. It was reread and copied perhaps, but for forty years it remained merely a letter written on a few sheets of papyrus in the handwriting of a professional letter-writer of Corinth.

Paul wrote many other letters. Shortly after the Thessalonians replied to his first letter, he wrote them a second one. Did he write them more than these two? This seems quite possible, though if he did the later Epistles have been lost. But the New Testament contains a superb collection of letters to other churches. From Corinth Paul made his way back to Jerusalem, stopping at Antioch. There, no doubt, he heard distressing news that caused him to write his Epistle to the Galatians. Before his journey into Macedonia and Greece, Paul and Barnabas had founded churches in Pisidian Antioch, Iconium, Lystra, and Derbe and had "opened the door of faith unto the Gentiles." During Paul's absence these churches in the Roman province of Galatia had been visited by teachers who saw Christianity as a sect of Judaism. They taught that Christianity must be entered through the gateway of Jewish Law and ritual. They thought that a Gentile must first be circumcised before he could become a Christian. Paul saw this for what it was, a dangerous challenge to his own teaching. Faith or the Law: this was the issue at stake. For Paul there could be no question about it. Since his tremendous experience on the Damascus road, his whole being was possessed by his faith in Christ which had made him free of the Law. This Faith he had preached to the Galatians. Now he wrote them one of his greatest Epistles, which explains his doctrine of the freedom of religion. He vindicated his own right to be called an Apostle and showed the difference between Faith and the Law. He clearly set forth the responsibilities of this Faith and described the fruits of the Spirit. Surely none of the narrow Judaizers could have matched the spiritual vitality and depth of Paul's teaching in this Epistle to the Galatians.

Paul spent three fruitful years in Ephesus with his friends Priscilla and Aquila, who were now settled here, and he founded a church which became one of the chief centers of Christianity in Asia. While in Ephesus news was brought to him by "Chloe's people" that all was not well in Corinth and that differences of opinion divided the church there. People had even begun to doubt Paul's authority and to prefer other leaders. Questions had arisen about such matters as lawsuits, the relationship of men and women, eating meat sacrificed to idols, women's behavior and dress in church, ecstatic speaking, and the Resurrection. As was his custom, Paul dealt with all these problems in his First Epistle to the Corinthians. If he had done only this, his reply to the Corinthians would have little value for us, but it is far more than this. He related these local problems to fundamental Christian principles and wrote one of the most valuable documents the Church possesses. It contains our oldest account of the Last Supper (I Corinthians 11:23-26), and of the Resurrection (I Corinthians 15:3-9), both written at least ten years earlier than Mark's account. Its best-known chapters are the thirteenth, with its superb poem on love, and the fifteenth, which ends with the majestic verses on immortality. It was passages like these which led Erasmus to exclaim: "Paul thunders and lightens and speaks sheer flame." This magnificent Epistle closes with brief personal messages and Paul's own autograph greeting:

> The salutation of me Paul with mine own hand.
>
> I CORINTHIANS 16:21

We know that Paul wrote at least four letters to the Corinthian church. Scholars believe that in the Second Epistle to the Corinthians are imbedded fragments of two short letters. The first fragment is II Corinthians 6:14 to 7:1 and is a warning against associating with immoral people. It contains the great sentence: "Ye are the temple of the living God." The second fragment, chapters 10 to 13, is Paul's self-defense against his enemies in Corinth. It is really a brief autobiography and contains an almost incredible catalogue of Paul's dangers and sufferings, which, as we know from Acts, were far from over at this time.

The main part of II Corinthians, chapters 1 to 9, was prob-

ably the fourth letter written to that church and it was most
likely written from Macedonia when Paul was planning to return to Corinth. The controversy that called forth the famous
self-defense in the third letter is now happily ended and Paul
is filled with thanksgiving. In this mood he opens his heart to
the Corinthians and gives them, in chapters 2:12 to 6:10, an
account of how and why he is preaching the Christian faith.
He was an ambassador of Christ who had come to him in the
blinding experience on the Damascus road. Paul had become
a new person and he preached that all men might enter into
this transforming experience.

> Therefore if any man be in Christ, he is a new creature: old things
> are passed away; behold, all things are become new. And all things are
> of God, who hath reconciled us to himself by Jesus Christ, and hath
> given to us the ministry of reconciliation.
>                                             II CORINTHIANS 5:17, 18

Reaching Corinth shortly after his fourth letter was delivered,
Paul looked out from her western harbor toward the Adriatic
Sea and Italy. He planned now to carry his message to Rome
and Gaul and distant Spain. Before he could do this, however,
he felt impelled to take the gifts of money contributed by his
Gentile churches for the poor of the Mother Church and bring
them to Jerusalem. After that he would go to Rome. In order
to prepare for his arrival in the imperial city and to acquaint
the Christians there with his doctrines, Paul at this time wrote
to the Roman church his greatest Epistle. It was written in
Corinth, about A.D. 55, and contains the heart of Paul's message compressed into a letter.

Righteousness is the theme of Romans. In the first two chapters Paul shows how both Gentiles and Jews "have sinned, and
come short of the glory of God." The third chapter states that
the only remedy for sin is faith in Christ. Paul explains in
chapter 4 how Abraham was justified by faith. In the next four
chapters Paul describes the Christian life ending in the well-
known eighth chapter with the triumphant assertion:

> Nay, in all these things we are more than conquerors through him
> that loved us. For I am persuaded, that neither death, nor life, nor

angels, nor principalities, nor powers, nor things present, nor things to come, nor height, nor depth, nor any other creature, shall be able to separate us from the love of God, which is in Christ Jesus our Lord.

ROMANS 8:37-39

Chapters 9, 10, and 11 contain his explanation of God's dealings with Israel, for Paul never forgot that he was a Jew. Next, he sketches a practical and helpful picture of how Christian people should behave. This section, 12:1 to 15:13, is like a Sermon on the Mount written for the Greek-speaking church. Paul ends with personal news and his hope:

That I may be delivered from them that do not believe in Judaea; and that my service which I have for Jerusalem may be accepted of the saints; that I may come unto you with joy by the will of God.

ROMANS 15:31, 32

From Acts we know what actually happened: the riot and arrest in Jerusalem, the long imprisonment in Caesarea, the shipwreck, and finally Paul's arrival in Rome in chains.

The oldest known copy of Romans is a papyrus manuscript written about A.D. 200. The final pages of this book are now at the University of Michigan. This ancient copy differs from the Romans we read in one significant aspect: it gives the great doxology, Romans 16:25 to 27, at the end of chapter 15 rather than at the end of the whole Epistle. Some scholars believe that Romans originally ended with chapter 15 and the doxology, and that chapter 16 is a separate letter that was somehow tacked on to Romans. This separate letter is a brief note of introduction for a certain Phoebe of Cenchreae who was about to embark for Ephesus, the city Paul had recently left. In this note he greets Aquila and Priscilla, who were undoubtedly at Ephesus rather than in Rome at this time, and "the church that is in their house," and also twenty-four other people. Paul could hardly have known so many people in Rome. This letter introducing Phoebe was written from Corinth at the same time as Romans, possibly by the same scribe. As Paul kept copies of his letters, the scribe had to write out both letters again. It is quite likely that he found space for them both on one papyrus roll, thus joining Phoebe's letter to the great Epistle of Romans of which it has been a part ever since.

Paul's last three letters, Philippians, Colossians, and Philemon were all written from prison. According to one theory Paul may have sent these Epistles from Ephesus during a period of imprisonment there. If this is true, they add three new titles to the list of Christian documents produced in Ephesus. Perhaps we shall never know whether to place these three letters in Ephesus or in Rome, from which tradition says they were written. The letter to the Philippians is a letter of thanks for aid they had sent Paul by their messenger, Epaphroditus. In his customary manner Paul transforms a letter on an ordinary subject into a supremely important Christian document and in a memorable sentence explains the secret of his heroic life: "For to me to live is Christ."

Colossians and Philemon were written at the same time and entrusted to two men traveling together. Tychicus carried the Epistle to the Colossians which deals with a new heresy and touches on the idea of Christ as the Logos or Word of God, an idea John the Elder was later to develop.

With Tychicus traveled a young slave named Onesimus who had robbed his master and run away from him. Though runaway slaves were usually crucified, Onesimus was now courageously returning to his master Philemon with a letter for him from Paul. Traveling in the company of Tychicus, Onesimus must have felt some misgivings as he wondered how Philemon would receive him. Philemon was a Christian, probably of Laodicea, and the Church there seems to have met in his house. As the runaway slave had now become a Christian also, Paul believed this created a new relationship between master and slave and made it safe for Onesimus to return to Philemon bearing Paul's letter. Did Christianity effect any change in the conditions of slavery, that hideous blot on antiquity? Did Philemon receive Onesimus back with Christian kindness? We do not know the actual outcome of this story, but the fact that this letter survived at all is sufficient proof that Onesimus was forgiven and that Christianity little by little improved the relations between masters and slaves.

Such are the nine Epistles of Paul which convey so much of "the unsearchable riches of Christ." Did he write any others? Though I and II Timothy and Titus were written long after Paul died, they undoubtedly contain parts of his genuine letters. To the problem of the authorship of Ephesians we shall turn in a moment. But the nine Epistles we have considered form the bulk of Paul's writing. We wish we might read the complete file of his correspondence, together with all the letters to which his Epistles were the answers. There is much in Paul's letters that is timeless and his deepest religious insights shine like jewels with little need of their ancient settings. But there are some things in his letters that are not clear to us. Even the writer of II Peter shared our difficulty:

> Our beloved brother Paul also according to the wisdom given unto him hath written unto you; as also in all his epistles, speaking in them of these things; in which are some things hard to be understood.

> II PETER 3:15, 16

We sorely need to clip together and file with Paul's letters the correspondence and the reports from which they arose. Many historians and scholars have tried to meet this need. In commentaries, encyclopedias, Bible dictionaries, and volumes of New Testament introduction, these students have stored the results of their study of the background of Paul's Epistles and they have lighted up many an obscure corner in this great series of Christian writings.

The Epistles with their wealth of spiritual insight remained merely letters for many years. Sometimes they were taken from the wooden chests in which they were kept and reread and studied by the local church to which each one had been addressed. In time the inevitable fate of letters would have overtaken them; the papyrus would become torn, the ink would fade, and church leaders with new ideas would find Paul a little old-fashioned. In a hundred years or so all the letters might easily have disappeared. Paul's mighty legacy could only be preserved for the future by the collection and publication of his Epistles. Fortunately, this was done. Who first published Paul's Epistles and when and why is one of the most interesting of New Testament problems. Professor Edgar J. Goodspeed in his *An Introduction to the New Testament* offers the following theory.

When Luke-Acts was published, probably in Ephesus about A.D. 90, men saw the tremendous part Paul had had in the spread of Christianity. This kindled enthusiasm for Paul and created the desire to know more about him. Someone, probably in Ephesus, knew of at least two letters Paul had written to the neighboring churches of Colossae and Laodicea (Philemon). A man named Onesimus was active in the Ephesian church at this time. Could this Onesimus be the same man who was once Philemon's runaway slave? If this is so, Onesimus would have had good reason to know about Paul's two most obscure letters. He and Tychicus together had brought Colossians and Philemon from Rome to their destinations. Philemon is really a personal letter and perhaps no one but Onesimus would have considered it important enough to be published in a collected edition of Paul's Epistles. With Colossians and Philemon in his hands, Onesimus, or whoever first assembled Paul's letters, traveled to the great cities mentioned in Acts, hoping to find letters of Paul in these places. In this he was not disappointed. Counting Philemon as a letter to the church of Laodicea, we discover that Onesimus assembled letters to seven churches. Then, with his mind saturated with Paul's ideas and words, he wrote an introductory letter as a preface for the published collection. This introductory letter we now call the Epistle to the Ephesians. This name, however, is probably incorrect, for the words of the salutation "which are at Ephesus" do not appear in our oldest manuscripts of this Epistle. Originally it was addressed simply "to the saints" everywhere and was thus a circular letter to all churches. Its enthusiastic statements of the value of Christianity abound in Paul's ideas and phraseology to such an extent that many scholars think it must come from Paul himself. Whether Paul, Onesimus, or someone else wrote it, it forms an appropriate preface to Paul's work and may well have stood first in the original volume of his collected Epistles.

It has been said that these letters take the roofs off the early Christian churches and let us look inside. We see that serious and often bitter problems endangered the first-century Church, for Paul often fought heresy, schism, and lapses into paganism. The evils accompanying a pagan civilization were not conquered in one round. If we are prone to put halos on the early Christians, these letters remove them. Paul's lists of the sins and failures of his converts are quite appalling. But turning from the dark side to the bright one, we find in his letters a wonderful picture gallery of early Christians. As we read his letters we gain a sense that Paul is describing something the world had never seen before. Here is a new society emerging, a spiritual fellowship ruled by love. Christ is the fountainhead of this new brotherhood which is indeed the "household of God." Paul's courtesy, his concern for each one of the brethren, his joy in their faith, his gratitude for their care of him—all this is the expression of the new fellowship in Christ. For all his mysticism Paul was a practical man, and one may assemble from his Epistles a valuable collection of rules to govern the lives and relationships of Christian people. Here is a source of much that is attractive in Christian civilization and characteristic of Christianity at its best.

In these letters Paul himself steps down from our stained glass windows and we see him more human than any imaginary painting can make him and at the same time, greater in stature than the most august idealization. His letters are full of autobiography. Even without Acts we might re-create his life and personality from these letters. We are amazed that Paul so often found it necessary to defend his right to be an Apostle and that his many opponents forced him again and again to present, as it were, his credentials. These were nothing less than his experience of Christ. Over and over again he tried to explain this experience which in its depth and breadth and intensity was incapable of being put into adequate words. But Paul's swift mind, his ready tongue, and his intense longing to communicate his Faith brought great areas of his experience within the comprehension of the men and women of his time and of all times. He spoke indeed with the tongues of men and of angels. His true epitaph is written in the words:

> I have fought a good fight, I have finished my course, I have kept the faith.
>
> II TIMOTHY 4:7

## 34

### Training Church Leaders

#### I AND II TIMOTHY, TITUS

THE three Epistles of I and II Timothy and Titus were probably written near the beginning of the second century by an unknown Christian leader of Ephesus. On the surface these letters seem to come from Paul, for the salutations are in his name. Most scholars agree that II Timothy and Titus include genuine fragments of Paul's letters. Titus apparently ends with four verses written by Paul, while II Timothy contains several of his short letters. One of them says:

> Only Luke is with me. Take Mark, and bring him with thee: for he
> is profitable to me for the ministry.
>                                                        II TIMOTHY 4:11

It also requests that the cloak which Paul left at Troas, together with "the books" and "especially the parchments" be brought to him. Scholars now believe that such fragments as these are Paul's, but that the letters as a whole are the work of an unknown writer. His style and vocabulary are different from Paul's. His ideas lack Paul's profoundly spiritual ring. The situation which called forth these Pastoral Epistles arose long after Paul's death.

If this unknown Christian writer lived in Ephesus, as is possible, we can imagine him climbing to the top of Mount Prion and looking toward the crowded harbor and the splendid city beneath him. The Temple of Diana was still the most impressive building of Ephesus, but here and there in back streets were plainly visible the roofs of houses where the Christian churches met. Since Paul's three years here with Aquila and Priscilla, Christianity had grown and flourished. From Acts and from Paul's Epistles we can draw up a long list of the men and women who labored to establish faith in Christ in this proud and wealthy capital. Luke had probably stopped here; Timothy may once have had charge of the entire Ephesian church. The Elder John had been one of its greatest and most beloved leaders. Now all these men were dead and our unknown Christian looked sadly down upon his city. The Temple of Diana seemed so large and the roofs of the Christian meeting places so tiny. There came to his ears the distant echo of marching feet as a Roman cohort paraded in the streets below. Paganism and imperial might were formidable enemies. There had already been serious persecutions and it was not unlikely that "all that will live godly in Christ Jesus shall suffer persecution." But it was not so much these external dangers that troubled the leader of Ephesus as the situation within the Church itself.

The Church had only recently begun to feel the need of a definite organization. It was torn with disputes. Heresies and "profane and vain babblings" filled the air. Men argued shrilly about new myths and fables which were fast turning the Faith into something Jesus, the Apostles, and Paul would not have recognized. In the rank and file of the Church were people who had not yet learned the great Christian virtues. They were "covetous, boasters, proud, blasphemers, disobedient to parents, unthankful, unholy . . . lovers of pleasures more than lovers of God." Many Church leaders were little better themselves. How could a Church like this withstand both paganism and persecution and grow in the religious traditions of the Apostles?

The unknown leader of Ephesus saw one answer, at least, to this urgent problem. The Church needed men like the Apostles and Paul and John and Timothy and Titus, for much of her weakness was directly due to the low moral quality of her leadership. Wherever the Church was strong there was usually to be found a leader who was:

> . . . blameless, as the steward of God; not self-willed, not soon angry, not given to wine, no striker, not given to filthy lucre; but a lover of hospitality, a lover of good men, sober, just, holy, temperate; holding fast the faithful word as he hath been taught, that he may be able by sound doctrine both to exhort and to convince the gainsayers.
>
> Titus 1:7-9

The unknown leader saw that in the present situation he must devote himself to the training of new leaders. He would draw up a list of the qualifications necessary for those who aspired to power in the Church. He could offer advice on how to conduct public worship, preach, teach, and admonish. He could warn against heresies, strife, and wrangling. He would lay down rules to govern the Church. Whether or not he gathered about him a group of young men for training we do not know, but we do know that he wrote three pamphlets to guide such a group of potential leaders. These are the three so-called Pastoral Epistles or I and II Timothy and Titus.

When we remember how popular the volume of Paul's collected Epistles was at this time, we are not surprised that this leader chose to deliver his message in the form of a series of letters. He may also have been prompted to use the letter form because he had in his possession several unpublished fragments of Paul's own letters. He decided to edit and expand these and issue a group of three letters in Paul's name. The main part of the documents would be from his pen, not Paul's, but the author felt that what he wrote might well have been written by Paul for it would express Paul's teachings. The author of Deuteronomy had done a similar thing when he put long speeches in Moses' mouth. This was not considered deception: it was a common literary device. In this case it awakened keen interest in the three new Epistles. Anything even remotely connected with Paul was eagerly read, and men still remembered Timothy and Titus, to whom the letters were supposed to be addressed, as ideal types of Church leaders.

The letters were particularly valuable to those on whom religious responsibility fell, but they also helped the entire Church to choose its leaders and set up its orderly government. Here were practical directions about how men should behave themselves "in the household of God." The mighty wind of faith that blows so freely through Paul's letters is almost absent from these and we have instead sound advice and careful instructions. These letters do not kindle, they protect and conserve. "Hold fast the form of sound words" and "Speak thou the things which become sound doctrine" advises this writer. He is very specific in his counsels.

> The servant of the Lord must not strive; but be gentle unto all men, apt to teach, patient, in meekness instructing those that oppose themselves.
>
> II TIMOTHY 2:24, 25

Such a man should be an example to others "in word, in conversation, in charity, in spirit, in faith, in purity."

In its earliest days Christianity had attracted "not many wise . . . not many mighty, not many noble." But now men of power and wealth were beginning to come into the Church. To these the unknown author wrote:

> Nor trust in uncertain riches, but in the living God, who giveth us richly all things to enjoy.
>
> I TIMOTHY 6:17

As he looked toward the troubled future and tried to equip leaders to guide the Church through the years to come he issued a trumpet call that might well have come from Paul himself:

> Fight the good fight of faith, lay hold on eternal life.
>
> I TIMOTHY 6:12

Reading Paul's Epistles and then these three Pastoral Epistles is a little like going from the Old Testament prophets to such books of wisdom as Proverbs. The Pastoral Epistles seem to reduce the faith of the Apostles and of Paul to a set of practical instructions, nevertheless it is a true Christianity that they teach. If we miss in them Paul's deeply-burning, inward faith, we gain from them a useful picture of the Christian life. From the beginning these three little documents must have been used as textbooks in church training schools, and in time they joined the Gospels and Epistles of Paul as sacred Scripture. But when their author wrote these lines he little dreamed that his own three books would one day themselves be "holy scripture" and as Scripture be included in his description:

> From a child thou hast known the holy scriptures, which are able to make thee wise unto salvation through faith which is in Christ Jesus. All scripture is given by inspiration of God, and is profitable for doctrine, for reproof, for correction, for instruction in righteousness: That the man of God may be perfect, thoroughly furnished unto all good works.
>
> II Timothy 3:15-17

## 35

### *Defending the Faith*

HEBREWS, I PETER, JAMES, JUDE, II PETER

IT was once thought that these five Epistles were written by Apostles: Hebrews, by Paul; I and II Peter, by the Galilean fisherman named Peter whom Jesus called the "Rock"; James, by the Lord's brother who became one of the leaders of the Jerusalem church; and Jude, by another brother of the Lord and of James. If these theories of authorship were correct the five Epistles would reflect the years before A.D. 65, for tradition tells us that James was murdered by the mob in Jerusalem in A.D. 62, and Peter and Paul died in Rome during Nero's persecutions in A.D. 64 and 65. We find, however, that the background of these Epistles is not the earliest years of Christianity but a period when the Apostles were dead and a new generation of Christians faced apathy from within, persecution from without, heresy, and schism. It is against the background of the years from A.D. 80 to 150 that these Epistles were probably written. They show Christianity defending the endangered areas of faith. After we discard the traditional theories of their authorship we find that these documents have lost little of their value, for their authority comes, not from the identity of their authors, but from the quality of the writings themselves.

Whoever their authors were, Hebrews and I Peter are among

the finest things in the New Testament. In searching for the
real author of Hebrews, scholars have suggested such people as
Apollos, Luke, Barnabas, Philip the Evangelist, and Priscilla
the wife of Aquila. Though we may never be able to name the
unknown writer of Hebrews, we know his style to be the most
polished and literary in the New Testament. His language is
brilliant and forceful and he follows a carefully thought-out
plan. In the eleventh chapter, with its catalogue of the heroes
of the Faith, he rises to a magnificently eloquent climax. But
the author of Hebrews was more than an accomplished writer:
he was a spiritual statesman as well. He saw Christians becoming lukewarm toward their glorious heritage. He also knew
that they wondered about the true relation of Christianity to
Judaism. Indifferent and puzzled Christians were no match for
Roman persecution, which was becoming a serious threat under
Domitian. Christians could be put to death for refusing to burn
the little piece of incense to the emperor. Foreseeing renewed
persecution, the unknown author wrote Hebrews to help the
Church meet this danger. It was a book designed to rekindle
Christian faith wherever it burned low.

Perhaps Hebrews was originally not a letter at all but a
sermon. Though it ends like a letter, it reads like a speech.
There is no salutation in the beginning, but it opens with a
bold announcement of its theme:

> God, who at sundry times and in divers manners spake in time past
> unto the fathers by the prophets, hath in these last days spoken unto
> us by his Son, whom he hath appointed heir of all things, by whom
> also he made the Worlds.
>
> HEBREWS 1:1, 2

We are at once reminded of the opening of John's Gospel and
of Paul's doctrine in Colossians. The author of Hebrews goes
on to explain Christ's nature and mission. He compares Judaism and Christianity and brings out the supreme value of the
latter. His picture of Jesus as the high priest whose sacrifice and
faith showed us the reality of the invisible world was a picture
especially attractive to those familiar with Judaism and the

Scriptures. They must have listened with pleasure to the many quotations from Deuteronomy, Psalms, Proverbs, Jeremiah, and Habakkuk. The unfolding argument paused now and again for practical exhortations, but even with this relief the sermon was an exacting one to follow and it demanded a high degree of intelligence from its audience. If any grew weary during the ninth and tenth chapters, their attention was captured by the eloquent chapter beginning:

> Now faith is the substance of things hoped for, the evidence of things not seen.
>
> HEBREWS 11:1

As the congregation heard the preacher set forth the glittering array of heroes of the Faith, there was rekindled in their hearts an answering faith strong enough to withstand persecution.

> Wherefore seeing we also are compassed about with so great a cloud of witnesses, let us lay aside every weight, and the sin which doth so easily beset us, and let us run with patience the race that is set before us, looking unto Jesus the author and finisher of our faith.
>
> HEBREWS 12:1, 2

Like Hebrews, I Peter is written against the background of the "fiery trial," which was probably the persecution under Domitian. If this is so, the Epistle must be dated about A.D. 95, too late to come from the pen of Simon Peter. Its unknown writer belongs, nevertheless, to the true company of believers. His book is one of the most beautiful in the New Testament and its message of patience, forgiveness, and hope breathes the spirit of pure Christianity. The Epistle opens with a salutation and closes with the customary personal messages, but these were probably written by a later editor. There is a theory that the editor had in his possession two valuable documents, a sermon and a letter, both by an outstanding Church leader.[1] In order to make these available to a wider audience he published them together in the form of an Epistle. This was easily done and the true author's name having been lost, the Epistle was circulated under the name of Peter.

The sermon apparently opens with: "Blessed be God the

---

[1] B. H. Streeter, *The Primitive Church* (Macmillan, 1929) , p. 121 ff.

Father of our Lord Jesus Christ," and closes with a doxology and amen in I Peter 4:11. It is the sort of address a church leader might have made to a group of newly baptized adults. He gave them a picture of the new life they had just entered and exhorted them to live worthy of it, not only in all the relationships of their lives, but even through suffering and persecution. His directions for living the Christian life are inspiring at any time, but they become even more moving to us when we picture those for whom they were first written. These were newly converted Christians, brought up in paganism and now facing the hostility of a world that worshiped a divine emperor.

The pastoral letter opens abruptly in I Peter 4:12 with: "Beloved, think it not strange concerning the fiery trial which is to try you," and ends with a doxology and amen in 5:11. It seems to be addressed to several churches and to their leaders or elders.

James, like Hebrews and most of I Peter, is a sermon later published in letter form and circulated among Christians everywhere. Its author is unknown, but he probably delivered this sermon about A.D. 100 to a congregation who needed definite instructions in moral living. He exhorts men to be "doers of the word, and not hearers only." Though this Epistle adds little to our understanding of Christianity, it is full of practical advice and occupies an honored place in the library of Christian ethical literature.

Jude was probably written by the Bishop of Jerusalem in the reign of Trajan, about A.D. 125. It is a vigorous denunciation of the heresy of a group of Christians who considered themselves so spiritual that they did not need to obey the ordinary rules of decent behavior. They thought that anything they chose to do would be right and that the usual moral laws did not apply to them. As a result of this they indulged in all kinds of sensuality until they became a scandal in the Church. Jude lashed out against these "ungodly men" calling them clouds without rain, trees without fruit, raging waves, and darkened stars. He wrote to exhort men "that ye should earnestly contend for the faith which was once delivered unto the saints." This phrase carries overtones of a Christianity that was now old and well established, but that still needed to be defended. Jude ended his Epistle with a doxology that is as beautiful as any in the New Testament.

II Peter cannot be by the same author as I Peter, nor is it by the Apostle Peter. Its date is probably A.D. 150 and this makes it the last New Testament document. II Peter exhorts men to stand fast in the faith, to avoid false teachers, and to continue in the hope of Christ's return. For us its chief value is the light it throws on second century Christian history. Its author read many of the Christian books popular in his day. Among these was the Epistle of Jude which the author of II Peter liked so much that he incorporated a large part of it in his own document. He knew the tradition that Peter is the authority behind Mark's Gospel. He had read I Peter, for he states that his is the "second epistle." He also gives evidence of knowing the four Gospels and the collected Epistles of Paul, some of which puzzled him. When he mentions Paul's Epistles in the same breath with "the other scriptures," he gives us a clue to the emergence of the New Testament. By A.D. 150 a new idea was appearing that there should be a New Testament to stand on an equal footing with the ancient Scriptures we now call the Old Testament. Before long, as we shall see, twenty-seven Christian documents written between A.D. 50 and 150 were to be collected, canonized, and published as the New Testament.

# ~ 36 ~

## Christianity Triumphant

### THE REVELATION OF JOHN

FIFTY miles offshore from Miletus in Asia Minor lies the rocky island of Patmos. Here, about A.D. 96, came a Roman galley with a boatload of prisoners. Roman guards herded them ashore and turned them over as slave labor to the quarry foreman on Patmos. These people were, for the most part, Christians from Asia Minor who had refused to worship the Emperor Domitian as a god and had therefore been condemned to exile on Patmos. It is thought that among the exiles was a man named John, not the Apostle John who had died years before, nor the Elder John of Ephesus who wrote in a different style. This John was a sensitive type of person, imaginative, poetic, a dreamer of dreams, one who often saw visions. He was well educated and, even though he had not been able to bring his books with him into exile, his mind was a storehouse of scripture, Jewish apocalypses, and Christian literature. The strongest fibre in John's being was his Christian conviction for which he had been willing to suffer persecution. Rather than compromise with Emperor worship, he had preferred banishment at hard labor in the quarries of Patmos. There, straining his eyes eastward toward the mountainous coast of Asia Minor, he wondered how his brothers in Christ fared. Were they strong enough to withstand tribulation? Now that the outlook seemed hopeless, were they deserting their Faith for the safety of the official religion of the Empire?

Then a strange thing happened to John and he tells about the beginning of it in these words:

> I was in the Spirit on the Lord's day, and heard behind me a great voice, as of a trumpet, saying, I am Alpha and Omega, the first and the last: and, What thou seest, write in a book, and send it unto the seven churches which are in Asia.
>
> REVELATION 1:10, 11

The visions John saw were not of this world. Some were beautiful and some were horrible. He saw the throne of God, angels with trumpets, the Son of Man with eyes as a flame of fire, grotesque beasts, a woman clothed with the sun, and four extraordinary horsemen. There were earthquakes, thunder, loud trumpeting, and song. The actions that took place in John's visions were like the events in a dream. All these sights and sounds held profound meaning, for they proved to him the reality of his Faith and justified his belief that Christianity would soon triumph. When the harshness of his exile was over and he could obtain writing materials, John wrote the substance of his visions in a book which we now call the Revelation of John.

Its purpose was to inspire hope, courage, and endurance among persecuted Christians. Hebrews and I Peter had been written with a similar purpose, but Revelation was an entirely different type of book from these. It is an apocalypse filled with strange visions of things to come. Throughout the New Testament we come upon brief apocalyptic passages which show the popularity of this form of literature in the first century. The Jews at this time also had their apocalypses, some of which may have influenced the author of Revelation. This is the only New Testament apocalypse, as Daniel is the only Old Testament apocalypse.

The opening chapter of Revelation introduces the author:

> I John, who also am your brother, and companion in tribulation, and in the kingdom and patience of Jesus Christ.
>
> REVELATION 1:9

It announces that the theme of the book concerns "things which must shortly come to pass." Next John writes in Christ's behalf seven letters to the seven Churches of Asia Minor whose names make haunting music: Ephesus, Smyrna, Pergamos, Thyatira, Sardis, Philadelphia, Laodicea. No doubt Paul's collected Epistles gave John his idea for using the letter form. In the letter to Laodicea, the probable church of Philemon and Onesimus, John wrote his beautiful description of Christ knocking on the door:

> Behold, I stand at the door, and knock: if any man hear my voice, and open the door, I will come in to him, and will sup with him, and he with me.
>
> REVELATION 3:20

After the letters comes the main action of John's vision which unfolds in three stupendous acts. The first act, in chapters 4 through 11, is laid in heaven where a book of fate sealed with seven seals is finally opened. Though we cannot understand exactly what is happening or what it means, we are shown the throne of God, twenty-four elders clothed in white, seven lamps, four beasts, angels, the Lamb who, as so often in a dream, turns into something else and becomes the Conqueror on a white horse. He also saw that:

> . . . a great multitude which no man could number, of all nations, and kindreds, and people, and tongues, stood before the throne, and before the Lamb, clothed with white robes, and palms in their hands.
>
> REVELATION 7:9

We learn who these people are and the blessedness to which they have attained.

> These are they which came out of great tribulation . . . They shall hunger no more, neither thirst any more; neither shall the sun light on them, nor any heat. For the Lamb which is in the midst of the throne shall feed them, and shall lead them unto living fountains of waters.
>
> REVELATION 7:14, 16, 17

In the second vision there is war in heaven between a great red dragon and Michael and his angels. The eighteenth chapter announces that "Babylon the great is fallen" and as we read this passage we realize that it is John's dream of the fall of hated Rome.

In the last four chapters triumph and rejoicings are heaped one upon another in the vision of the New Jerusalem. The heavens open and a white horse appears whose rider can be no other than Christ. He is not like the Christ of the Gospels but a Divine Being whose name is "The Word of God." With his sharp sword He smites the nations and rules them with a rod of iron. John saw "a new heaven and a new earth" and "the holy city, new Jerusalem, coming down from God out of heaven." He heard a great voice proclaiming the goal of human striving. Here is the culmination of all the prophets' longings and the Church's prayers.

> Behold, the tabernacle of God is with men, and he will dwell with them, and they shall be his people, and God himself shall be with them, and be their God. And God shall wipe away all tears from their eyes; and there shall be no more death, neither sorrow, nor crying, neither shall there be any more pain: for the former things are passed away.
>
> REVELATION 21:3, 4

This holy Jerusalem was a city with twelve foundations and twelve gates, and a high wall, all shining in a many-colored blaze of jeweled splendor.

> And the city had no need of the sun, neither of the moon, to shine in it: for the glory of God did lighten it, and the Lamb is the light thereof. And the nations of them which are saved shall walk in the light of it: and the kings of the earth do bring their glory and honour into it.
>
> REVELATION 21:23, 24

The Bible opened in a garden, but it ends in the Holy City, the new Jerusalem. There were two people in the garden, but here there are multitudes of God's people from all nations. Instead of the river that flowed out of Eden, John saw "a pure river of water of life, clear as crystal, proceeding out of the throne of God and of the Lamb." And the tree that grows here in paradise is one whose leaves are "for the healing of the nations."

This book of visions and symbols, of unearthly music, and unconquerable hope must have stirred the people for whom it was first written. Where we grope for its meanings, they understood clearly what John was trying to tell them. He was dealing with their tribulations and persecutions, their bitter conflict with Rome. The very stuff of his vision came from the books they read and the apocalypses which were so popular among them. John knew how dark the present was with suffering, fear, and hopelessness. Against this darkness he painted the Bible's most radiant picture of heaven. He proclaimed that the time for its coming was at hand and Christians must endure and stand fast.

If John had lived longer, he would have become a disillusioned old man, for history did not bear out his promises. Rome did not promptly fall; the Holy City, the new Jerusalem, did not come down out of heaven; and Christ and His saints did not begin their thousand-year reign. This troubled some church leaders so much that they refused to accept Revelation into the New Testament canon. "What did John really mean?" they asked, and their answers often took them into strange places. With its mystic numbers, its cloudy symbols, and its unfulfilled promises, Revelation is a perfect mine for those who delve in occult speculations. John probably meant to symbolize Nero when he wrote about the beast whose number is 666, but this has not deterred people from interpreting the beast at different times as Luther, the Pope, Napoleon, and even Hitler. It was doubtless speculations such as these which led one old commentator to remark that Revelation either finds a man mad or leaves him so! Revelation cannot be interpreted in terms of the future. It was written as a tract for its own time and its meaning must lie in the first century. It is there that we must search for clues to its symbols and ideas. Fascinating as it is to try to solve the riddles of John's meanings and to trace the sources of his dreams in first-century life and literature, the real value of Revelation for us does not lie in these, but in John's cry of triumph out of the dark night of persecution.

Revelation stands high among the creations of the human imagination. Though its interpretation is vague and its prophecies failed to come true, this book is an imperishable Christian heritage. Poets and artists under the spell of its extraordinary power have created some of the world's finest literature and art. It gave the Church its dream of heaven and its assurance of blessedness. Many a triumphant hymn is clothed in its phrases and images: "Ten thousand times ten thousand, in sparkling raiment bright." "I heard a sound of voices around the great white throne." "Hark! the sound of holy voices, chanting at the crystal sea."

Fortunately Revelation is not the only book Christians possess. If it were, there would probably be no Christianity, for it represents only one aspect of our heritage. Here are none of the historical records of the synoptic Gospels. We miss in it Paul's transforming faith and the spiritual insight of John, the Elder of Ephesus. But a glory shines from the pages of Revelation that can be found nowhere else in the New Testament. Here stands an unshakable conviction that God reigns and that Christ's message is the truth. Though Rome's power seemed unconquerable, nevertheless:

> The kingdoms of this world are become the kingdoms of our Lord, and of his Christ; and he shall reign for ever and ever.
>
> REVELATION 11:15

From an exile on the island of Patmos came this poem of triumph. The long Bible story which began in Eden here comes at last to its fitting end with heaven shining in jeweled splendor and all the trumpets sounding.

## ✤ 37 ✤

# Forming the New Testament

## THE CANON

THE Bible of Jesus and the Apostles was the Old Testament. Jesus often referred to the ancient Scriptures of His race; Peter used Old Testament quotations to prove his points; and Paul "reasoned with them out of the scriptures." During the Church's early years this was the authoritative Book read whenever Christians assembled. We are told that zealous converts "searched the scriptures daily." Very soon, as we have seen, the Church produced books, not to rival or supplant the Old Testament, but to meet Christianity's own definite needs. Little did Paul realize on the day in A.D. 50 in Corinth, when he began dictating his letter to Thessalonica, that he was composing the first book of a New Testament. Many of the Apostles still lived. Christian traditions and teachings were still in their oral period. The need for an official collection of writings to define and preserve Christianity had not yet become urgent.

The first hint of such a need comes from the preface to Luke's Gospel written about A.D. 75 or 90.

> Forasmuch as many have taken in hand to set forth in order a declaration of those things which are most surely believed among us . . . it seemed good to me also . . . to write unto thee in order . . . that thou mightest know the certainty of those things, wherein thou hast been instructed.
>
> LUKE 1:1-4

It was doubtless the publication of Luke-Acts and the resulting interest in Paul's career that led to the collection and publication of the ten Epistles of Paul about A.D. 90. This was followed by the collection and publication of the fourfold Gospel about A.D. 115. These two collections were well known by A.D. 150 when a nameless author wrote II Peter. He bent over his papyrus sheet and added his final sentence: "But grow in grace, and in the knowledge of our Lord and Saviour Jesus Christ. To him be glory both now and for ever. Amen." Then he put down his pen never imagining that with his words the writing of the New Testament was ended. In the hundred years between A.D. 50 and 150 Christianity produced its twenty-seven imperishable books. Though the New Testament as we know it did not appear in its entirety for another two hundred years, by A.D. 150 all the books had been written and some had even been brought together and published in two short collections. In a later chapter on the discovery of papyrus books we shall find confirmation of this theory.

The factors that led to the formation of the New Testament are elusive, and the history of the two hundred and fifty years during which the canon emerged is a complicated one. The twenty-seven books of our New Testament are only a fraction of the volumes written in the first creative period of Christianity, and it therefore required time to sift this great mass of literature and to decide which documents should be considered canonical. As it is impossible to trace all the details of the history of the canon in one chapter, we shall now turn to five brief stories which will serve as windows through which we may observe the New Testament coming into being as a collection of sacred Scripture.

The Church was forced to make one of its first decisions about the New Testament by a heretic named Marcion. He was a wealthy shipowner of Pontus who journeyed to Rome in A.D. 140 with a burning conviction that Christianity was being polluted by its Jewish background. He failed to see in Judaism the historical preparation and the nursery of Christianity. It did not occur to him that the Old Testament showed the growth and development of men's ideas about God. Christianity taught that God was a loving Father, but the Old Testament often records the words and acts of a jealous God demanding blind obedience instead of faith. To end this confusion Marcion advanced the simple plan of rejecting the Old Testament entirely. In its place he proposed that the Church adopt his "Bible" or "New" Testament. This was a slim volume edited by Marcion himself, containing only Luke's Gospel and Acts, ten of Paul's Epistles, and a treatise written by himself. These were the only Christian writings Marcion found relatively free of Hebrew ideas, but even from these he had deleted a number of passages tinged with what he considered Jewish heresy.

The Church decided it was Marcion's doctrines rather than the Old Testament books that were heretical, and it would have nothing to do with his New Testament. Undaunted by this rebuff Marcion withdrew from the Church and founded a rival sect of his own which used his first anemic little New Testament. Heretic though he was, Marcion made a valuable contribution to the Church upon which he turned his back He introduced the idea of a New Testament. He raised the issue of the Old Testament and forced the Church to decide that Christianity must not be torn from its ancient roots. And he forced Church leaders to act in the controversy about which books were truly inspired.

Marcion's sect still offered serious rivalry to the Church in Rome when Tatian was converted about A.D. 150. Tatian's conversion to Christianity was almost a denial of Marcion's stand. Curiously enough, Tatian says he became a Christian through reading the Old Testament and finding in it the prediction of events that later actually happened. Before long he was in the midst of preparing the story of Jesus to use in his missionary work in the Kingdom of Edessa. In this independent country northeast of Syrian Antioch people did not speak the Greek and Latin of the Roman Empire, but a language called Syriac akin to Hebrew and Aramaic. In the Syriac language Tatian prepared a Gospel in an odd way. With copies of the four Gospels of Matthew, Mark, Luke, and John before him he borrowed now a story from this Gospel, now a sentence from that, until he had completed one connected story of the life of Christ. Tatian's Syriac Gospel is nicknamed the "Scissors and Paste Gospel." He called it the *Diatessaron,* meaning the "Concordance of Four" or "Four Gospels in One." Here was a mosaic composed of small bits quarried from our four Gospels and carefully fitted together to make a portrait of Christ. Tatian did to the four New Testament documents what the editors of the Pentateuch had done to the original writings underlying Genesis, Exodus, Leviticus, Numbers, and Deuteronomy. Though the *Diatessaron* remained popular in Edessa for many years, elsewhere the individual Gospels were never plowed under and thus escaped the fate of such old records as the J and E histories which all but lost their identity in the composite document of the Pentateuch.

Tatian could have used other gospels such as the *Gospel of Peter,* the *Gospel According to the Hebrews,* or the *Gospel According to the Egyptians.* The Gnostic sect had by this time produced many strange and sometimes charming gospels. Some of these contained stories of a fantastic, Christmas-card quality, utterly different from the sober records undergirding the Christian faith; while others were filled with definitely unchristian teaching. The fact that Tatian in A.D. 170 rejected all other gospels and used only our four shows that by this time Matthew, Mark, Luke, and John had already been chosen to head the list of sacred writings. To be sure they had not yet put on their halos, for Tatian felt free to cut, edit, and publish them in a new form. In the end our four Gospels won over all other rivals, and in the second half of the second century they were chosen for the position they have occupied ever since. They became the four cornerstones of the Christian faith.

Our third story took place in a Roman courtroom in Carthage, North Africa. It was July, A.D. 180. Seven men and five women were on trial for their lives. They were all Christians from the nearby town of Scilla, and the accusation brought against them was that they practiced an unlawful religion and refused to acknowledge the divinity of the Roman Emperor, Marcus Aurelius. The trial dragged on until finally the Proconsul Saturnius addressed a question to Speratus, the spokesman for the accused Christians: *"Quae sunt res in capsa vestra?"*

He leaned forward to hear the answer, believing that if he knew what sort of documents these Christians kept in their church chest he would have evidence on which to condemn them to death.

Simply and directly Speratus replied: *"Libri et epistulae Pauli, iuri iusti."* By this he meant: the Gospels and the letters of Paul, a just man.

There, in a North African bookbox, in A.D. 180, lay evidence that Christians already placed Paul's letters beside the four Gospels as books to be treasured above all others and to be read in the services of the Church. Though the chest itself and all its precious manuscripts were probably burned on July 17 when the twelve Scillitan martyrs met their death, the evidence of a Roman trial provides one more fact on which to reconstruct the formation of the New Testament.

Before the end of the second century the main books of the New Testament had taken their places: Matthew, Mark, Luke, John, Acts, Romans, I and II Corinthians, Galatians, Ephesians, Philippians, Colossians, I and II Thessalonians, Philemon, I Peter, and I John. But what of the others? These were the disputed books and for many years remained on the fringe of the canon. They included: Hebrews and Revelation; the Pastoral Epistles: I and II Timothy and Titus; the Epistle of James; II Peter; II and III John; and Jude. With these were associated such books as *The Shepherd of Hermas,* the *Didache,* the *Epistle of Barnabas,* the *Epistle of Clement,* and others popular in their own day. Finally, people began to say that a book was scriptural if its author was an Apostle or closely associated with an Apostle. Then by a sort of pious fiction the names of Apostles were attached to anonymous books thought to be inspired, and the books were included in the canon. Hebrews was attributed to

Paul; the Epistles of James and Jude, to the brothers of the Lord; the Epistles of John and Revelation, to the Apostle John; and the Epistles of Peter to Simon Peter. In this way arose the misleading traditions of authorship which the scholars of our own day attempted to put right.

Our last story concerns the great Christian scholar and leader, Athanasius, Bishop of Alexandria. It was his custom to send an Easter letter to the clergy of his diocese. When Athanasius sat down to write his annual letter for the year A.D. 367, he decided to include in it a list of all the Christian writings which he thought rightly belonged to the canon. The list he sent included twenty-seven books and it was the first official list to correspond exactly with the table of contents in our New Testament. Thus the Festal Letter of Athanasius of A.D. 367 is a landmark in the history of the canon. At various Church councils in the years that followed, Athanasius' list was widely adopted.

There is an amusing old legend that attempts to tell how the canonical books were chosen. According to this story there was once a council whose members were deadlocked on the question of the canon. In this quandary they placed all their books at the foot of the altar and prayed that God would show them which were the inspired volumes. Thereupon, with one accord, all the truly inspired books hopped upon the altar! However convenient such a method of choice might be, the Church decided, of course, in an entirely different way what books to include in the canon. The choice was not quickly made, and fortunately no board of experts was able to impose its opinion upon the Church. Even Athanasius and the councils did little more than ratify a choice that had already emerged after years of experience. Ultimately, we owe the New Testament canon to multitudes of Christians everywhere who listened to the Scripture readings Sunday after Sunday and weighed what they heard on the scales of life itself. It was the final judgment of the whole Church after two and a half centuries of use that selected out of the great mass of literature the twenty-seven books which are the bulwark of Christianity.

PART III

*The Bible Through the Centuries*

## 38

### Bibles Copied by Hand

#### ROLLS AND CODICES

CHRISTIANITY with its enormous vitality spread quickly throughout the Roman world. The pagan gods had nothing with which to meet its challenge. It broke old bonds of cruelty and degradation, and in its presence fear and despair shriveled away. It set hearts to singing. It made men unafraid to die. The darkness of paganism gave way to the shining splendor of Christianity. Christ is "the true Light, which lighteth every man that cometh into the world" and He came that men "might have life, and that they might have it more abundantly." This was the good news the Apostles proclaimed.

By A.D. 150 the apostolic age was over. All the men and women who had known Jesus on earth were dead and the voices of the Apostles and their immediate followers had now fallen silent. But the written records of the apostolic age remained and through the Gospels and Epistles the great leaders still spoke to the Church which carried on in their stead. In the books written during the first period of creativeness the Church found ample material for its preaching and teaching. These twenty-seven books were to help the Church spread its gospel far and wide.

Wherever the new religion went, the Christian writings accompanied it. Before setting out for distant places missionaries packed books in their traveling bags. Paul in prison begged Timothy to bring him the books and parchments he had left behind in Troas. Sometimes in the mail pouch of a ship putting in at the harbors of Ephesus, Corinth, or Rome there would be a letter from Paul. Copies of the Gospels packed in saddle-bags must have been carried over many a Roman road to far outposts of the Empire. Perhaps among the freight unloaded from a Roman galley at one of the great Mediterranean seaports there would be a small package consigned to a local Church. It might contain a few books: an edition of the Gospels, a volume of Paul's collected letters, a copy of the Septuagint.

At first the books were all written on papyrus imported from Egypt. There, papyrus is a reed which still grows along the banks of the upper Nile. From time immemorial the pith of this papyrus reed was cut into thin strips which were then laid side by side. A second layer of strips was placed on top and at right angles to the first. When soaked in water, hammered, dried in the sun, and finally polished, a tough, smooth sheet was obtained. Twenty or more sheets pasted together formed the roll upon which the scribes of the ancient world copied their books. They wrote in solid columns several inches wide, with only a narrow margin separating the columns. A book of average size required a strip of papyrus about thirty-five feet long, and when this was rolled up it formed a bulky object. When not in use the roll was stored in a capsa or bookbox similar to a large can with a lid or in one of the pigeonholes of an old bookcase. Such were the books of the ancient world and from them many of our words about books are derived. The word "paper" comes from papyrus. "Volume" comes from the word describing the opening and closing of a scroll, namely *volumen* meaning "to roll." The very word "Bible" reminds us of the early papyrus rolls, for the Greeks called papyrus *Biblos,* in honor of the Phoenician seaport where they purchased it.

While Christianity was still young, a change came in the form of books and this change had a marked influence on the New

Testament. The time-honored roll began to be replaced by a book with leaves or pages. Such a leaf book was called a codex and this word gives a clue to its origin. For their brief notes the Romans used wooden tablets coated with a thin layer of wax in which they cut letters with a stylus. Several tablets would be bound together along one edge, perhaps with leather thongs threaded through holes bored in the wood. These bound edges looked like a section of a tree trunk which in Latin was called a *caudex*. A bound collection of wooden tablets began to be called a caudex or codex. Soon, in place of wooden tablets, a stack of folded papyrus sheets were used. These sheets were fastened together in quires by sewing through the center fold, and the leaf book so obtained was also called a codex. Some of these early papyrus codices, preserved for centuries beneath the dry sands of Egypt, have recently been discovered, and among them there are far more Christian books than Greek, Roman, or Hebrew. Probably the early Christian Church, unfettered by synagogue custom or literary habit, became the pioneer in using the newest book form. From every point of view the codex was more convenient than the roll. It was easier to turn over pages than to unroll yards of papyrus. A roll usually has writing on one side only, while the sheets of a codex have writing on both sides. It is obvious that twice as much material will fit in a codex as in a roll having the same amount of papyrus. It was, moreover, possible to make a fairly thick codex, but too bulky a roll could not be conveniently handled.

As each of the Gospels is about the right length to fill a roll, no doubt they were originally written as roll books. But in the second century when Church leaders desired to issue all four Gospels together, they found that this could be conveniently done by using the codex book. Probably Paul's collected Epistles were already being published in the codex form. As early as the second century, then, Christian publishers were offering their reading public two codices: the Gospels and the Epistles of Paul. This may have had no small influence on the formation of the canon.

Book publishing was a thriving business in the Greco-Roman world where an abundance of slave labor took the place of modern printing presses. A Roman publishing house was similar to those in the Jewish quarter of Alexandria where we have already watched Septuagints being made. Instead of the roar and clatter of our presses there was only the droning voice of a reader dictating to a battery of copyists. With seventy-five slaves working on a book that required eighteen hours to complete, a publisher could produce an edition of one thousand copies in a single month. That of course meant that the slaves worked steadily at the rate of sixty hours a week. After the book was copied and proofread, its sheets or quires were sewed together and often placed between wooden boards. They were now ready to be put on sale in booksellers' shops in the market places of Ephesus, Alexandria, and Rome.

How soon Christian books were published and sold through the usual trade channels we do not know. The poverty of the early Church and the persecutions it suffered doubtless prevented New Testament books from being as freely manufactured and sold as the Greek and Roman classics. But in spite of all obstacles, ways were found to copy and distribute them. Where professional copyists could not be hired, amateur copyists took over and zealously labored the long hours necessary to produce a single volume. Unfortunately these amateur copyists left a plentiful harvest of errors in their manuscripts. Strict accuracy was apparently not their goal, and the text at this time suffered many corruptions which modern scholars have taken great pains to sift and remove.

By the end of the second century, the written records of Christianity were distributed far and wide. In libraries, in the capsa or bookboxes of private homes, and in the wooden chests of early Christian churches lay copies of New Testament books side by side with the Old Testament in Greek. Sometimes the only property a church possessed was a wooden chest kept in someone's house. In this chest would be stored the sacred vessels, the Septuagint, and a few books of the New Testament.

The Scillitan martyrs of A.D. 180 had the Gospels and the Epistles of Paul in their chest. Church chests in great centers like Antioch, Caesarea, Ephesus, Corinth, Alexandria, and Rome must have held many treasures. There were the widely distributed twenty-seven books we know so well, together with other books popular in their own day but now forgotten. Some churches must have possessed original manuscripts. Possibly Roman Christians whose grandfathers had known Mark still kept the autograph of Mark's Gospel which had now lost its ending and stopped abruptly with the words: "for they were afraid." Perhaps one of the Galatian churches still treasured the letter from Paul which contained his own distinctive handwriting in the words:

Ye see how large a letter I have written unto you with mine own hand.

GALATIANS 6:11

Eighteen centuries have come and gone since wooden chests held the original manuscripts of the New Testament. What would we not give to find one of these! As we shall see in a later chapter, a few priceless fragments of second and third-century books have been dug out of the Egyptian sands, but not a single original New Testament manuscript written by the author himself is known to exist today. Constant use and the effects of time wore out the papyrus of the earliest books and they literally crumbled and vanished away. How many Christian documents perished in the flames of persecution that burned so often in the early centuries, no one can say. But somehow the New Testament survived. Perishable though the material substance of the books was, their message was imperishable and passed on from one copy to another in an unbroken chain.

In this there lurked a danger. It is a rare copy that is exactly like its model, for even the most conscientious scribe made careless little copying mistakes when he was tired. But that is not all. In the early years teachers and missionaries did not hestitate to edit, omit, or add to the original book. Their chief purpose was, not to guard the purity of the text, but to adapt it to the needs of their listeners. The writings were not protected by copyright laws nor by the idea that they were sacred. We have already seen what Marcion did to Luke's Gospel and Paul's Epistles and what Tatian did to the four Gospels in his *Diatessaron*. What was there to prevent the records of Christianity from being transformed by this chain of copying and editing into something entirely different?

The Church itself was planted firmly athwart this dangerous tendency to alter the Christian message. Had the Church relied solely on copies of copies of copies of her documents there is no telling how her message might have been transformed after the lapse of centuries. But the Church had other sources of authority: these were her traditions and teachings. These checked any serious changes in her written documents as they passed from copy to copy and thus protected the basic historical record and the main doctrines of her Faith.

It must be admitted, however, that hundreds of minor variations did creep into the New Testament text. Though hardly any of these involve major points, today's Bible reader wants each word and phrase to be exactly as it left the pen of the author and before a thousand successive copyings had their chance to alter the original. This is the goal toward which modern textual experts labor. They assemble many old manuscripts and compare the variations. Studying these and sifting all the evidence, scholars begin to discover what the original text must have been. Their work is like an elaborate puzzle and as they solve it bit by bit the true text of the New Testament emerges. In a later chapter we shall learn of the discovery of some of the ancient manuscripts with which these experts work.

A new writing material was beginning to replace papyrus. Tradition says that in the second century B.C. the King of Egypt learned that King Eumenes II of Pergamon was building up a library that bid fair to surpass his own royal library at Alexandria. To end this rivalry King Ptolemy laid an embargo on papyrus, which Eumenes had been importing in large quantities from Egypt. Thereupon, Eumenes ordered his craftsmen to find a substitute. They took the skins of sheep, goats, or calves, washed, scraped, and stretched them and finally rubbed them with pumice until a smooth writing surface was obtained. Because Pergamon was its traditional place of origin, animal skins processed for writing were called in Latin *charta pergamena* or in English "parchment." The finest quality of parchment was made from calf skin and took its name from the calf or "veal"; it was called "vellum." Parchment or vellum was far more durable than papyrus; it was likewise more expensive. But by the fourth century the Church began to use this superior writing material.

The infancy of the New Testament was its most hazardous period. By the fourth century it entered upon a new era of relative safety when the Emperor Constantine declared Christianity to be the official religion of the Empire. The fires of persecution died down. Churches could now afford to buy parchment instead of papyrus for their books. Amateur copyists gave way to professionals. The foremost scholars of the period turned their attention from the Greek and Roman classics to the Bible and edited its manuscripts in order to produce a reliable text. All this change is summed up in the story of the first large Bible order.

In A.D. 332 Constantine placed an order with Eusebius of Caesarea for fifty copies of the Bible to be given to the churches of Constantinople. They were the first of a long line of Bibles given as royal gifts, and this was the first large Bible order on record. The Emperor specified that they were to be made on vellum by trained scribes copying the best text available. His letter to Eusebius further ordered that two public "carriages" were to be commandeered to bring the finished volumes to the Emperor, and he promised a liberal reward to the deacon who supervised this shipment.

From the fourth century come the two oldest and finest Greek manuscript Bibles now in existence. One is the Codex Vaticanus now in the Vatican Library and the other is the Codex Sinaiticus in the British Museum. If these famous Bibles are not themselves two of the fifty copies made for Constantine in A.D.

332, they are doubtless similar to them. From now on the Bible was safe. Soon beautiful editions written in silver or gold on parchment stained with purple dye began to appear. Some of these sumptuous volumes, which St. Jerome criticized as useless luxuries, are in existence today.

With the fall of the Roman Empire the publishing business declined and the Church took over the production of Bibles. Monasteries throughout Europe set aside a room called the scriptorium where monks patiently copied books by hand. They began to decorate their manuscript books, first with pen drawings and later with painted illustrations and illuminations of remarkable beauty. The artists of the Middle Ages lavished some of their most exquisite work on manuscript Bibles, many of which still survive in the museums and libraries of Europe and America. Today when we see the delicacy of the miniature illustrations, with their intricate ornamentation and their clear, jewel-like colors, we realize that all this is part of the homage the Middle Ages paid to the Bible.

## ❧ 39 ❧

### *Translating the Bible*

CONSTANTINE'S beautiful vellum codices had been in use about fifty years when the Bible reached a new mile-stone. About A.D. 375 a party of Roman scholars on a "grand tour" of the Mediterranean reached Antioch, the city in which the followers of Christ had first been called Christians. Antioch was in the midst of a severe outbreak of fever which one of the Roman tourists contracted and of which he died. A second one also lay dangerously ill of the fever. This was Jerome, perhaps the most brilliant and learned member of the little group. He had been born in Dalmatia of wealthy Christian parents who gave their son the best education of the day in grammar, rhetoric, law, philosophy, and Latin poetry. Jerome was baptized by the Pope himself, but his interest in Christianity was only lukewarm. He enjoyed searching through the catacombs of Rome for martyr's graves and he was clever at deciphering inscriptions carved on tombs, but Jerome disliked reading the Scriptures. In his day these had been translated from the original Greek into a crude Latin which offended the ear of a scholar like Jerome accustomed to the majestic cadences of the Latin poets. The Old-Latin version of the Bible suffered in comparison to Virgil, Horace, and Cicero.

One night in Antioch while Jerome's fever was at its height

he dreamed that Christ stood beside his bed and reproached him, saying: "You care more about being a follower of Cicero than of Me."

Stung by this rebuke Jerome cried: "O Lord, thou knowest that when I read secular books I deny Thee!"

When Jerome recovered from the fever he decided to turn from the Odes of Pindar to the Psalms of David and to devote his life to the Holy Scriptures instead of Greek and Latin classics. Immediately he began to learn Hebrew and to perfect his Greek, and as a further evidence of his change of heart he was ordained to the priesthood.

On his return to Rome he was introduced to Pope Damasus. At this time many others besides Jerome criticized the Old-Latin translation of the Bible. The Pope himself was concerned about this and was searching for someone to revise the Old-Latin translation for him. Jerome was just the man he needed for this task and Damasus immediately commissioned him to carry it out.

In A.D. 383 Jerome completed his revision of the Latin Gospels and published it in Rome with a dedication to Pope Damasus. The following year the Pope died and Jerome was mentioned as his successor, but, as nothing came of this he returned to his lifelong work of revision and translation.

From Rome he journeyed to Palestine, followed by a wealthy Roman widow, Paula, her daughter, and a group of their friends. These matrons were enthusiastic members of Jerome's Bible classes in Rome. Now he conducted them on a tour of the sacred sites of Palestine. Finally, they all settled down to live in Bethlehem, the ladies in three nunneries built by Paula, and Jerome in a monastery. Here Jerome once more plunged into his work of translation. He was no longer satisfied with the Septuagint version of the Old Testament but desired to translate directly from the original Hebrew text. In this undertaking Rabbi Ben Anina helped him, coming to Jerome's study secretly at night under cover of the darkness, for fear of the Jews. Doubtless Jerome's Jewish teacher showed him that the Apocrypha was not in the Hebrew Scriptures and convinced him that it should not be included in his Bible. But the Church did not agree to this. Though it is not clear exactly how much of the new Latin version Jerome completed before he finally laid down his pen, it is fairly certain that the major portion of it is his work. He certainly translated the canonical Old Testament books from the Hebrew, the Psalms from the Septuagint, and he revised the Old-Latin version of the Gospels and possibly other New Testament books as well. The common people who could not read Greek now had an excellent version of the Bible in their own tongue. For this outstanding service the Church gave Jerome the title of saint.

At first men were slow to accept Jerome's work, for they were so accustomed to the Old-Latin phrases that any change in them seemed irreverent. According to one story a bishop read Jerome's version of Jonah to his congregation. In the Old-Latin version the word for the vine under which Jonah sat had been translated "gourd" or "pumpkin." Jerome translated this "ivy." When the bishop read the new word "ivy," his congregation rose in a body and indignantly left the church vowing never again to listen to the reading of such heresy!

In time the hostility that always greets a new version began to die down as people learned to appreciate the superior quality of Jerome's work. Until the seventh century, the Roman church used both the Old-Latin version and Jerome's, though Pope Gregory the Great said he preferred Jerome's. Jerome called his work *Translatio Nova,* the New Translation, but by the thirteenth century it had earned another name. In those days the word "vulgar" had not fallen from its original, high meaning: "widespread" or "common." Jerome's version was universally read throughout Western Europe in homes, schools, churches, monasteries, and cathedrals and because of this widespread use it was accorded the title of the Vulgate.

Ten years before St. Jerome died in Bethlehem in A.D. 420, the city of Rome was captured and sacked by Alaric the Goth. The civilization of the Roman Empire was submerged by invading barbarians and there followed the long dark night of the

Middle Ages. Through all that time the Vulgate remained a shining beacon of civilization and Christianity, and for a thousand years its Latin words were read, recited, chanted, sung, and spoken in prayer all over Western Europe. Upon it depended the literature and art of Europe from the fourth century to the Reformation. It inspired Dante, Giotto, Leonardo da Vinci, Raphael, Michelangelo, and the sculptors of Chartres. It provided subject matter for glassmakers, ivory carvers, enamel workers, tapestry weavers, jewelers, woodcarvers, stonecutters, and all the artists and artisans of Europe. At last, when printing was invented, the first book believed to have come from the press of Johannes Gutenberg of Mainz about 1456 was no other than a copy of St. Jerome's Vulgate.

Though the Vulgate was by far the most important Bible version issued by the fifth century, there had been many others. Any translation from the original languages of the Bible, Hebrew for the Old Testament, Greek for the New, is technically known as a version. The Septuagint was the first version of the Old Testament and the Old-Latin was doubtless the first version of the New Testament. Tatian's Syriac *Diatessaron* was another version and this was followed by translations of the separate Gospels in Syriac made before A.D. 200. As we shall see in a later chapter, these ancient Syriac Gospels, lost for centuries, were discovered in modern times and have helped scholars reconstruct the original Greek text of which they were very early translations. Coptic is the Egyptian language written in Greek letters, and Coptic versions are known to have existed by A.D. 250. In the fourth century peoples living in the widely separated lands of Armenia, Abyssinia, and Gaul had Bibles in their own languages. An alphabet had to be invented for the Scriptures in Armenian, for no written literature then existed in that language. In their classical Ethiopic language the black people of Abyssinia possessed a Bible a thousand years before there was one in English.

When Ulfilas began to convert the Goths he needed a Bible in their language. About A.D. 300 he made a Gothic translation of the entire Bible with the exception of the Book of Kings which he feared might encourage the warlike spirit of his converts. This Gothic Bible is the oldest surviving piece of literature in the great Teutonic family of languages to which both German and English belong. One of the finest manuscripts of this Gothic version is called the Codex Argenteus, for it is written in silver letters on purple-stained vellum. Made in North Italy in the fifth or sixth century, it belonged for a time to the monastery of Werden in Germany. From there it was taken to Sweden as part of the booty of the Thirty Years War. Now it is one of the great treasures of the University Library at Upsala.

A thousand years after Ulfilas' Gothic Bible there appeared in the fourteenth century the first complete English version. This, as we shall see, was the translation made by John Wycliffe and his associates who gave English-speaking people the first Bible in their own tongue.

There is a curious old stone in China at Chang 'an in Shensi Province. This stone bears an inscription in both Chinese and Syriac and it is believed to have been set up by Nestorian Christian missionaries who visited China in A.D. 781. The inscription states that in the New Testament there are twenty-seven books. Later Marco Polo found a string of Nestorian churches along the trade routes from Baghdad to Peiping. Did the Syriac-speaking missionaries who founded these churches bring Bibles with them and did they ever translate these Syriac Bibles into Chinese? Such an early Chinese version is an interesting possibility, though if it ever existed it has now perished. Today's Chinese Bibles stem from a different lineage.

Thus the Bible began to span the gulfs separating peoples of different languages. The Septuagint and the Old-Latin Version were the first Greek and Latin bridges, but for Western Europe for a thousand years St. Jerome's Vulgate became the chief bridge. Besides the Syriac, Coptic, Armenian, Ethiopic, and Gothic versions more and more languages and dialects were added until, by 1948, the entire Bible or portions of it existed in 1,090 different languages.

# 40

## The Early History of the English Bible

### CAEDMON, BEDE, THE LINDISFARNE GOSPELS, AND WYCLIFFE'S BIBLE

THE story of the arrival of the Bible in Britain is lost in obscurity. Tradition says that thirty years after the Crucifixion Philip the Apostle went to Britain and founded the Church at Glastonbury to which Joseph of Arimathea brought the Holy Grail, the cup used at the Last Supper. These legends, however, fail to mention the Bible. Perhaps the first copy of the Scriptures came to this distant outpost of the Roman Empire in the baggage of some Christian legionary. There must have been at least one copy of the Vulgate in St. Augustine's traveling bag when he landed in England in A.D. 596 with orders from Pope Gregory the Great to preach the Gospel to the Angles and Saxons. His mission was successful, and before long there was established on English soil a Church whose Bible was the Vulgate. This Latin version remained the bulwark of English Christianity for centuries and not until the time of Chaucer in the fourteenth century, when the English language began to emerge in its present form, did the entire Bible appear in English.

How then did the common folk of Britain learn Bible stories and teachings during the many centuries when Latin was the language of the Church? Answers to that question can be found in three stories: of Caedmon, of the Venerable Bede, and of the Lindisfarne Gospels.

Caedmon was a simple, unlettered herdsman who sat one night at a feast in a great hall where each guest in turn was expected to sing a song. Dreading the moment when the harp would be handed to him and he would have to sing, Caedmon fled to the barn and lay down in the straw to sleep. He dreamed that a stranger appeared and said to him: "Sing of the beginning of created things."

The song he composed in his dream remained in his memory and the next morning as he sang it to the steward of the monastery of Whitby, Caedmon knew that he was no longer a poor, dumb herdsman, but a singer and a poet. The steward took him to Hilda, the Abbess of the monastery, and there the learned brothers taught him Bible stories. They translated the Latin stories into Anglo-Saxon, and Caedmon transformed these into songs. So popular were Caedmon's songs that other singers imitated him and thus turned a large part of the Bible into verse. These songs or poems were not actual translations but paraphrases, for they gave the idea of the original without keeping strictly to its words. They served to bring to the people of Britain a knowledge of the Bible.

Caedmon's story appeared in *Ecclesiastical History of the English People,* written by the Venerable Bede at the monastery of Jarrow. At the end of his manuscript someone copied Caedmon's Hymn of Creation, which is perhaps the very song he composed in his dream. Scholars think it was written about A.D. 665 and they consider it to be the oldest surviving fragment of native English song.

The Venerable Bede himself belongs with Caedmon among those who helped to bring the Bible to the people. Unfortunately his version of the Gospel of John, which was probably the first Anglo-Saxon prose translation of any part of the Bible, disappeared long ago. In a letter written by one of his friends there is a story of how Bede finished his translation just before his death. It was Easter time, about A.D. 735. Though Bede had been ill and felt his end fast approaching, he continued his work of translating John's Gospel. The young scholar who acted as his scribe feared that the one chapter remaining might be too difficult for his master's failing strength.

"It is easy," replied Bede. "Take your pen and write."

During the day his friends came to his cell to bid him farewell. Finally, as darkness fell Bede's scribe reminded him of the translation.

"Dear master, one more sentence still remains unwritten."

"Write quickly," the dying man said.

"Now it is ended," said the young man as he wrote the final words.

"Well you may say: it is ended. Take my head in your hands and lay me down where I have been wont to pray, that I may call upon my Father."

Lying on the floor of his cell the Venerable Bede died with the *Gloria* upon his lips.

Other translations of portions of the Scriptures followed that of Bede. King Alfred is said to have translated the first fifty psalms as they appear in the famous *Paris Psalter* now in the National Library in Paris. Moreover, Alfred's Dooms or Book of Laws opened with the Ten Commandments and closed with the Golden Rule. About A.D. 1000 the four Gospels were translated into the West Saxon dialect, and Abbot Aelfric translated many portions of the Old Testament. Though Aelfric tried to provide religious instruction in simple English for the common people, he had misgivings about translating the Old Testament, for he did not believe that all of it was suitable for them.

The Venerable Bede was still working on his translation of John's Gospel when Eadfrith became Bishop of the island of Lindisfarne. In honor of St. Cuthbert, patron saint of Lindisfarne, Bishop Eadfrith made a copy of the Latin Gospels. So beautiful was this book that his successor, Ethelwold, ordered a cover made for it of gold inlaid with jewels. A goldsmith named Billfrith did this work. For over a hundred years this beautiful book of Eadfrith, Ethelwold, and Billfrith remained safely in the Lindisfarne library, and then one day the Danes came pillaging and burning towns along the Northumbrian coast. Snatching up their treasured Gospel book in its golden case and the shrine containing St. Cuthbert's bones, the monks of Lindisfarne fled before the invaders, but their ship capsized in a storm and their valuable book slid into the water. It seemed a miracle to the monks when they later found their Gospels on the sands at low tide. Years later, about A.D. 950, when the book was once more safely back at Lindisfarne, a monk named Aldred wrote between the lines of the old manuscript the Anglo-Saxon meaning of each Latin word. This is not a translation, for it cannot stand by itself as an independent narrative. Aldred's work is called a gloss and it was a common device to help a priest, who was none too sure of his Latin, explain the Scriptures. Today one of the treasured manuscripts of the British Museum is the Lindisfarne Gospels. In the course of its many adventures Billfrith's jeweled case was lost, but you may still see Eadfrith's seventh-century handwriting and Aldred's tenth-century, Anglo-Saxon, interlinear gloss, and here and there the edges of the pages still show water stains.

England had to wait until the fourteenth century for the first complete Bible in English, which was the version prepared under the leadership of John Wycliffe. It appeared about 1383 while Richard II reigned and Geoffrey Chaucer was at work on his *Canterbury Tales*. A change had come over the English language. People no longer sang Caedmon's paraphrases nor read the old prose translations of the Gospels, nor listened to a priest reading the interlinear glosses of the beautiful manuscript Bibles, for Anglo-Saxon was no longer spoken. Since the Norman Conquest of 1066, a new language had emerged, fashioned out of the old Anglo-Saxon and the French of the conquerors. The first great literary works in this new English language are Chaucer's *Canterbury Tales* and the Wycliffe Bible.

John Wycliffe, one of England's most powerful reformers, was a university man and the master of Balliol College at Oxford. He protested against the wealth and power of the Church, saying that it no longer taught the true message of Christ and the Apostles as contained in the Scriptures. Together with Nicholas of Hereford, and probably other scholars of his reform movement, he translated the entire Bible into English so that people might see for themselves how far the Church had fallen from the teachings of its Founder and how much its worldliness needed to be reformed. "To be ignorant of the Scriptures is to be ignorant of Christ," said Wycliffe. He organized groups of preachers who traveled throughout the country preaching and reading the Scriptures wherever they went. Members of this reform movement were called Lollards. Their number increased rapidly, especially among poor people heavily burdened by the demands of the Church. The clergy became alarmed and forbade the Bible to be translated. The Church banned Wycliffe's version and burned its readers at the stake with their copies hanging from their necks. Wycliffe himself died a natural death, but the authorities dug up his bones and scattered his ashes.

Persecution failed to stop the circulation of this first complete English Bible. People were so eager to read it that some who could not afford an entire Bible gave a load of hay for a few chapters of Paul. The book was expensive, costing more than two hundred dollars, for each copy had to be laboriously written by hand. Even so, many copies were evidently made, for a hundred and fifty of them still survive. In the Bodleian Library at Oxford the original manuscript of the Wycliffe Bible is carefully preserved. Its five different handwritings are probably those of Wycliffe, Nicholas of Hereford, and three other translators who worked with them. Their translation was an almost word for word rendering of the Vulgate into English. When a new edition was issued in 1397 by John Purvey, the translation was revised and the language made more readable.

Such is the story of the Bible in England until the sixteenth century. From Caedmon to Wycliffe it was a handwritten book. Soon after the invention of printing in the fifteenth century, the English Bible entered a new epoch. The old translations were made from the Vulgate, but scholars were discovering Greek and Hebrew texts far more accurate than the Vulgate, which was now filled with the copying errors of a thousand years. In the universities men were studying Hebrew and Greek and there were many who could read the first printed Greek Bible. This was prepared by Erasmus in 1516 at the behest of the enterprising printer of Basel, Johann Froben. By this time Wycliffe's ideas were bearing fruit and everywhere people were asserting their right to read the Scriptures for themselves. Furthermore, the English language had now reached a new level of development and Wycliffe's and Purvey's English was already antiquated. The time was ripe for a new English version. The art of printing, the Greek and Hebrew texts, the popular demand, and the perfection of the language all awaited a translator with enough skill, determination, and above all courage to render the Bible into English.

## 41

## The Father of the English Bible

### WILLIAM TYNDALE

IN Gloucestershire, at Stinchcombe near the border of Wales, there was born a child destined to become one of the most important men in the history of the English Bible. This was William Tyndale. About two years before his birth, on October 12, 1492, the lookout on Columbus' ship the *Niña* had cried "Land Ho!" and the New World loomed up before the weary eyes of Old World pioneers. Like Columbus, Tyndale was a pioneer. His interest lay not in ships, maps, oceans, and continents, but in changing dead languages into the speech of living men. Columbus led the way to the shores of an undiscovered continent, while Tyndale opened the unknown realms of the Bible to English-speaking people and laid the foundations of our English versions. This earned for him a title as proud as any man bears, for he is called the Father of the English Bible.

William Tyndale felt the stir of the Renaissance while still a student at Oxford and Cambridge. The spirit of adventure and the eagerness for new things which unfurled the sails of the *Niña,* the *Pinta,* and the *Santa Maria* blew like a mighty wind through the universities and the Church. The fall of Constantinople to the Turks in 1453 had resulted in the flight of scholars to Western Europe. They brought with them a rich heritage from classical civilization which acted like a match to the fuse of the Renaissance. Scholars everywhere lectured on the new learning, while the Church rocked under the impact of fresh ideas. The greatest humanist and theologian of the Renaissance was the Dutch priest Erasmus whose lectures at Oxford were still remembered when Tyndale became a student there. In 1516, as we have noted, Erasmus published his epoch-making Greek Testament with a fresh Latin translation beside it. He dedicated this volume to Pope Leo X who accepted the dedication, little realizing that this Greek text of the New Testament was to challenge the accuracy and authority of the Vulgate. The Church was disturbed by this wave of interest in the Bible and feared lest comparative study and criticism of the time-honored words of the Vulgate, which were now considered sacred, might weaken the authority of the Church. As a candidate for the priesthood Tyndale was forbidden to read the Bible without special authority from his bishop, but even so he seems to have devoted himself to the study of the Scriptures and to the mastery of the Greek language, thus preparing himself for what was later to become his life's work.

After Tyndale was ordained he went to Little Sodbury near Bristol to become the tutor for the children of Sir John Walsh, one of the courtiers of Henry VIII. While he was living in Sir John's household Tyndale's enthusiasm for the Bible began to crystallize into a determination to translate it into English. He was a scholar by training but a reformer at heart. As a scholar he knew both Greek and Latin and this knowledge made him aware of the many differences between the original Greek text and the Vulgate translation. Wycliffe had rendered the Vulgate into English, but as yet no one had translated the Greek text of Erasmus into English. Here was Tyndale's opportunity. As a reformer, Tyndale desired to bring the Church back to the pure religion of an earlier day and he felt that the best way to do this was to put into men's hands a Bible they could read. Most people did not understand the Latin Scriptures, and often the priests themselves did not know the meaning of the words they read.

Church leaders were suspicious of a reformer like Tyndale, and he was often entangled in arguments with them and accused of heresy. One day in fiery indignation he burst out against one of his learned opponents: "If God spare my life, ere many years I will cause a boy that driveth the plough shall know more of the scriptures than thou dost." He was as good as his word.

In 1523 William Tyndale left Little Sodbury for London, hoping to secure the patronage of the great scholar, Cuthbert Tunstall, then Bishop of London. Bishop Tunstall put Tyndale off with the excuse that his palace in St. Paul's churchyard was full and there were already more in his household than he could well support. Undiscouraged by this failure, Tyndale found a sympathetic patron in one of the aldermen of London. This was Humphrey Monmouth, a wealthy cloth merchant, in whose house near the Tower of London Tyndale spent six months working day and night on his translations. For his hospitality to Tyndale, Monmouth later suffered arrest, imprisonment, and the loss of his fortune.

Tyndale soon realized "not only that there was no room in my lord of London's palace to translate the New Testament, but also that there was no place to do it in all England." Accordingly, in the spring of 1524 he set sail from England never to return. He landed at Hamburg and from here on his story becomes the record of an underground movement, for even on the continent his work met opposition and he was often in danger of arrest at the hands of Church authorities.

By 1525 his first translation of the New Testament was ready for the printer. Six thousand copies were ordered but the printer, Peter Quentel of Cologne, was afraid of risking so many and began work on three thousand copies of quarto size. Only ten sheets of this edition had come from the press when Tyndale heard a knock at his door and a whispered warning that the work had been discovered by Johannes Cochlaeus, one of the bitterest enemies of the Reformation. Cochlaeus had invited the printers to his tavern and had treated them to wine until their tongues became loosened and they openly boasted of the

English New Testament they were printing. Thereupon Cochlaeus issued an order stopping the work. Tyndale's warning came just in time. He hastened to Peter Quentel's shop, gathered up the ten finished sheets and escaped with them by boat up the Rhine to Worms. A fragment of this quarto edition, consisting of the twenty-two chapters of Matthew snatched from under Cochlaeus' hand, came to light about a hundred years ago and is now in the British Museum.

At Worms Tyndale found another printer willing to work for him. This was Peter Schoeffer the younger, whose father had helped Gutenberg develop the art of printing at Mainz seventy years before. Tyndale and Schoeffer decided to set aside the quarto sheets and to issue an octavo edition, for this would be smaller and consequently easier to hide than the Cologne quarto.[1] This was a wise precaution, for by the time the books were finished in December, 1525, and began arriving at the English ports, the authorities were on the watch for them. John Cochlaeus had written to Henry VIII warning him of this impending "invasion of England" and advising him to guard his ports against the "pernicious merchandise." But in spite of this the first New Testaments printed in English were quietly smuggled into England. They were hidden in bales of cotton, in sacks of flour, and in bundles of flax, and once past the officials they found a ready market. At the universities of Oxford and Cambridge the New Testaments were eagerly purchased and in London weavers, blacksmiths, servants, bakers, and wealthy men, all willingly paid from four to twelve dollars for a single copy. No wonder the Church authorities were alarmed. It was not so much the New Testament itself that they feared as Tyndale's notes and comments printed in the margins of the text. In these he sharply criticized the Church and its officials, and pointed out to his readers how far the religion of their day had departed from Christ's teachings. Following in the steps of

---

[1] A quarto is a volume made from sheets of paper folded twice so as to give four leaves (eight pages). In order to make a book which is half the size of a quarto the sheets are folded three times. This gives eight leaves (sixteen pages) and the volume so obtained is called an octavo.

Wycliffe and Luther, Tyndale used the Bible as a weapon with which to reform the Church.

Bishop Tunstall was furious and declared that Tyndale "with crafty trickery translated the holy gospel of God into our vulgar English tongue, intermingling certain articles of heretical depravity and pernicious erroneous opinions, pestilent, scandalous, and seductive of simple minds." He ordered all copies turned over to the authorities under penalty of excommunication and he lighted a bonfire of the books at St. Paul's Cross in London. The battle was joined.

Booksellers were fined; readers were haled into court and imprisoned. Still the books were eagerly bought, circulated, and read. The authorities bought up as many copies as they could find and destroyed them, but this, as Tyndale gleefully remarked, only put more money in his pocket to finance another edition. So successful were the authorities in their destruction of this first New Testament printed in English that today only two copies of it are known to exist. One is a fragment now in the library of St. Paul's Cathedral. The other lacks a title page but is otherwise the only perfect copy surviving of the three thousand first issued at Worms in 1525. It is owned by the Baptist College in Bristol, and of all printed English Bibles this is surely the greatest treasure. It came to light in the seventeenth century when someone found it and sold it to Lord Oxford for his "Harleian" Library. Lord Oxford paid only ten pounds for the book, but so highly did he value this unique volume that he settled an annuity of twenty pounds for life upon the man who had discovered it.

The storm that greeted Tyndale's first translation of the New Testament did not deter him from continuing his work. Though he was in constant danger and often moved to escape arrest, he continued translating in Worms, Hamburg, and Antwerp, turning his eleven years of exile into fruitful years. He took up the study of Hebrew so that he might translate the Old Testament, as he had the New Testament, from its original language. The first printed edition of the Hebrew Old Testament was older by a few years than Erasmus' edition of the Greek New Testament of 1516, for the Hebrew Bible had been issued at Soncino in 1488 and it may have been this edition that Tyndale used for his translation of the Pentateuch. Misfortune dogged him, for his Deuteronomy was lost in a shipwreck off the coast of Holland and he had to retranslate it. With the help of Miles Coverdale he issued an English version of the Pentateuch and the Book of Jonah. Although John Hoochstraten of Antwerp printed the Pentateuch and shipped it to England in the summer of 1530 his name, probably for reasons of security, does not appear in the book. After revising Genesis, Tyndale resumed work on his New Testament, for he was not entirely satisfied with his first version and wanted to rewrite large portions of it, smoothing out rough passages, deleting old-fashioned words, and perfecting the rhythm of the sentences. It is on his revised New Testament of 1534 that his fame as a translator chiefly rests. This is the only book whose title page bears his name:

> The Newe Testament dylygently corrected and compared with the Greke By Willyam Tindale: and fynesshed in the yere of oure Lorde God A.M.D. & XXXIIII in the moneth of November.

Of the twelve or more surviving copies of this edition perhaps the most interesting is the volume now in the British Museum. This is printed on vellum and decorated with woodcuts and illuminated capitals. Its gold edges are inscribed in red letters with the words: *Anna Regina Angliae,* for this copy once belonged to Anne Boleyn, wife of Henry VIII. Anne had aided one of the English merchants who was accused of selling Tyndale's first edition and this presentation copy of the second edition may have been Tyndale's way of returning thanks for the Queen's favor.

At Antwerp Tyndale lived at the headquarters of the merchant adventurers in the English House where he gathered a group of his fellow countrymen each Sunday to listen to his readings from the Bible. Two days a week Tyndale visited the poor and sick to relieve their troubles with generous gifts. One of the people he helped finally betrayed him to the authorities and in 1535 he was arrested and imprisoned.

For sixteen months he suffered boredom and cold as a prisoner in Vilvorde Castle outside Brussels. In a letter written to the authorities at this time he made his pitiful requests for a warmer cap and coat and for a piece of cloth to patch his leggings. He asked to be allowed to have a lamp in the evening, saying it was wearisome to sit alone in the dark. Most of all he begged for his Hebrew Bible, grammar, and dictionary so that he might pass his time in study.

In spite of his friends' efforts to save him, he was tried for heresy, condemned, and on October 6, 1536, he was strangled and his body burned at the stake. His last words were the cry: "Lord, open the King of England's eyes!"

Tyndale's dying prayer was nearer to being answered than he knew, for in that very year his New Testament was printed on English soil for the first time, and from then on to our own day a steady stream of English Bibles has issued from the presses. Tyndale's cause had triumphed.

When Tyndale began his work there were a surprising number of Bibles in existence, among which were translations in: French, Spanish, Italian, Danish, Bohemian, Dutch, Slavonic, Russian, Swedish, German, and Wycliffe's English Bible. Except for the German version, all these had one thing in common: they were all translations of the Vulgate. Tyndale broke with this custom of translating the Vulgate, and for this reason he did not use Wycliffe's version nor the other versions based on the Vulgate. Only Luther's German translation made in 1522 influenced Tyndale. The New Testament of this German Bible, like Tyndale's English one, was a translation, not of the Vulgate, but of the Greek text.

Tyndale's work became the cornerstone of the English Bible, and all the translators following him built upon his foundation. As his goal was accuracy and complete faithfulness to the original Greek or Hebrew he became independent of all other renderings, however honored. His work was honest and scholarly, revealing on every page his basic integrity. There was a mingled simplicity and grandeur in his sentences that stemmed from Saxon directness and Latin majesty. He possessed a sense of poetry and his ear was delicately attuned to the music and rhythm of phrases. His magical harmonies persisted through successive editions and can still be heard in the Authorized Version, ninety per cent of which, it is estimated, comes from his translation.

Here is Tyndale's translation of Hebrews 1:10-12. Its extraordinary felicities of expression and rhythm are preserved almost intact in our Authorized Version:

> And thou Lord in the beginning hast laid the foundation of the earth. And the heavens are the works of thy hands. They shall perish, but thou shalt endure. They all shall wax old as doth a garment: and as a vesture shalt thou change them, and they shall be changed. But thou art the same always, and thy years shall not fail.

The history of this fragment from Hebrews is a curious one. The verses in Hebrews are a quotation from Psalms. When Coverdale translated Psalm 102:25-27 he remembered Tyndale's beautiful translation from Hebrews and used it. Coverdale's Psalms were incorporated in the Great Bible of 1539 and the Great Bible's Psalms were used in the *Book of Common Prayer.* Thus, though Tyndale himself never translated Psalms, his translation of a quotation in Hebrews is preserved today in the Psalter of the *Book of Common Prayer.*

We owe to Tyndale many a familiar phrase like these which have become part of the very texture of the English language: the burden and heat of the day; eat, drink, and be merry; in Him we live, move, and have our being; he cannot serve God and Mammon; consider the lilies of the field, how they grow; a prophet hath no honor in his own country. It is interesting to note that Tyndale introduced the word Jehovah as the name for God. Where he learned this word we do not know. Tyndale's error persisted in translation after translation, acquiring such an aura of sacredness that it is now almost impossible to discontinue the use of Jehovah and substitute for it the more accurate Yahweh.

Here is Tyndale's rendering of Matthew 6:9-13, the first English translation of the Lord's Prayer directly from the Greek:

O oure father which art in heven, halewed be thy name. Let thy kingdom come. Thy wyll be fulfilled, as well in erth, as hit ys in heven. Geve vs this daye oure dayly breade. And forgeve vs oure treaspases, even as we forgeve them whych treaspas vs. Lede vs nott into temptacion, but delyvre vs from yvell. Amen.

When the spelling is modernized and a word or two changed this becomes the Lord's Prayer of the English-speaking world. With this example before us we can see why William Tyndale, the English clergyman, scholar, and martyr is known as the Father of the English Bible.

## 42

# The Lineage of the English Bible

## SIX IMPORTANT BIBLES

WITH William Tyndale the English Bible put eight hundred years of experiment behind and entered upon a century of great achievements. In the seventy-five years after Tyndale's death six important Bibles appeared: Coverdale's, Matthew's, the Great Bible, the Geneva Bible, the Bishop's Bible, and the Rheims-Douay Bible. Edition followed edition, and it often seemed as though the printing presses would never satisfy the demand. Men risked their lives to bring out the Scriptures; kings and bishops hastened to issue authorized editions; printers enlarged their shops and bought new equipment; rival religious parties printed their own versions. From the reign of Henry VIII to the accession of James I the English Bible passed through a period of amazing activity.

Why were Bibles so much in demand at this time? The answer to that goes back to the state of the Church. Even loyal churchmen realized all was not well. Many of the clergy were ignorant. People were superstitious. Religion consisted largely of masses, confession, prayers to the saints, and the buying of indulgences. Of the Bible only those portions of the Gospels and Epistles used in the liturgy were known, and these were intoned in an unintelligible Latin. A few learned theologians in the monasteries read the rare copies of the Bible, but for the lay people of Western Europe it had become an almost unknown Book. Then came Erasmus' Greek text and its accompanying new Latin translation, together with a whole series of modern language versions. The printing presses of Europe produced these Bibles, and enterprising merchants distributed them far and wide. The result was a religious upheaval. Men everywhere read about Jesus and His disciples and they rubbed their eyes in amazement. Could their religion with its Borgia Pope, its superstitions, and its worldly clergy be the religion founded by Jesus? The Reformation spread like wildfire among men who asked such questions. Men caught up in this movement read the Bible and created a demand for more and more copies of it. All this was behind the immense translating and printing activity of the sixteenth century.

To Miles Coverdale belongs the honor of bringing out the first printed English Bible complete from Genesis to Revelation. This was in 1535. The sheets were printed abroad, probably in Zurich, and sent to James Nicholson, a Southwark printer, for binding and distribution. This Bible, dedicated to Henry VIII, "defendour of the fayth and under God the chefe and supreme heade of the Church of Englonde," escaped seizure and burning and was allowed to circulate freely. Though Coverdale was by no means as great a scholar as Tyndale, he was a master of stately English prose. He revised the translations of other men, creating many passages of delicate harmony and solemn beauty which have been preserved in our modern version. Coverdale helped in the translation of three other Bibles: Tyndale's Old Testament, and later the Great Bible and the Geneva Bible, but his version of 1535, which is known as the Coverdale Bible, is the only one bearing his name.

In order to meet the continuing demand, two London booksellers, Richard Grafton and Edward Whitchurch, published the so-called Matthew Bible in 1537. The work of preparing this edition was supposed to have been done by a certain Thomas Matthew, but as no such person seems to have existed, the name was evidently an assumed one used to hide the identity of the real translator. This is believed to be none other than Tyndale himself. After his death his friend and literary executor, John Rogers, assembled all Tyndale's Bible translations in this one volume called the Matthew Bible. Rogers used Tyndale's New Testament, his Pentateuch, and his hitherto unpublished translations of Joshua through Chronicles made during his imprisonment. Tyndale had not translated the books from Ezra through the Apocrypha, and for these Rogers used Coverdale's translation. For the first time all of Tyndale's work could be obtained in one volume. The Matthew Bible was printed in Antwerp and a royal license for its sale was issued by the English king who was unaware that he was authorizing the circulation of Tyndale's work. John Rogers suffered a fate similar to that of his friend Tyndale. When Queen Mary came to the throne he was the first martyr to be burned at Smithfield. Among all the early translators only Coverdale died in his own bed.

Following the three private publications of Tyndale, Coverdale, and "Matthew," came England's first authorized Bible, the Great Bible of 1539. This was a revision of the Matthew Bible and it was made by Coverdale. It was a handsome folio volume, beautifully printed on the best quality of paper. The court painter Hans Holbein, who probably designed the title page, left no doubt in anyone's mind that this book was fully authorized, for he showed King Henry VIII seated on a throne distributing copies of it, while a crowd of his subjects are pictured with open mouths out of which come streamers with the words "Vivat Rex." The engraving also shows Cranmer, Archbishop of Canterbury and author of the preface, together with Thomas Cromwell, the High Chamberlain of England and the man chiefly responsible for the book. Both these men later fell from the high estate in which Holbein pictured them. Cromwell was beheaded in the Tower because of his opposition to Henry VIII's policies, and Cranmer was burned at the stake in Mary's reign for his religious views.

The story of how the Great Bible was made shows that even a king could have trouble printing the Scriptures in the sixteenth century. English printers at this time did not have the equipment with which to print the sort of volume Henry VIII desired, and he therefore asked the King of France for the help of his famous printer Regnault. This was granted and the work was begun in Paris under Regnault's direction with the Englishmen, Grafton and Whitchurch, assisting. Officers of the Inquisition, learning what was going on, halted the presses and confiscated the sheets. Some of these they burned and others they sold to a Parisian milliner for wrapping paper. Fortunately the English ambassador in Paris rescued a large number of the sheets and succeeded in smuggling them out of France and sending them to England where the book was finally completed.

As evidence of the great change which had taken place in the English church since Tyndale's day, clergymen were now ordered to set up this Bible "in sum conuenient place wythin the said church that ye haue cure of, where-as your parishioners may most comodiously resorte to the same and reade it." At St. Paul's Cathedral in London no less than six copies were chained to six of the pillars and all day long these were surrounded by crowds of people earnestly listening while someone read from the new book. The reading caused many an argument in which voices rose so high and the crowds became so noisy that Bible reading had to be forbidden whenever there was a service in the Cathedral. Far and wide throughout England copies of the Great Bible were distributed. Today, after four hundred years, there is at least one little country church that still treasures its original copy of the first authorized English Bible, the Great Bible of 1539. Though its text was superseded by later translations, the Psalter of the Great Bible is still used in the *Book of Common Prayer.*

The Bible and its friends fared badly at the end of Henry VIII's reign when the versions of Tyndale and Coverdale were banned by act of Parliament and it was decreed that "no woman unless she be noble or gentle woman might read to herself alone, and no artificers, apprentices, journeymen, servingmen . . . husbandmen, or labourers" should read the Scriptures under penalty of fines and imprisonment. During Queen Mary's reign religious persecution flared up again. The Bibles set up in churches were burned and no longer was the English Bible read in church services. It was at this time that both John Rogers and Cranmer suffered martyrdom and Coverdale was forced to flee to Geneva. With him went nearly eight hundred refugees from religious persecution.

The next three Bibles were rival volumes put out by different religious parties: the Puritans, the English Bishops, and the Roman Catholics. In the Swiss city of Geneva lived the group of English Puritans who had fled from home during the persecutions under Queen Mary. These refugees issued a Bible in 1560, edited by William Whittingham and named for the city in which they had found safety. This became the Bible of the Reformation and of John Calvin and John Knox. It was a scholarly revision with helpful notes in the margin. This was the first Bible to divide its chapters into numbered verses thus making them convenient for reference and quotation. It was smaller in size than the Great Bible and less expensive. All these things made the Geneva Bible popular for two generations as the family Bible of England. Moreover, this was the Bible which the early colonists brought with them to America. It is said that its phrases echo in English literature from Shakespeare to John Bunyan. It was commonly called the "Breeches Bible" because the translation of Genesis 3:7 reads: "They sewed fig leaves together and made themselves breeches."

Few books are popular enough to require reprinting but from 1560 to 1640 the Geneva Bible was issued in one hundred and fifty editions. If it had not been for this great popularity, the Bishops' Bible of 1568 might never have appeared. Matthew Parker, Archbishop of Canterbury, was alarmed to see a Puritan version containing many controversial notes, supplanting the authorized Great Bible of the Church. He knew that people found the Geneva volume cheaper and more convenient to use in their homes and that they often criticized the Great Bible, which was appointed to be read in churches, as an inferior translation. To remedy this the Bishops' Bible was prepared and printed. It was a magnificent folio volume bearing on the title page a rather ugly portrait of Queen Elizabeth holding the scepter and orb. This was the official Bible which every bishop was supposed to set up in his hall for the use of servants and strangers. As single copies cost nearly a hundred dollars it never supplanted the smaller and cheaper Geneva Bible in English homes.

So far all the English versions belonged to the Tyndale "family," being either revisions of his text or based on his work. The next version to appear was issued by the Roman Catholics, who heartily disapproved of the current English versions. While this Roman Catholic version did not belong to the Tyndale group it was nevertheless influenced by his work. The translator was a former Oxford scholar named Gregory Martin who fled to France with many other Roman Catholics when Elizabeth succeeded to the throne of England. The refugees settled in the French city of Rheims and later moved to Douay. They established a college in which Gregory Martin became lecturer in Hebrew and Holy Scripture. He set himself a stint of translating two chapters a day and by 1582 the Rheims New Testament was finished. The complete Rheims-Douay Bible did not appear until 1609.

In a footnote to history we learn that the question of which Bible version to use was a burning issue in the sixteenth century. On the night before her execution Mary Queen of Scots swore her innocence on a copy of the Rheims New Testament, but the Earl of Kent declared her oath was invalid because the book was not a proper translation.

The Rheims-Douay Bible was translated directly from the Vulgate and many of Jerome's old Latin words reappear in it. Here is a typical passage:

> Our Father which art in heauen, sanctified be thy name . . . Guie us to day our supersubstantial bread.

Its characteristic Latin flavor and sonorous music influenced the next translation, the King James Version of 1611. This was to gather together all the excellencies of previous Bibles and produce what is undoubtedly the finest version of the Bible in any language.

## ◆ *43* ◆

## *The Authorized Version of 1611*

### THE KING JAMES VERSION

ON Monday, January 16, 1604, a group of solemn Church leaders filed into the council chamber at Hampton Court Palace for a meeting with the new king, James I, to settle difficulties between two rival groups: the High Church party and the Low Church or Puritan party. In this very palace during the Christmas season just ended James had entertained the far more picturesque group of the King's Company of Actors to which belonged a certain William Shakespeare. The players had performed six plays in the Great Hall. But the Christmas festivities were over and in place of the actors, a group of bishops and clergy now awaited the arrival of His Majesty.

James came in, took his seat, and opened the conference. In appearance he was anything but regal, for the quilted doublet he wore as a protection against assassination made him seem more ungainly than he really was. The assembled leaders looked in vain for a likeness between him and his beautiful mother, the ill-fated Mary Stuart, Queen of Scots. Unfortunately the King's manners were as disappointing as his appearance. He rudely scolded the Puritans and declared that he would force them to accept his point of view or else drive them out of his kingdom. The conference seemed doomed to failure.

At this point, when deadlock promised to be the only result, Dr. John Reynolds rose and made a suggestion. Everyone listened to him intently, for Reynolds was the spokesman for the Puritan party, besides being a famous linguist, scholar, and the president of Corpus Christi College at Oxford. He moved that a new translation of the Bible be made because those being used at that time were, as he said, "corrupt and not answerable to the truth of the Original."

Taken by surprise at this unexpected proposal and feeling perhaps a touch of remorse for his rudeness to the Puritans, James quickly agreed to the motion. He was himself something of a Bible student, having translated the Psalms into verse and written a paraphrase of Revelation. He declared that special pains should be taken to produce a uniform translation and he drew up rules for the translators to follow, adding that he had never yet seen a Bible well translated into English.

The Hampton Court Conference adjourned without accomplishing the purpose for which it met; nevertheless, from the point of view of the English Bible it was one of the most important conferences on record. Soon fifty-four of England's greatest scholars were appointed for the work of translation, though only forty-seven of these can be identified. They were divided into six companies, two working at Oxford, two at Cambridge, and two at Westminster. In the Oxford company were Dr. John Reynolds who had suggested the undertaking, and Dr. Miles Smith who "had Hebrew at his fingers' ends." Among the Cambridge group were John Bois, "a precocious Greek and Hebrew scholar," and Andrew Downes, described as a man "composed of Greek and industry." The Westminster company was presided over by Lancelot Andrewes, later Bishop of Winchester, of whom it was said that he "might have been interpreter-general at Babel." This group also included the greatest Arabic scholar of the day, William Bedwell.

The three companies of translators were guided by elaborate rules which instructed them to follow the Bishops' Bible as far as the truth of the original permitted, but allowed them to use

Tyndale's, Coverdale's, Matthew's, and the Geneva Bible wherever these translations were better. Actually, we know that they used the Rheims New Testament as well, for many of its phrases are incorporated in their work. For more than two years the scholars translated, revised, corrected, and copied: As soon as one group finished its assigned portion, a copy of it was sent to the other five companies for criticism. In those days many thick Bible manuscripts must have shuttled back and forth between Oxford, Cambridge, and Westminster. Slowly a new translation emerged, based upon the best work of a generation of translators and perfected by the painstaking labor of the foremost scholars of the day. Speaking for all translators Dr. Miles Smith wrote in the preface:

> Truly (good Christian Reader) we never thought from the beginning, that we should need to make a new Translation, nor yet to make of a bad one a good one . . . but to make a good one better, or out many good ones, one principal one, not justly to be excepted against; that hath been our endeavor . . . To that purpose there were many chosen, that were greater in other men's eyes than in their own, and that sought the truth rather than their own praise.

At length, in 1611 there issued from the London press of Robert Barker the first edition of this Bible. On the engraved title page amid pictures of Moses, Aaron, the four evangelists, and other saints, appears a statement of what this volume actually is:

> The Holy Bible, Conteyning the Old Testament and the New: Newly translated out of the Originall tongues and with the former translations diligently compared and revised by his Maiesties speciall comandement. Appointed to be read in Churches. Imprinted at London by Robert Barker, Printer to the Kings most excellent Maiestie. Anno Dom. 1611.

Copies of this large, beautifully printed, first edition of the Bible of 1611 still exist, and book collectors offer large sums for them. If you ever see a very old King James Bible, turn to the third chapter of Ruth. If the fifteenth verse reads: "He measured six measures of barley and laid it on her and *he* went into the citie," you may know that you hold in your hands the historic first edition which came from Robert Barker's press in 1611. "He" was a misprint which was corrected in later editions to read "she went into the citie." From this misprint came the name by which this rare first edition is known among collectors: the "He" Bible.

The first edition of 1611 is thought to have numbered twenty thousand copies, a large gain over Tyndale's first three thousand copies. How many copies of the Authorized Bible have been printed since 1611 no one knows, but it is certainly many millions. If the words: "Authorized King James Version" appear on the title page of your Bible it is one of the many editions of the great 1611 version. The Authorized Version has been the Bible of the English-speaking world for more than three hundred years.

Many Authorized Bibles printed today contain the original dedication to James I. Instead of being very brief, in the style of modern dedications, this is a veritable jungle of flattering words offered to the King. The translators praise him as "the sun in his strength" and "the principal Mover and Author of the work," while they say of themselves "we are poor instruments to make God's holy Truth to be yet more and more known unto the people." Today we see all this in a different light. The King's part in the undertaking appears very small to us, for, aside from his initial encouragement, he did nothing for it and, as far as we know, he did not contribute one penny toward the expenses. It is ironic that this is named the King James Version. In unconscious tribute to the quality of this Bible, people sometimes misname it the "St. James" Version. Nothing, however, could be farther from the truth than this and James I would surely be amazed to hear himself so canonized. This incorrect title led to the following conversation between a bookseller and his customer.

"I want a St. James Bible," said the customer.

"I suppose you mean the King James Version," murmured the bookseller.

"No I don't," snapped the customer, "I don't want any of

those newfangled things at all. What I want is the Bible just as St. James himself originally wrote it!"

It is not to King James but to the translators that the highest possible praise belongs. They brought to their work not only their knowledge of Hebrew, Greek, and many other tongues but their mastery of the English language as well. In their hands this became an instrument capable of expressing mankind's highest dreams and aspirations. Their phrases possess a melody, rhythm, and strength that has never been surpassed. They took the vivid, majestic translations of Tyndale, Coverdale, and the rest, and out of these created the final splendor of the Authorized Version. The Latin and the earlier English versions influenced them greatly, but the subtle music pervading their work is their own glorious achievement. Who can say how it was done? One can only compare and marvel.

In the following comparisons modern spelling has been introduced.

*Tyndale:* Come unto me all ye that labor and are laden and I will ease you.

*Authorized Version:* Come unto me, all ye that labour and are heavy laden, and I will give you rest.

MATTHEW 11:28

*Coverdale:* Her ways are pleasant ways and all her paths are peaceable.

*Geneva Bible:* Her ways are ways of pleasure and all her paths prosperity.

*Authorized Version:* Her ways are ways of pleasantness, and all her paths are peace.

PROVERBS 3:17

*Matthew:* Open your gates, O ye princes, let the everlasting doors be opened.

*Authorized Version:* Lift up your heads, O ye gates; and be ye lift up, ye everlasting doors.

PSALM 24:7

*Coverdale:* When the morning stars gave me praise, and when all the angels of God rejoiced.

*Matthew and Bishops':* When the morning stars praised me together, and all the Children of God rejoiced triumphantly.

*Authorized Version:* When the morning stars sang together, and all the sons of God shouted for joy.

JOB 38:7

*Coverdale and Matthew:* So that they shall break their swords and spears, to make scythes, sickles and saws thereof. From that time forth shall not one people lift up weapon against another, neither shall they learn to fight from henceforth.

*Authorized Version:* They shall beat their swords into plowshares, and their spears into pruninghooks: nation shall not lift up sword against nation, neither shall they learn war any more.

Isaiah 2:4

These comparisons help us to understand why the Authorized Version supplanted the older translations and soon won first place for itself wherever English is spoken. For more than three centuries it reigned supreme, becoming the Bible of both home and Church. Scholars pored over its text; preachers expounded its meanings; choirs chanted its words; children learned to read from its pages; humble men and women read it, their only book. Its ideas entered into the substance of our thoughts. Its expressive phrases were incorporated into everyday speech. Its brilliant music helped create the rhythms of our English language. People are apt to listen to a passage of harmonious, polished, majestic prose and say: "It *sounds* like the Bible." English literature from 1611 traces the ancestry of its harmonies, its rhythms, and its vocabulary back to the Authorized Version. It can be said of this as of no other book that it is woven into the fabric of our life. This Bible is indeed part of the very warp and woof of our civilization.

# 44

## The Discovery of Ancient Manuscripts

### CODICES AND PALIMPSESTS

ONE day in 1628 a package from the East was unloaded at an English port. It had been sent by the Patriarch of Constantinople, Cyril Lucaris, and it contained a gift for Charles I. Inside the package the King found an old handwritten Greek Bible consisting of nearly eight hundred vellum leaves, each measuring ten by twelve inches and containing two columns of beautifully written Greek. So far there was nothing unusual about it; the libraries of Europe were full of manuscript Greek Bibles. Not sharing his father's interest in the Scriptures, Charles I turned his book over to the scholars. They were amazed when they saw its distinctive handwriting. All the manuscript Bibles they had ever seen before had been written in a running hand called "cursive" or "miniscule," a style of writing adopted in the ninth century. This manuscript, however, was written in capital letters known as "uncials." Clearly, this Greek codex from Constantinople was older than any other they had previously known, for it must have been made before the ninth century. Exactly when and where had it been written: that was the question.

Handwriting experts were now consulted. The clue to the date of a manuscript is its style of writing. These styles change from century to century and from country to country as much as do fashions in clothes. From their study of manuscripts whose date and place of origin are known experts can accurately determine these facts for a particular manuscript. The experts said that this Greek codex was written in the style employed in Alexandria in the fifth century. It was, therefore, named the Codex Alexandrinus. Charles I had it bound in four volumes decorated with the royal arms and the letters "C R" and he placed it in his library at Abingdon House, Westminster.

There it had a narrow escape. One night a fire broke out in the library and this priceless manuscript was saved only by the prompt action of the custodian, the famous classical scholar, Richard Bentley. A bystander described how Bentley, clothed only in his nightgown, his great wig awry, rushed from the burning building with the Codex Alexandrinus under his arm. When the royal library was presented to the nation, the codex was deposited in the British Museum where it is today.

Seventeenth-century English scholars realized what a valuable manuscript this codex was. When Erasmus issued his epoch-making Greek New Testament in 1516 he had copied the text from Greek manuscripts written in the cursive hand, the oldest of which was an eleventh-century text. As the Codex Alexandrinus was six hundred years older than the texts Erasmus used, scholars had good reason to be enthusiastic about it. They now possessed a text written before the thousands of copying errors of the Middle Ages had produced wide variations. It was unfortunate that it arrived in England just eighteen years too late to be used in preparing the Authorized Version.

The Codex Alexandrinus came first in the long parade of ancient manuscripts. It awoke a new interest in the Greek text of the Bible and it fired experts with zeal to find older and better manuscripts. All over Europe they ransacked old libraries and explored shelves and cupboards where manuscripts had been collecting dust for centuries. Many cursive and a few uncial manuscripts came to light. Some of these had been rescued from Constantinople by Greek scholars who fled before the invading Turks in 1453.

One of the manuscripts brought from Constantinople was a twelfth-century book of sermons of the Syrian Father, Ephraem. Catherine de Medici bought this old book in Florence and added it to her collection which was later given to the Royal Library at Paris when she became Queen of France. There it remained unrecognized until about 1700 when the French scholar, Pierre Allix, noticed a faint writing underneath the words of Ephraem's sermons. It is not unusual to find books written on sheets from which the original writing has been partly erased. As vellum was expensive, many an old book was taken apart, its original writing washed and scraped off, and its sheets used for another book. Ephraem's sermons had been written on just such secondhand sheets. A vellum book containing writing superimposed on older writing is called a "palimpsest."

The French scholars at the Royal Library were not interested in Ephraem's sermons, but they were exceedingly curious about what was written underneath. By applying chemicals they revived the older writing and to their astonishment saw that this was as great and rare a treasure as the Codex Alexandrinus. The underneath writing was a fifth-century Greek copy of the New Testament. It was not easy to decipher the faded underneath writing of the Codex Ephraemi, but a hundred years later this was brilliantly accomplished by Count Tischendorf, of whom we shall hear more later.

Before long two other Greek Bibles came to light even older than the Codex Alexandrinus or the palimpsest of Ephraem. One of these is the Codex Vaticanus, generally considered the most important manuscript Bible in existence. Like the Codex Alexandrinus it is believed to have been made in Egypt at Alexandria, but it was written a hundred years earlier and scholars date it before A.D. 350. No one knows its long history nor how it finally come to rest in the great library of the Vatican.

It was doubtless originally made for some important person or some great church in Constantinople, where it remained until the Turks captured the city in 1453. Who brought it to Rome we do not know. By 1481 it was safely stored and catalogued in the Vatican Library, but for the next three hundred years no one seems to have realized what a superb manuscript it was. When Napoleon conquered Italy he carried this codex off to Paris with his other loot. There, a certain Leonhard Hug examined it and realized its great age and its unusual textual purity. After Napoleon's fall, France was required to return this valuable fourth-century codex to the Vatican, and before long its entire text was reproduced in photographic facsimilies for the use of scholars. Today the Codex Vaticanus is recognized as one of the oldest and best authorities in existence for the Greek text of the Bible, and it is the supreme treasure of the Vatican Library.

The story of our other fourth-century codex is one of the romances of Biblical scholarship. The man responsible for its discovery was Count Tischendorf, the German Bible scholar who deciphered the Codex Ephraemi. Whenever he visited ancient libraries in remote corners of the world he always searched for old Greek manuscript Bibles. In the month of May, 1844, he visited the Monastery of St. Catherine at the foot of Mount Sinai, near the southern end of the triangular-shaped peninsular of Sinai. One day in the great hall he saw a basket full of old parchments which the librarian told him were about to be burned as trash. Tischendorf looked these over and to his amazement found a pile of sheets from a Greek Bible older than any he had ever seen. The uncial handwriting indicated that this book belonged to the fourth century. Here was an incomparable treasure about to be destroyed! From Tischendorf's undisguised excitement the monastery authorities realized their mistake and gathered up the pile of old sheets. Forty-three of them, including Chronicles, Jeremiah, Nehemiah, and Esther, they allowed Tischendorf to take away, but the others they kept at Sinai.

The memory of the other sheets haunted him for fifteen years until finally he returned to St. Catherine's Monastery, hoping to see them again. He spent several days in the chilly, dark library without finding the great treasure he had once saved from the fire. Perhaps it had been burned after all, he thought, or some other scholar had carried it off. As his visit had proved a failure and as nothing was to be gained by remaining longer, he ordered his Bedouin to bring the dromedaries to the gate the next morning so that he might return to Cairo.

The evening before he left, Tischendorf was invited by the steward of the monastery to his cell for refreshment after their walk. Their conversation eventually came around to the subject of Greek Bibles.

"And I, too, have a Septuagint," said the steward, taking from the shelf over his door, where extra coffee cups were stored, a large volume wrapped in red cloth. Removing the cover, Tischendorf saw the very book for which he had been searching. Here were the fragments he had rescued from the basket fifteen years before, and here also were other parts of the Old Testament and the New Testament. Trying to disguise his great joy, Tischendorf asked if he might examine the book in his own room. Permission was granted and all night long in his cold, dimly lit cell Tischendorf studied this ancient and important manuscript.

In return for a favor, the monks of St. Catherine's Monastery gave this fourth-century codex to the Czar of Russia. A Bedouin brought it by camel from Sinai to Cairo, and from there Tischendorf carried it to the Summer Palace at Tsarskoye Selo where it was presented to their Imperial Majesties in November, 1859. The scholarly world was electrified by Tischendorf's discovery and one learned Bible student was heard to remark:

"I would rather have discovered the Sinaitic manuscript than the Koh-i-noor [diamond] of the Queen of England."

The text was immediately printed for the use of scholars, and photographic facsimiles were made, but the manuscript itself remained in Russia until 1933. In that year the Soviet Government sold it to the British Museum for the equivalent of half a million dollars, part of which was raised by public subscription. It remains in the Museum with the Codex Alexandrinus, the two outstanding manuscript Bibles in England.

The Codex Sinaiticus is now bound in two volumes measuring thirteen by fifteen inches. Of an original 730 leaves only about half survive; of these 347 are in the British Museum, while the 43 Old Testament leaves first obtained by Tischendorf are in Leipzig. When the volumes are opened eight columns of beautiful uncial writing are spread out, four to a page, giving the effect of an exposed section of a roll book. Three different scribes can be identified from their handwriting and from their characteristic spelling mistakes. One was a good speller, another only fair, while the third was very poor. As most of their spelling errors can be traced to an incorrect hearing of sounds, it seems likely that the scribes wrote from dictation and that other codices were made simultaneously with this one.

Whether or not the Codex Sinaiticus was one of the fifty Bibles ordered by Constantine, it must have originated between A.D. 300 and 350. It was surely made before the New Testament canon was finally decided upon, for it contains two non-canonical books: the *Epistle of Barnabas* and the *Shepherd of Hermas*. The text of this great fourth-century uncial codex together with that of the Codex Vaticanus push back our knowledge of the Greek text of the New Testament to A.D. 350 at least, thus bypassing the copying mistakes of the thousand years that followed.

We should mention two important fifth-century codices which aid scholars in restoring the original Greek text of the New Testament. One of these is the Codex Bezae consisting of the Gospels, Acts, and some of the Epistles. It was rescued from the sack of Lyons in 1562 by the Reformation scholar, Theodore Beza, and presented by him to Cambridge University. The second codex was purchased in Egypt by C. L. Freer. It is an important fifth-century copy of the Gospels on parchment.

Today this codex is in Washington and it is called the Codex Washingtonianus.

The Bible possesses a curiously living quality which makes it far more like a growing thing than an inert monument carved in stone. Through the centuries its roots grow deeper as scholars discover older and more trustworthy manuscripts. Bending over timeworn codices with their faded writing, or modern reprints, or photostatic copies of old manuscripts, comparing this word with that, and this translation with some other, they begin to discover what the original text was. Theirs is an exacting study requiring a knowledge of many ancient languages, and the patience to advance slowly word by word and phrase by phrase. This study has more fascination than a crossword puzzle or a game of anagrams. Though we are farther from the original authors of the Bible than any other generation, it is safe to say that we know more about its origins than our predecessors did, and that our knowledge of the text far exceeds that of St. Jerome, Erasmus, Tyndale, or the translators of 1611.

Deeper roots mean higher branches. New knowledge of the original text created demands for new and better translations. As we shall see in the next chapter, Bible editing and translating did not cease in 1611.

# 45

## Translating Continues

### THE REVISED AND OTHER VERSIONS

THOUGH the Authorized Version with all its stately beauty and splendid imagery reigned supreme for more than two and a half centuries, other translations were made under its august shadow. Even the Authorized Version, which has been called the "noblest monument of English prose," was itself constantly improved and corrected. Its spelling was modernized, its punctuation revised, and several thousand other changes were introduced. This, however, was not enough. The English language is constantly discarding old words, introducing new ones, changing meanings, and altering forms. This fact together with the new Bible discoveries soon prompted people to ask for new translations.

As early as 1755 John Wesley published a revised New Testament "for plain, unlettered men who understand only their Mother Tongue." Using a different Greek text from that employed in 1611, he made a careful translation that includes twelve thousand variations from the Authorized Version.

When Dr. Edward Harwood made his translation in 1768 he declared that he would be rewarded "if men of cultivated and improved minds, especially YOUTH, could be allured by the innocent stratagem of a *modern style,* to read a book, which is now, alas! too generally neglected and disregarded by the young and gay." Possibly the "young and gay" of the eighteenth century were attracted by his style, which he says he tried to make a thing of "freedom, spirit, and elegance." The 1611 translation of Matthew 5:17 is: "Think not that I am come to destroy the law, or the prophets: I am not come to destroy, but to fulfil." For this Harwood wrote:

> Do not think that the design of my coming into the world is to abrogate the law of Moses, and the prophets—I am only come to supply their deficiencies, and to give mankind a more complete and perfect system of morals.

He wove this baroque eighteenth-century prayer to replace "Give us this day our daily bread":

> As thou hast hitherto most mercifully supplied our wants, deny us not the necessaries and conveniences of life, while thou art pleased to continue us in it.

Benjamin Franklin proposed that the Authorized Version be revised and its language brought up to date, but little seems to have been done about this in America until the end of the eighteenth century. Then the first American translation was made by Charles Thomson, an Irish-born immigrant who arrived in America in 1727 and became the first secretary of the United States Congress. It was Thomson who presented George Washington with the letter notifying him that he had been elected first President of the United States. One day in Philadelphia Charles Thomson bought a strange old book at an auction. Even the auctioneer admitted it was written in "outlandish letters" and Thomson himself, though greatly intrigued by it, had no idea what the book was. When he discovered that the letters were Greek and the book was the Septuagint, he learned Greek and translated his volume. In 1808 his version was published in Philadelphia by a woman publisher named Jane Aitken. Twenty-six years before, her father, Robert Aitken, had published the first English Bible in America with a title page bearing the date, 1782, and stating that copies could be bought at Robert Aitken's shop "at Pope's Head, Three Doors Above the Coffee House, in Market Street."

We must return to England for the most noteworthy translation made after that of 1611. When Bishop Wilberforce rose to make a motion in the Convocation of the Province of Canterbury on February 10, 1870, he had three things on his mind: the new Bible discoveries, the improved Greek dictionaries and grammars, and the antique language of the 1611 Bible. It was high time, he thought, to correct and improve the King James Version. Accordingly, he made a motion that the New Testament be revised. This was amended to include the Old Testament and was quickly passed. When the Province of York was invited to cooperate with Canterbury, it declined, saying that it deplored any change in the text of the Scriptures. Elsewhere the project was received more favorably. Though scholars of the Church of England formed the majority in both the Old and New Testament companies, Presbyterian, Baptist, Congregationalist, Methodist, and Unitarian scholars assisted them.

On the morning of January 22, 1870, the twenty scholars of the New Testament company met in Westminster Abbey and, in preparation for their work, celebrated Holy Communion in the beautiful Henry VII Chapel. Proceeding through the Abbey, past the tomb of Edward the Confessor and the high altar where the kings and queens of England are crowned, past the Poet's Corner and by way of the Great Cloisters, they came to the historic old room in the Deanery where Henry IV died. There beneath tapestries which give to this room its name of Jerusalem Chamber, the revisers began their long labor.

For ten years they worked four days each month from eleven in the morning until six in the evening. The doors of Jerusalem Chamber used to be closed to visitors on those days and to anyone curious enough to ask why, the attendant replied: "The New Testament is sitting, sir."

Unhurriedly these eminent scholars studied each passage, proposed corrections, weighed the evidence for and against each change, and made their decisions. Each day they completed about thirty-five verses. At the same time the Old Testament company met in Westminster Chapter Library and for fourteen years they worked in a similar manner.

Meanwhile in America a company of translators met in Bible House in New York and received advance copies of the proposed English revision. After study and discussion they sent their comments and corrections back to London where the English translators again studied the revision and considered all the American proposals. No wonder that it was ten years before the revisers ended their labors and on November 11, 1880, met in the Church of St. Martin's-in-the-Fields in London for a service of thanksgiving.

The enormous task of printing the Revised Version of the New Testament was completed on May 17, 1881, by the Oxford and Cambridge presses working at top speed. The Oxford Press had already received advance orders for a million copies and the Cambridge Press nearly as many more. Public interest in this New Testament was greater than for any book ever published. All that day of May 17 wagons and lorries filled with Bibles choked the streets around Paternoster Row in London where the Oxford Press was located. Every London bookseller clamored for copies and the railway stations and wharves were piled with boxes of Bibles ready to be shipped to every English town and to almost every place in the world where English was spoken.

The first copies of the Revised New Testament reached New York by fast ocean steamer on Friday, May 20. Subscribers to the Chicago *Tribune* and the Chicago *Times* woke up on the morning of May 22 to find the entire Revised New Testament printed in their Sunday paper. In order to accomplish this feat the 118,000 words of the Gospels, Acts, and Romans were telegraphed to Chicago from New York as soon as the new Bible was received there from England. The remainder of the New Testament in book form reached Chicago on the evening of May 21 in time to be set up in type for the next morning.

Meanwhile, the Old Testament company kept steadily at their longer labor and on May 19, 1885, the Revised Old Testament was published with the Revised New Testament. The Apocrypha was not completed until ten years later.

The American scholars were somewhat disappointed that the more conservative English revisers had not seen fit to incorporate many of their suggestions in the text itself but had printed these in an appendix. It was also true that the English revisers had used certain typically English expressions unfamiliar to American readers. Because of these facts the American scholars prepared their own independent edition, and Thomas Nelson and Sons published this as the American Standard Version in 1901. The title page sets forth its ancestry.

The
HOLY BIBLE
containing the
OLD AND NEW TESTAMENTS
Translated out of the Original Tongues
Being the Version Set Forth A.D. 1611
Compared With The Most Ancient Authorities And Revised
A.D. 1881-1885
Newly Edited by the American Revision Committee
A.D. 1901
Standard Edition
New York
Thomas Nelson & Sons

The American Standard Version, stemming directly from the original Hebrew and Greek, is largely the King James Version of 1611 which, as we already know, was itself ninety per cent the work of Tyndale. All the English versions were studied by the American committee. From Tyndale's first printed New Testament of 1525 the weighing and comparing, the winnowing and sifting, the correcting and rewriting had gone on for nearly four hundred years, each successive group of scholars building upon the vast labors of its predecessors.

What was the result of all this labor? How were the English Revised and the American Standard Versions received? At first the revisions were greeted with outcries of protest. Favorite passages had been reworded and time-honoréd phrases cut out. Some people went so far as to say that the very word of God had been changed. When the outcries died down people saw that the revisions clarified many an obscure passage, and that on the score of correctness the new versions were superior to the beloved King James Version. But in the quest for a perfectly faithful translation the revisers had often spoiled the majesty and rhythm of the old sentences. The revisers had not laid hands on the Authorized Version in ignorance of its beauty, for in their preface they paid tribute to its "simplicity, dignity, and power," to "the music of its cadences and the felicities of its rhythm."

Though there can be no question of the superior beauty of the King James Bible, every serious Bible student consults one of the revised versions. There he finds the old verses of 1611 swept away and the text printed in the paragraphs of modern prose. The footnotes remind him that the translation of many words and phrases is still uncertain and that even the "ancient authorities," such as the Codex Vaticanus, the Sinaiticus, and the Alexandrinus, sometimes disagree. English-speaking people were indeed fortunate to have not only the great literary masterpiece of the King James Bible, but the outstanding scholarly achievements of the Revised Versions as well. Before long they became heirs of further Bible riches.

## 46

### Buried Treasure

#### NEW BIBLE DISCOVERIES

TISCHENDORF'S discovery of the Codex Sinaiticus did not end the search for Bible manuscripts nor the enthusiastic hunt for buried treasures of any kind that might shed new light on the Bible. People asked questions about the authenticity of the Scriptures. They said: "How do you know that the Greek text of the Codex Vaticanus and Codex Sinaiticus is not hopelessly different from the original text written more than two hundred years before them?" To answer this question scholars needed to find earlier manuscripts. But where could they look?

People also asked: "Are you sure that you are translating the Greek of the New Testament correctly? After all, it is a peculiar Greek and quite different from that of the classical writers." One scholar thought that this "Biblical Greek" was probably the everyday language spoken in the first and second centuries, but he needed to find such things as ordinary letters and business reports of this period to prove his theory. Such nonliterary writings as this usually end on a trash heap. There was little hope that documents of this nature survived.

A third question involved the contents of the Bible itself. "How accurately do the historical statements in the Old and

New Testaments conform with authentic historical facts?" **Perhaps**, thought the archaeologists, if we dig near the sites mentioned in the Bible we might unearth evidence to support Bible statements.

In these three areas of text, translation, and historical accuracy new knowledge was earnestly sought and at length found, most of it buried under old writing, or hidden beneath the sands of Egypt, or unearthed from forgotten cities. This was a period of buried treasures.

People did not dream that manuscripts older than the two great codices written before A.D. 350 still survived, for as late as A.D. 303 Emperor Diocletian ordered all Christian churches destroyed and all Bibles burned. Scholars considered themselves fortunate to have texts as old as the Codex Vaticanus and the Codex Sinaiticus. To be sure, there was a long gap between fourth-century copies and first and second-century originals, but there was little expectation of finding a manuscript to bridge this gap.

Then one day in February, 1892, two ladies arrived by camel at the monastery of St. Catherine at Mount Sinai made famous by Count Tischendorf's discovery. Their native camel drivers must have wondered why two English women had journeyed all the way from Cambridge to Sinai and why they had brought cameras. The ladies were Mrs. Agnes S. Lewis and her twin sister, Mrs. J. Y. Gibson, both students of Oriental languages and, like Tischendorf, in quest of ancient manuscripts. The librarian of the monastery brought out an armful of these from a little chest in a dark closet and carried them into the daylight for the English ladies to examine. Mrs. Lewis was the first to see the palimpsest. It was an unattractive object, grimy and stained, and its pages were stuck together with some greasy substance. The sisters boiled water in a kettle and with great care and patience managed to steam the pages open. The upper writing, dating from about A.D. 697, contained the biographies of women saints. This did not especially interest the two Englishwomen, for in a palimpsest it is, of course, the underneath writing that arouses curiosity. Mrs. Lewis brushed the faintly visible, older writing with hydrosulphide of ammonia and revived the ink enough to see that underneath the saints' lives was a copy of the Gospels in Syriac. As Syriac was one of the first languages into which the New Testament was translated, she thought this palimpsest might prove interesting. Mrs. Lewis and her sister photographed all its vellum leaves and took their photographs home for careful study.

When the difficult feat of deciphering the underneath writing had been accomplished, scholars were amazed at the unexpected treasure Mrs. Lewis had brought to light. This Syriac copy of the Gospels, though made at about the same time as the Codex Sinaiticus, was derived from a much older Greek text. This was its great importance. By translating the Old Syriac Gospels back into Greek, scholars obtained a Greek text used in the second century, possibly as early as A.D. 150. This text brought them very near to the time when the Gospels were actually written. Scholars believe that of all the manuscripts we now possess the Old Syriac palimpsest of Sinai alone preserves the original reading of some Gospel passages. This ancient Syriac palimpsest may well be one of the most important copies of the Gospels in existence. It forms a bridge between the fourth-century codices and the first-century originals. Today this book remains in the Convent at Mount Sinai in the mahogany box Mrs. Lewis had made for it and presented to the monks. The box is lined with cedar and has two lids, one of glass through which the contents may be seen without being handled. The words inscribed on its silver label are translated:

> The four Holy Gospels in Syriac. Agnes, the foreigner, has given this casket for the Sacred Scriptures not without gratitude to the famous monks.

It required hydrosulphide of ammonia to bring out the buried writing of the Syriac palimpsest but it took archaeologists' shovels to unearth buried manuscripts. Scholars knew that books made earlier than the two fourth-century vellum codices were papyrus books. Papyrus rots in the dampness or crumbles when exposed to wear and dryness. Was there any place in the East where climatic conditions made the survival of papyrus books a possibility? As early as 1778 Egyptian natives, digging in the hot dry sand near Fayum on the Nile, had come upon some large brown papyrus rolls, which, having no value to them, they had burned! This story of rolls preserved in the Egyptian sands gave a clue to two Oxford men, B. P. Grenfell and A. S. Hunt. In 1897 they made excavations around Oxyrhynchus in Egypt and unearthed an ancient rubbish pile filled with papyri. Enormous interest was aroused when a sheet of hitherto unknown sayings of Jesus was found among these papyri. Besides this third-century document they found a fragment of the Gospel of Matthew from the same period and many other documents to which we shall return later.

The most amazing discovery of all was a torn papyrus sheet unearthed by Grenfell and Hunt in 1920 and sold to the John Rylands Library at the University of Manchester, England. It is only a tiny fragment containing the five verses of John 18:31 to 33, 37, 38, but its importance far overshadowed its size. When its handwriting was analyzed, experts gave it a date before A.D. 150. This, then, is the oldest known fragment of any part of the New Testament. Its writer might have spoken to men who had seen Jesus. The great age of this fragment silences critics who once tried to prove that the Gospels were late second-century books and therefore unreliable. John's was undoubtedly the last of the Gospels to be written. If copies of it were being made in far-off Egypt before A.D. 150, the book itself was most likely written about A.D. 100. The text of this ancient fragment gives us renewed confidence in the authenticity of our later Bibles, for these verses from John reproduce a text identical with that of later manuscripts. This shows that there was not as much tampering with the text between A.D. 150 and 350 as we had feared.

The most sensational of all Bible discoveries was made by Egyptian natives digging in an old Coptic graveyard near Fayum. They unearthed a quantity of jars containing some

well-preserved papyrus books which may once have been part
of the library of an ancient religious community in Egypt.
Chester Beatty, an American living in England, bought most of
these papyri, though some now belong to the University of
Michigan and to other owners. When the books were deciphered and their contents announced in 1931, scholars were astonished. Here were three New Testament papyrus codices from
the third century. The first codex, though fragmentary, contained the four Gospels and Acts; the second codex contained
Paul's Epistles, including Hebrews, but excluding the Pastoral
Epistles; the third codex consisted of ten leaves of Revelation.

This was a find of immense importance. Though the sheets
are brittle and torn, enough of them remain to give us a good
idea of the appearance of the Bibles read by Christian people
from A.D. 200 to 250. At this period the Hebrew Scriptures and
the classical Greek and Roman books were still being written
on papyrus rolls, but Christians evidently preferred to use the
new papyrus codex which was a transitional book form between
the papyrus roll on one hand and the vellum codex on the
other. These New Testament codices show us that though there
was no such thing as a one-volume New Testament in the third
century, the various New Testament documents were beginning
to come together and to form two chief collections: first, the
Gospels and Acts; second, the Epistles of Paul. Meanwhile
other books, like Revelation, were circulating separately. Not
only do these New Testament codices show us one of the stages
in the formation of the canon, but they also provide us with
a Greek text a hundred years older than the Codex Vaticanus
and the Codex Sinaiticus.

In the Chester Beatty collection of Biblical papyri there are
a number of codices of Old Testament books. As these were
found with the New Testament documents they probably belonged to the same library. They bear witness to the importance
of the Old Testament in the early Church and they show that
Marcion's point of view about Hebrew religion was not adopted
in Egypt. In this collection there are fifty leaves of a codex

containing Numbers and Deuteronomy written in the middle of the second century, a little earlier than the John Rylands fragment from the Gospel of John. These leaves of Numbers and Deuteronomy were long thought to be from the oldest known copy of any book of the Bible.

Now, however, we have a Bible manuscript four hundred years older than this. It is, of course, a fragment from an Old Testament book, for it was written in the second century B.C. This makes it the oldest manuscript in any language of any part of the Bible. The story of its discovery is a curious one. Egyptian mummies were often encased in a kind of *papier mâché* cartonnage made from torn bits of discarded papyrus rolls. The papyrus fragments were glued together, coated with plaster, and the entire mummy case decorated with painted designs. A few broken pieces of such a cartonnage were purchased by the John Rylands Library. When the papyrus fragments were separated, they were found to be from written rolls of the most famous books of antiquity. One was part of the first book of the *Iliad*. Glued to this was a fragment from a Greek roll of Deuteronomy written about 150 B.C. For scholars the importance of this ancient Bible fragment lies in its text which agrees with that of the Codex Alexandrinus copied more than six hundred years later. Again the reliability of our fourth and fifth-century codices is demonstrated.

Lying beneath the dry sands of Egypt or wrapped around a mummy there may be other ancient papyri older than those we have. But if older documents are never found, we now have far more facts about the text of the Bible than any previous generation. We also have a better foundation for the text of the Bible than for any other ancient book. More than 170 papyrus manuscripts of the New Testament have been found, some of them, of course, only fragments. We have over 200 uncial manuscripts and more than 2,400 cursives. No other Greek book exists in so many ancient copies. Moreover, the Bible manuscripts are not as far removed in time from the original writings as are the Greek and Roman classics. The earliest known manuscript of Virgil was written 350 years after his death and this is the best record for any ancient book except the Bible. The oldest Horace manuscript was copied 900 years after his death and the oldest manuscript of Euripides, 1,600 years later. But for the Greek Bible we have the outstanding fifth-century codices; Alexandrinus, Ephraemi, Bezae, and Washingtonianus; the great fourth-century Codex Vaticanus and Codex Sinaiticus; the Chester Beatty third and second-century papyri; the Syriac palimpsest Gospels translated from a second-century Greek text; the second-century John Rylands fragment of John; and finally, the second-century B.C. fragment of Deuteronomy. These are indeed incomparable treasures. They show us that however far back we go we find a Greek text which agrees fundamentally with the text reconstructed by modern scholars from the best manuscripts. It had been feared that some important Christian doctrine or some event in Christ's life might depend upon a reading not included in the earliest texts. But this is not so. The second-century New Testament books agree with the later manuscripts and we can be satisfied with the authenticity of the New Testament. The "title-deeds of our faith" rest on secure foundations.

How well have we translated these title-deeds? Here again the papyri unearthed by Grenfell and Hunt are valuable. The two Oxford scholars found in their rubbish heap masses of non-Biblical papyri including such things as: business accounts, personal letters, wills, receipts, birth notices, leases, and invitations. These discoveries show what everyday life in New Testament days was like, but more important still, they provide samples of the kind of Greek spoken by ordinary people in the first and second centuries. This everyday Greek differed from the language of the classical authors, but, surprisingly enough, it was found to be identical with the Greek of New Testament writers. Scholars used to puzzle over what they called "Biblical Greek" and wonder why Paul, Luke, Matthew, and the others did not employ a more literary language. Now this problem was solved. The New Testament authors wrote, not in a unique jargon of their own, but in the common spoken language of their day. They were not writing for literary effect but simply to be understood by their contemporaries. These non-Biblical papyri showed scholars how to translate the New Testament more accurately.

Finally we must ask what the recent archaeological discoveries show as to the historical accuracy of the Bible itself. Volumes have been written on this subject, and the ancient sites from Egypt to Mesopotamia have yielded much evidence. Such places as: Tel el-Amarna, Ras Shamra, Ur, Babylon, Jericho, Lachish, Bethshean, Megiddo, Sinai, Jerusalem, Capernaum, Antioch, Ephesus, and Corinth, have been excavated and have disclosed a wealth of written tablets, broken pottery, burned bricks, bones, jewelry, inscriptions, foundation stones, and other remains of antiquity which archaeologists know how to translate into historical facts. While few of these discoveries concern the Bible narratives directly, most of them fill in the background and prove that Bible writers reported their times with a remarkable degree of accuracy. Though they were not primarily historians they usually succeeded in recording ancient facts correctly. Archaeology has not undermined the reliability of the Old and New Testaments. Instead, it has reinforced it. Many of the buried treasures brought to light have been of inestimable value in increasing our understanding of the text, the translation, and the authenticity of the Bible.

## 47

### The Bible Today

#### A LIVING BOOK

IN the last chapter we wandered through a graveyard of history where writing is buried under other writing, papyrus is hidden beneath the sand, and broken bits of stone and pottery lie among the debris of dead cities. In this limbo of vanished civilizations, where few but scholars come, lie most of the books written between 1200 B.C. and A.D. 150 when the Bible came into being. Here lie Canaanite books, Egyptian literature, the forgotten Aramaic literature, and many a work by Greek and Roman authors. But the Bible is not buried with these, for today it is a living Book, entering creatively into modern life. It issues in an endless stream from roaring presses; it speaks over the radio; it is typed on the movie director's script; it is recorded for phonographs; it stands beside the typewriters of modern authors ready to supply them with titles, ideas, phrases, and stories; and finally, it is read and preached and taught in every Christian Church throughout the world. Here, of course, is its most real and effective life. No other ancient literature can boast of such continuing vitality and it is indeed a rare modern book that challenges the Bible's popularity.

By 1948 the entire Bible had been translated into 185 languages or dialects and the New Testament into 241 additional languages, and a single Gospel or other selection into 664 more, making the unbelievable total of 1,090 tongues in which some part of the Bible exists. The languages added to the immense list of Bible translations in 1946 and 1947 were: Yipounou and Nantcheri of French Africa; Maya of Yucatan; Ancash Quechua of Peru; Maguindanao of the Philippines; and Totonac, Mixteco, Mazateco, Tarahumora, and Chol, all spoken by different groups of Indians in Mexico. There is perhaps in the world today no one with the ability to read who cannot find a Bible in his own language. Nor will he have to search far to obtain a copy, for printing plants manufacture Bibles in enormous quantities. In one year the American Bible Society has issued as many as 11,394,200 copies. Since its foundation in 1816, the Society has published more than 360 million copies. Large as these figures are they represent only a partial report, for, beside the American Bible Society, a dozen or more publishing companies print hundreds of thousands of copies every year. No one would dispute the statement that there are more copies of the Bible in existence than of any other book.

The Bible in English illustrates the living quality of the Scriptures. Though people agree that the King James Version of 1611 is one of the finest works in English prose literature, even this stately monument of the Stuart period could not entomb the Bible itself. Translation after translation continued to be made in English as manuscripts with better texts were discovered, problems in the Greek language were solved, old words died or changed meaning, and new words were born.

The new translations challenged and stimulated modern readers and gave them a better understanding of many an obscure sentence. All too often the matchless phrases of the King James Version slide along a well-worn groove in our minds and fail to engage our attention. The new translations cut new channels in men's thinking. What the Bible lost in majesty and power in the new translations, it gained in accuracy, readability, and clarity. Though some people deplore any change in the familiar phrases of the 1611 Version, few would agree with the enthusiastic but inaccurate statement of the person who said:

"A Bible that was good enough for St. James is good enough for me!"

Three of the many new translations proved very popular. In 1902 Dr. Richard Francis Weymouth published his *New Testament in Modern Speech*. This excellent rendering has passed through many editions and has been revised twice. More notable still were Dr. James Moffatt's translations. In 1913 he published his *New Testament: a New Translation*, followed eleven years later by *The Old Testament*. Dr. Moffatt's style was colloquial and he tried to present the Bible in effective, intelligible English. How well he succeeded is indicated by the fact that his New Testament was reprinted seventy times in twenty-five years. His translation of Paul's Epistles is particularly noteworthy, for it divests Paul of the stately garment of pompousness with which the King James translators clothed him and reproduces his ideas in understandable English. The revised and final edition of Dr. Moffatt's work was issued by Harper & Brothers in 1935 with the title, *The Bible: A New Translation*.

In 1923 Dr. Edgar J. Goodspeed published *The New Testament: an American Translation*. His aim was to present the New Testament in modern English so that it could be "continuously read and understood." This was followed by a translation of the Old Testament by a group of American scholars under the editorship of Dr. J. M. Powis Smith, and by the translation of the Apocrypha by Dr. Goodspeed. Finally, these three readable and excellent versions were published in 1939 by the University of Chicago Press under the title, *The Complete Bible: An American Translation*.

An eagerly awaited event in Bible history came in 1946 with the publication of The Revised Standard Version of the New Testament. This stems from the long line of the English Bibles and is the latest fruit of centuries of translating, revising, and scholarly study. It traces its lineage back to William Tyndale's first English translation of 1525 and it counts among its ancestors: Coverdale's Bible, the Matthew Bible, the Great

Bible, the Geneva Bible, the Bishops' Bible, the Rheims-Douay Bible, the King James Version, the Revised Version of 1881, and the American Standard Version of 1901. It is the work of a committee appointed in 1929 by the International Council of Religious Education representing forty Protestant denominations. Among the nine outstanding Bible scholars who worked on this version were the two well-known translators, James Moffatt and Edgar J. Goodspeed.

In publishing this important New Testament, Thomas Nelson and Sons and the Bible committee solved many printing problems. They followed the style of the other recent translations and substituted logical, readable paragraphs for the separate verses of the Authorized Version which so often cause one to lose the thread of the narrative. They introduced modern punctuation. They printed poetry as such. They swept distracting symbols from the text and grouped cross references and notes at the bottom of the page. All these details add enormously to the pleasure and convenience of the reader.

The Revised Standard Version is a splendid achievement of American Biblical scholarship. We miss in it some of the beautiful harmonies of the Authorized Version with all its obscurities and antique words. But this Version avoids that literal, word-for-word rendering of the Greek that makes the reader of the English Revised or the American Standard Version aware that he is reading a translation rather than an English book. In revising the English New Testament in the light of the best ancient manuscripts and the latest Greek discoveries, the revisers tried to make a version that would speak directly to people of today in plain, meaningful language. When the Bible-reading public gives its verdict on their accomplishment it will surely be a "Well done!"

The Bible is a Book used in many different ways. Some people would forge it into iron links to chain us to bygone years. Others are content to keep the Bible safely locked up like a hoard of family jewels inherited from a magnificent past. These people know by hearsay the fabulousness of the gems, but they rarely take them from the vault and look at them in the light of day.

For the majority of Christians, however, the Bible is neither an iron chain nor a hoarded treasure. To most of us it is a great river of spiritual reality rising out of Israel's remote past and continuing to flow more deeply and powerfully through succeeding centuries. It is fed by many rushing streams and mighty torrents and into it has flowed the spiritual wisdom and insight of twelve centuries. Countless men have poured their genius into it: David's biographer, the J and E historians, the author of Deuteronomy, the priestly compilers of history, Amos, Hosea, Isaiah, Micah, and all the prophets. Others have made their contributions: the singers, proverb makers, and story-tellers of antiquity, the authors who made Ruth and Jonah live, and the writer who created Job. Finally, the river enters a new reach where its waters flow over unfathomed depths. Here are the inspired writers of the Gospels and Epistles, the men who beheld the glory of the Word that was made flesh and dwelt among us.

The long river of the Bible is broad and very deep, and the Spirit of God moves upon the face of its waters. Here men that thirst come to drink of the water of life. The power of its on-rushing current turns many a wheel. It gives direction and continuity to our individual understanding of spiritual things. Following the shores of this river, no man need lose his way in jungles of speculation nor deserts of spiritual dryness. It is like the ancient river that "went out of Eden to water the garden," for it is a river that enriches the soil of our civilization. The river of the Bible has broadened out, and sometimes its waters seem to rush less vigorously than they once did through the rocky gorges of the Reformation. Though it flows more quietly today, the Bible is a deep and unfailing stream. It is for us:

> . . . a pure river of water of life, clear as crystal, proceeding out of the throne of God and of the Lamb . . . And let him that is athirst come. And whosoever will, let him take the water of life freely.

> REVELATION 22:1, 17

# Bible Readings

In addition to the Bible passages quoted or mentioned in the text, the following selections illustrate the history and help to support the theories discussed in Part I and may well be read with it. They offer, however, only a brief taste of the Old Testament and Apocrypha, and it is hoped that the reader will go on from these examples to discover for himself more of the ample riches of the Bible.

No reading list is given for the New Testament as this can easily be read in its entirety.

## Chapter 3. THE OLDEST WRITINGS IN THE BIBLE

## Chapter 4. THE FATHER OF HISTORY

## Chapter 5. THE EPIC OF ISRAEL

## Chapter 6. A RELIGIOUS HISTORY OF ISRAEL

## Chapter 7. THE FIRST BOOK OF PROPHECY

| | |
|---|---|
| The story of a reluctant missionary | Jonah, entire |
| Ruth, the Moabite girl who became David's great-grandmother | Ruth, entire |

### Chapter 19. FIRST EDITIONS OF THE BIBLE

| | |
|---|---|
| A summary of the second-century B.C. Bible | Ecclesiasticus 44—49:10 |

### Chapter 20. AN OLD TESTAMENT MASTERPIECE

| | |
|---|---|
| The old folk tale | Job 1, 2, 42:7-17 |
| Job curses the day of his birth | Job 3 |
| An ode to wisdom | Job 28 |
| Job's story of his life | Job 29, 30 |
| The highest moral standards in the Old Testament | Job 31 |
| The Lord speaks | Job 38, 39 |

### Chapter 21. WISE MEN OF ISRAEL

| | |
|---|---|
| In praise of wisdom | Proverbs 3:13-26 |
| The ideal wife | Proverbs 31:10-31 |
| The sadness of life | Ecclesiastes 1:1-11 |
| Life's end | Ecclesiastes 11:9—12:8 |

### Chapter 22. ISRAEL'S GOLDEN TREASURY

Among the best-loved Psalms are: 8, 19, 23, 24, 27, 42, 46, 51, 67, 84, 90, 91, 95, 96, 100, 107, 121, 122, 125, 126

### Chapter 23. THE LITERARY HARVEST OF A CENTURY

| | |
|---|---|
| David prepares to build the Temple | I Chronicles 22:2-19 |
| How Temple music was organized | I Chronicles 15:16-28 |
| Is this history or opera? | II Chronicles 20:14-30 |
| The Temple is rebuilt and Ezra goes to Jerusalem | Ezra 5:1—7:10 |
| Mixed marriages | Ezra 9:5-15; 10:2-8 |
| How Ezra read the Law to the people | Nehemiah 8 |
| A Hebrew love song | Song of Solomon 2:8-17 |
| Four young men are loyal to their faith | Daniel 1 |
| The furnace does not burn the three youths | Daniel 3 |
| A great feast at which handwriting appears on the wall | Daniel 5 |
| A miracle in a lion's den | Daniel 6 |
| The adventures of a Jewish heroine | Esther, entire |

### Chapter 24. THE BOOKS THAT WERE LEFT OUT

| | |
|---|---|
| The prayer of Tobit, a pious Jew | Tobit 3:1-6 |
| Religion or "the fear of the Lord" is wisdom | Ecclesiasticus 1 |
| In praise of famous men | Ecclesiasticus 44:1-15 |
| Ancient craftsmen who supported "the fabric of the world" | Ecclesiasticus 38:24-34 |

| | |
|---|---|
| Songs to Jerusalem | Baruch 4, 5 |
| A cry of Penitence | Manasses, entire |
| The reward of righteousness | Wisdom 3:1-9 |
| The story of Judith | Judith 8—16 |
| A contest between three members of the royal bodyguard | I Esdras 3, 4 |
| Elephants are used in a battle against Judas and his Maccabean patriots | I Maccabees 6:28-46 |

# A Selected Bibliography

The books suggested below have been chosen from the vast field of Biblical literature for their interest to the general reader. They are, for the most part, readable, and not too technical and they offer guidance for further study.

## GENERAL

Bailey, Albert E. *Daily Life In Bible Times*. New York: Scribner's, 1943.

Finegan, Jack. *Light From the Ancient Past*. Princeton University Press, 1946.

Manson, T. A. *A Companion to the Bible*. Edinburgh: Clark, 1939.

## OLD TESTAMENT

Bewer, Julius A. *The Literature of the Old Testament*. New York: Columbia University Press, 1938.

Goodspeed, Edgar J. *The Story of the Old Testament*. Chicago: University Press, 1934.

James, Fleming. *Personalities of the Old Testament*. New York: Scribner's, 1946.

Pfeiffer, Robert H. *Introduction to the Old Testament*. New York: Harper, 1941.

Robinson, Theodore H. and Oesterley, W. O. E. *A History of Israel*. Oxford: Clarendon Press, 1932.

Smith, J. M. Powis and Irwin, William A. *The Prophets and Their Times*. Chicago: University Press, 1941.

## APOCRYPHA

Goodspeed, Edgar J. *The Story of the Apocrypha*. Chicago: University Press, 1943.

Oesterley, William O. E. *An Introduction to the Books of the Apocrypha*. New York: Macmillan, 1935.

Torrey, Charles Cutler. *The Apocryphal Literature*. New Haven: Yale University Press, 1945.

## NEW TESTAMENT

Fowler, Henry T. *The History and Literature of the New Testament*. New York: Macmillan, 1925.

Goodspeed, Edgar J. *The Formation of the New Testament.* Chicago: University Press, 1926.

——. *Christianity Goes to Press.* New York: Macmillan, 1940.

——. *An Introduction to the New Testament.* Chicago: University Press, 1937.

Lake, Kirsopp and Lake, Silva. *An Introduction to the New Testament.* New York: Harper, 1937.

Lyman, Mary Ely. *The Christian Epic.* New York: Scribner's, 1936.

Riddle, Donald W. *The Gospels: Their Origins and Growth.* Chicago: University Press, 1939.

Scott, Ernest F. *The Literature of the New Testament.* New York: Columbia University Press, 1936.

Streeter, Burnett H. *The Four Gospels.* New York: Macmillan, 1925.

## THROUGH THE CENTURIES

Bell, H. I. *Recent Discoveries of Biblical Papyri.* Oxford: Clarendon Press, 1937.

British Museum publication. *The Codex Sinaiticus and the Codex Alexandrinus.* 1938.

Goodspeed, Edgar J. *The Making of the English New Testament.* Chicago: University Press, 1925.

Kenyon, Frederic G. *The Story of the Bible.* London: John Murray, 1936.

Robinson, H. Wheeler. *The Bible in Its Ancient and English Versions.* Oxford: Clarendon Press, 1940.

Weigle, Luther A. and others. *An Introduction to the Revised Standard Version of the New Testament.* Chicago: International Council of Religious Education, 1946.

Westcott, Brooke Foss. *A General View of the History of the English Bible.* New York: Macmillan, 1916.

# Index